D1617433

RENDERING
FRENCH REALISM

LAWRENCE R. SCHEHR

Stanford University Press
Stanford, California 1997

Stanford University Press
Stanford, California

© 1997 by the Board of Trustees of the
Leland Stanford Junior University

Printed in the United States of America

CIP data are at the end of the book

Original printing 1997
Last figure below indicates year of this printing
06 05 04 03 02 01 00 99 98 97

For David Bell and Franc Schuerewegen,
compagnons de route

Acknowledgments

Some of this material has appeared in earlier form in the following articles: "Flaubert entre l'indécidé et l'indécidable," *Les Lettres romanes* 45.4 (1991): 293–306; "Balzac's Dyslexia," *Nineteenth-Century French Studies* 21.1–2 (1992): 1–26; "Quoin of the Realm: *La Muse du département*," *L'Esprit Créateur* 31.3 (1991): 78–87; "Stendhal's Pathology of the Novel," *French Forum* 15.1 (1990): 53–72. I should like to thank the editors of those journals for their interest in my work through their original publication of it and for their permission to reuse the material in this volume.

I should also like to thank, both for their work on this volume and on two previous volumes, the indefatigable Helen Tartar and Peter J. Kahn of Stanford University Press. Their advice and wisdom have been immeasurable. And again, Ann Klefstad has brought a magic hand to copyediting this work.

The University of South Alabama has provided me with release time over the years in order to conduct my research, and has given me, in particular, a Faculty Service and Development Award in order to complete this project. I should like to thank my chair, Bernard J. Quinn, the Dean of Arts and Sciences, Larry Allen, and the Assistant to the President, John Morrow, for their invaluable support on this project.

To some, it may seem odd to thank a conference, that many-headed collective, but over the years, the annual conference on Nineteenth-Century French Studies has provided me with the opportunities to participate in so much stimulating conversation and to hear so many thought-provoking talks. The influence and help of that collective body, as well as the annual celebration of the field, have been of invaluable inspiration. I would modestly add that I was able to present some of this material to the group over the course of the years, and that the feedback was of great help to me as I prepared this book.

As always, I have been able to count on a group of friends to provide critical readings, stimulating conversation, acute observations, corrections, and a myriad of other useful suggestions. Let them be thanked here in the most simple and heartfelt way for their help, suggestions, and support: the late George Bauer, Frank Paul Bowman, Ross Chambers, Mary Donaldson-Evans, Diane Fourny, Jean-François Fourny, Rodolphe Gasché, Michal Peled Ginsburg, Mette Hjort, Paisley M. Livingston, Caryl L. Lloyd, Allan S. Pasco, Laurence M. Porter, Gerald Prince, Rima Drell Reck, Joerg Ruthel, Murray Sachs. Their help has been invaluable.

Charles Stivale in particular made numerous helpful comments on the penultimate version of this manuscript. His remarks have aided me in the final preparation of the manuscript.

And lastly, I should like gratefully and quietly to thank the two dedicatees, David Bell and Franc Schuerewegen, whose ongoing friendship and whose gifts of reading *as* friendship, can never be measured.

L.R.S.

Contents

Rendering French Realism

Introduction:
De te textus

For the past quarter century we have been living in the age of the text. As I glance randomly at my bookshelves I see *The Pleasure of the Text*, *Textual Power*, *Is There a Text in This Class?*, *Saving the Text*, *Le Texte du roman*, *Sexual/Textual Politics*, and *The Reader in the Text*. We—academic literary critics—used to put great stock in individual generic categories by which we distinguished odes from pastoral poems, novels from plays, and history from fiction. More recently we have subsumed all of them under the all-inclusive category of "text," which is loosely defined as something, or anything, written. Instead of the confining generic categories that came laden with explicit or implicit codes and paradigms, the text overflows the restrictions of normalizing, canonizing reading and praxis. Instead of the artificial distinction between canonical high culture and marginal writing or popular culture, we have the all-inclusive term "text."

As Roland Barthes says in *S/Z*, the work that undoubtedly made the most of this concept of textuality, "*text, tissue*, and *tress* are the same thing" (166). Using the word "text" implies the weaving of the word's etymology, the tissue of its fellow derivatives, the infinite extension of its strands of words and strings of sentences somewhere toward a great beyond of context and intertext. This interwoven context and intertext is simultaneously immanent, for a text has meaning, and transcendent, for a text exists in the world of semioticity, deconstruction somewhere beyond meaning, expectation, and interpretation. A text weaves voices and writings, signs and symbols, subjects and meanings. Indeed, for Roland Barthes, the text is "woven" of voices (*S/Z* 28). And the voices intertwine, harmonize or sing in counterpoint, scat or do riffs, and fade in and out, as the text endlessly remakes itself.

It is not that the other words have disappeared. But now that we have the "text," the word and category of "book" seem so material, so bourgeois, and so derivative of the world of production and dominance. In the world of the text, generic lines seem more questionable and presuppositions seem more open to investigation; formats and paradigms seem somewhat less resistant to the critic's eye. The weave of the writing seems more pliable or unknottable; in any case, it is more easily deciphered. In the days before the easily named, yet elusively defined, concept of a "textuality" that Barthes developed in *S/Z* and then canonized in *Le Plaisir du texte* with the post-Freudian benediction of bliss (*jouissance*), the textual was by and large the realm of people preparing variorum editions and scholars looking at "textual" emendations.

Parisian structuralism and its aftermath in what is loosely called "poststructuralism" in North America raised the word "text" to a lofty status by redefining it, expanding it, and breaking the ties of the word and others like it, such as "discourse" and "writing," to author and authority. Even Michel Foucault, who took great pains to distinguish himself from the structuralist enterprise, asked the question "What is an author?" (*Dits* 1:789–821) in his 1969 essay of that name. It is here where he most clearly discusses the articulation of discourses and the disappearance of the subject. In this work discourse is seen as being related both to Jacques Derrida's concept of writing in a work like *De la grammatologie*, from 1967, and Barthes's concept of the text in *S/Z*, his 1968–69 seminar published in 1970.

Text or discourse or writing exists "out there." And since the structuralist and poststructuralist revolutions, and following the immeasurable impact of feminism, deconstruction, and gender studies on literary studies, we have moved away from an inherited, all-too-static, defining, and constricting view of what a text is. We can no longer see text as the normalized compromise and the summary or re-creation of the author's intention.[1] At its edges, whatever or however they are defined, the text entwines with context in a vague intermixing of borders and sides; there is a bleeding of one fabric into another caught in the literary wringer. Calling this "thing" in front of the reader a text means redefining what qualifies as a text, what can be read, reread, written, rewritten, unread and unwritten in our times, and indeed who can or cannot, may or may not read. Images too are texts, and the language of the visual arts has often been translated into textual metaphors during the past quarter-century.

Texts weave in and out, creating their own structures and patterns, escaping from, undoing, and "deconstructing" generic norms, the roles of the subject, the gaze of the reader, and the mark of the author. The text remakes (the) language itself, as it calls into question what we consider proper and improper and what we see as fit to read and not fit to read. With textuality comes a slippery relation between *parole* and discourse, between the individual instance of language and the general dictionary, encyclopedia, grammar, primer, or breviary of the language as a whole, if in fact it exists as a whole. Textuality calls wholes and parts into question, reorients the placing of desire, knowledge, and the subject itself.

The era of textuality will have been a liberating moment in the history of literary criticism. The practices and even the theories, now often discarded unread, that surrounded the discovery of textuality as the subject of our individual and collective endeavors, have given literary studies a new lease on life in several ways. New contexts for reading and writing literature have arisen, among which are feminism, literary theory (as opposed to criticism), cultural studies, and gender studies. New relations have arisen: the philosophical text and the literary text seem inseparably interwoven with one another in complementary or mismatched patterns, by and large thanks to the seminal work of Gilles Deleuze, Jean-François Lyotard, Michel Serres, and especially Jacques Derrida, who speaks of "the metaphor in the philosophical text," a subtitle he gives to his very influential essay "White Mythology" ("La Mythologie blanche," in *Marges*). Intertexts and contexts, the first popularized by Julia Kristeva in *Le Texte du roman*, her study of *Le Petit Jehan de Saintré* and the second reinvigorated by New Historicism, have allowed readings of the world heretofore unimagined. Indeed, textuality will have been a liberating and fecundating moment.

Though the concept of the text has contributed so enormously to this liberation of our individual and collective endeavors, thereby inspiring in many a false sense of freedom from canon, meaning, practice, and history, it does not mean that textuality is itself free. Within the text, constraints are endlessly at work defining who the reader may be, defining what is readable, and eschewing certain discourses. Similarly, on the outside, general discursive practices, as Foucault has so often shown, determine to a great extent what a text is and what is considered to be a "text." These textual constraints are matched by a phantom constraint, a mythology of textuality: the weaving and unweaving of Penelope, the web of Arachne, the thread of Ariadne, or even the frantic knitting needles of Dickens's Madame Defarge. Desire is sewn into the very lining of the concept. Desire moves the shuttle along to create Gogol's *Overcoat*, James's "Figure in the Carpet," and the upholstery on Goethe's *West-Östlicher Divan* and Crébillon's *Sopha*, finally to be gathered in Jacques Lacan's *points de capiton*.

The text is made of threads woven into a pattern binding warp and woof. The threads leading in various directions are the solid stuff, the texture, weaving, tissue, indeed the object itself. The holes in the text are a by-product of that weaving process. Holes are formed between the threads, produced when two pair of parallel threads cross at right angles. They are safe, well-defined holes whose engulfing power is limited by the strong threads that form the web of the work. Textuality is solid and strong; it is in control of its own emptinesses produced as a by-product of writing and its reading. We read the undecidabilities and absences, the *Leerstellen* or gaps of which Wolfgang Iser writes (*Prospecting* 3–30), as secondary to, or subsequent to, the act of weaving and writing that makes a text.

Deconstruction, as we know, seized the opportunity created by those absences in textuality. As Jacques Derrida has shown in so much of his work, including *De la grammatologie*, the essays on Mallarmé and Plato in *La Dissémination*, and "La Mythologie blanche" included in *Marges*, to name just a few salient and influential early studies, these openings and undecidabilities themselves form the text and are neither previous to nor subsequent to the manufactured object that is a text. Seeing where those holes appear and where the text is rent may rob the work of its materiality, may shake the foundations of the model-builders, but deconstruction persists in performing its act of discovering the holes that are "always already" in the text. Forced into cubbyholes and sequestered in margins, the nascent atoms of gender and genre theory (ultimately the same thing, as Philippe Lacoue-Labarthe and Jean-Luc Nancy point out presciently in "La Loi du genre") burst out, tearing away the spiders' webs that keep radical interpretations safely at bay.

Over the past quarter-century, reading literature through the optics provided by what has come to be known as "theory" has produced points of view that have engaged literary works in new ways and that have called into question fundamental methods of reading. As I have already noted, various important movements in contemporary theory—multiple versions of post-structuralism, deconstruction, feminism, reader-response theory, Lacanian psychoanalysis, as well as the anthropological approaches of René Girard, the scientific epistemology of Michel Serres, and Michel Foucault's analyses of power—have yielded a new vision of the literary work. No longer the idealistic object of traditional humanistic inquiry nor the privileged, airy artifact of various formalistic and phenomenological approaches, the literary work has become one discourse interacting with others, not the least of which is the critic's own theoretical approach.

In a general sense, these interactions have been fruitful since they have led to a radical reunderstanding of the literary work. Two of these theoretical discourses merit particular attention for the studies of nineteenth-century French literature that follow this introduction: feminism and poststructuralist theory in general and deconstruction in particular. I am using both words heuristically, collectively, and loosely for reasons that shall soon become clear. By "feminism" I mean nothing more than the idealized name for a whole host of possible readings, many (but not all) of which can be grouped under a rubric relating to the theorization of women's studies as they relate to the humanities. By putting such a wide variety of works under one general, impossible rubric, I do not mean to slight differences; I mean rather to underline the general effect that this work has had. By "poststructuralist theory" I mean the varied body of work that

arose in the aftermath of critiques of the "structures" of structuralism. Again, I am understanding deconstruction heuristically as that
body of work, within the manifold possibilities of the poststructuralist enterprise, that has been influenced by the work of Jacques Derrida and of Paul de Man, and which, of course, includes their work as
well.

Feminism, for example, has brought to the literary scene not only
a revision of thematics and a poetics of repression but also a fundamental revision in our ontology of the reading and writing subject.
What feminism has indicated, most clearly, is the systematic repression of the female subject in the praxis, history, and reception of literature. It is no longer possible blithely or naively to assume the
transparent (that is to say, male) nature of the literary subject. By refusing the hierarchic division of the subject in which the male dom-
inates and in fact fully eclipses the female subject, feminism has demonstrated that the value systems that literature repeats and inscribes
are exchange systems in which the sign of the feminine is itself a
phantom commodity.

During the 1970's, deconstruction in particular, and numerous
poststructuralist points of view in a wider sense, seized the linguistic
object, both literary and philosophical, for itself, and radically revised
our understanding of literary and philosophical writing. Following
the cues and overcoming the limitations of structuralism, the theorists of deconstructive readings exchanged certainty for ambiguity
and logic for the tropes of irony and reversal. The logic of the textual object, and even of the philosophical subject seen as an object of
study, was seen to be an insoluble opposition, fictionally transformed
into a hierarchy in which one member of a seemingly logical binary
pair was often repressed for the benefit of the other. From that original discovery, deconstructive theorists undertook a reading of the series of repressions operating within literary works that elaborately
covered up the initial difference with tropes of meaning, metaphors
of presence, and shifts of metaphysical prestidigitation.

In his famous work, "Structure, Sign, and Play in the Discourse of
the Human Sciences" ("La Structure, le signe et le jeu dans le discours des sciences humaines"), included in the collection *L'Ecriture
et la différence*, Jacques Derrida briefly sketches out what he considers to be the three critical moments in the radical revision of knowl-

edge: Nietzsche's concept of truth as game, Freud's concept of the unknowability of the subject, and Heidegger's radical critique of ontology (250). These three are the spiritual ancestors of what came to be known as deconstruction, for which in turn this article became the rallying cry and indeed almost the manifesto. Deconstruction enters the American academy in the 1970's, and even in the tamer form of institutionalized reading, it offers, along with feminism, one of the two most salient radical critiques of institutionalized discourse. Whereas Nietzsche, Freud, and Heidegger provided singular critiques of received knowledge, deconstruction and feminism have offered, in the past twenty years, institutionalized and systematic critiques of basic structures and paradigms.

The difference between the more radical versions of deconstruction and feminism on the one hand and the tamer institutionalized versions should not be minimized.[2] The proliferation of these two critiques as transmissible discourses has had certain effects. Most important, the institutionalized received versions of deconstruction and feminism depend on their readability. No matter how thorny the work, it is categorically assumed at this point—the last decade of the twentieth century—within the academy that these double radical discourses are teachable, transmissible, and applicable. Thus, separate and apart from their radicalness, and in fact in spite of it, there is a presumption of both readability and writeability for the two theories. There is an obvious effect of taming: in "Structure, Sign, and Play," Derrida indicates the impossibility of writing about metaphysics from a position outside of metaphysics; in so doing, he points to the failure of all brands of logical positivism. Yet in academic criticism, the subsequent institutionalized version of his discourse seems often to have forgotten the radical nature of that assumption. Similarly, the institutionalization of feminist discourse a few years after the boom of deconstruction, an event that led to a reradicalization of deconstruction through feminism, has often consigned the radical nature of a true feminist critique to oblivion. Specifically, what has been forgotten is that there is no discourse outside phallocentric discourse and that every discourse, certainly every institutionalized discourse, is tainted by phallocentrism. Just as for metaphysics in the Derridean sense, the object of feminism cannot be critiqued by means of a pure, feminist metadiscourse. In the zeal of some in the academy to incorporate the discourse of the other, even to the extent of including the radical alterity of this discourse, the double initial lesson of the foundational discourses may have been forgotten by their transformation into tame, teachable academic reason.

This normalization is problematic if one considers the validity of the radical discourse within the academy. And whatever the institutional pressures that urge conformity, it must be said that the push toward normalization and thus toward readability came from the very people who were the apostles of the new. Whereas the ramifications of this normalization will have significant repercussions in the teaching of humanities and thus in the future of the profession, the concern here is with the initial object of these theoretical discourses: the literary (or philosophical) works themselves.

The normalization of these most radical of critical theories, what is being called here their readability, has reordered the available means of reading works. Whatever the advances provided by these approaches, they have, in their current forms, shown themselves to have a significant blind spot: they have led to the assumption, ultimately the most conservative one imaginable, that the literary or philosophical work is readable. What does this mean? Basically it says that the literary or philosophical work can be fully understood by the theoretical discourse. But this is only true insofar as the theoretical discourse has forgotten its own radical undecidability and, just as important, insofar as it has now forgotten the undecidability of the literary work as well. For every haunting specter or undecidability of friendship offered us by Derrida as he continues his radical critique, we have scads of papers, articles, and books by others purportedly explaining ambiguities, translating them into an understandable rhetoric or ideology, refashioning them into a simple opposition.

Traditional criticism stressed making the text readable, that is, understandable, through the imposition of copious notes and commentaries. Even to the extent that one can name a figure "ambiguity," one is delimiting the possible readable meanings of the text. Contemporary criticism started from a point at which this ambiguity was not even nameable in the traditional sense: names like *différance* or *trace* were given to this radical ambiguity, but these names did not name anything as much as they described a flight from fixed names and readable contracts with the reader of texts. As this criticism became institutionalized, though, this subtle difference from a traditional concept of naming and readability seemed more and more to disappear. Thus literature is viewed as a series of understandable differences from a fully readable, ideal text.

The two theories in question have approached this normalization in opposing ways. Feminist discourse has spent much time discussing realism; deconstruction has by and large avoided it because of the assumption that the realist sign is readable. The readability of Austen, Balzac, or Dickens illuminates the exchange system that is the operative model within feminism; rather than being a metonymic figure of the subject, the sign of femininity is, within realism, the figure of the exchange system at a real or symbolic level. It is precisely because the realist work is presumed to reflect a reality of either a superficial or a deep level that this model can be drawn from the literary artifact.

Remarkable affinities abound between realism and feminism, as the work of Doris Kadish, Peggy Kamuf, and Naomi Schor amply shows. Kamuf even has a chapter on Virginia Woolf in *Signature Pieces* that recalls the great weaver herself: "Penelope at Work" (145–73). Thanks to the acute perceptions of these critics, to mention only three among many writing on French literature, there has been a revolution in our reading and a drastic revision of the very idea of canonicity. Realism finds a sympathetic reading in Lacanian psychoanalysis and in its reversal in the schizoanalysis developed by Deleuze and Guattari: the realist novel, as we normatively define it, finds its material, historical, and ideological base in the very structures that allow for the psychoanalytical interpretation in the first place.

Conversely, since deconstruction still seems to seek the unresolvable point that is the undecidability of the work, it has by and large eschewed forays into the nineteenth-century novel, since the latter is presumed to be readable in almost a vulgar fashion. What difference there is can be understood as an ideological troping of reality by Balzac on the right or Zola on the left. Ostensibly heteroreferential, the realist novel seems the antithesis of Romantic poetry or the epistemological tract in philosophy, both of which have elicited sympathetic readings in deconstruction.

Realism, as the abbreviation for a set of often contradictory literary praxes in the nineteenth and early twentieth centuries, depends on verisimilitude, a version of which we often continue to accept as the proper way of telling a story today. Realism appears always to be looking toward an elsewhere, even when it seems, as in the case of Zola's *Le Docteur Pascal* or Balzac's *Illusions perdues*, to be talking about its own material origins. In other words, realism itself is predicated on its difference from what it describes and on the consistency of the determination of its praxes from without, by the world it describes, and not, like self-reflective poetry or philosophical argument, from some internal consistency. The consistency of realism, one would surmise, is supposed to come from the consistency of its object.

Without picking an individual realist novel in particular, for doing so might bring out some of the contradictions in the specific work that resist reading, one might hypothesize a method of applying postmodern thought, and specifically deconstruction, to the realist novel—or the realist *text*—in general. Schematically put, the postmodern reading of a realist novel would go as follows: the realist novel purports to verisimilitude, so let us follow that until we reach the contradictions of that reading. Once found, the contradictions tell us about the ideological bias of the materialism and the bourgeois ethic that arise with the rise of the novel itself; or about the sexual bias of targeting the female reader through the controlling hand of the male writer. The contradictions are thus out there, in some place beyond the *text*. We follow the weave and the pattern, see where it fits, and determine where there is an unsightly bulge or even a seductive patch of naked flesh, the seductive, erotic gap of the cloth mentioned by Barthes in *Le Plaisir du texte*: "Isn't the most erotic spot of a body where there is a gap in the clothing? [*L'endroit le plus érotique d'un corps n'est-il pas là où le vêtement bâille?*]" (19).

To my mind, realism has resisted a full-fleshed deconstructive interpretation because of several assumptions that are part of the *mise-en-pratique* of the writing process of a realist novel read as a realist *text*. Most important for the study at hand is not this gradual normalization of the theoretical project, but, pragmatically, the existence of a literary corpus that seems already to have traced this path of normalization and readability for itself. It happens that this fully readable ideal work has a very palpable figure in literature: broadly defined, it is realist narrative. Implicitly or explicitly, it is against the supposedly clear sign systems of realism that all of the following are measured: the fragmentation and forgetting of romanticism, the difference from reason in the passions of the Enlightenment, and indeed the writeability of the modern literary artifact. In reading the works of realism through deconstruction and feminism, the now enforced readability taken as gospel blocks the outrageous fact that realism questions the nature of truth, as does Nietzsche; it questions the knowability of the subject, as does Freud; it questions the very nature of the subject and object, as does Heidegger. The rhetoric by which postmodern thought has congratulated, institutionalized, and normalized its own discourse has often blinded it to the radical questions in the supposedly normal and readable works of realism.

The radical nature of the realist enterprise, its inherent deconstructability, has been hidden because of the nature of realist representation and our continued belief in the possibility of representation. First of all, the only models of self-reflexivity or recursiveness offered by realism depend on mimetic reflection, realism's greatest rhetorical device. In other words, the kinds of self-reflexivity offered by realism, say in a work like Zola's *L'Oeuvre* or Stendhal's *Le Rouge et le Noir*, are of a scene of learning that parallels the construction of the writer's concept of his or her own craft. The scene is not ironic; for lack of a better term, it is mechanically mimetic. By dint of practicing, the artist creates the work until the final work is reached.

This model is of course an ideological construct, and as readers like Fredric Jameson, Richard Terdiman, and Terry Eagleton have shown, this "ideology of the aesthetic" is fundamental to the realist endeavor. Indeed, this ideology and its concomitant aesthetic accurately reflect the reified concepts of production, construction, and exchange found in the society that the realist novel reflects in its own structures. It is therefore wholly consonant to find a mechanism of production that is modeled *grosso modo* on the capitalist system of exchange and value. Even Balzac's ironies can be subsumed under the aegis of the dialectical reading of this aesthetic production that reflects its own roots.

The ideological problem posed by realism is the following: to the extent that the ideology is visible in the writing, the literary work is seen as having failed to attain the goal of realist writing founded on

logic, continuity, and reason. Whether it is Balzac's royalist and reli-
gious politics or Dickens's caricatural or carnivalesque reading of
London in the industrial age, the ideology deforms the work and the
supposed neutrality of the project—which neutrality, of course, is itself an ideological position. Now we can see two reasons for the
work's deformation through ideology, one of which is exterior to the
work, as a political motivation. Ideology disturbs both the form and
contents of a work because the author betrays or invokes his or her
own class consciousness as an unfounded reason for his or her supposedly transparent view of the world. Such is the critique leveled by
Georg Lukács, for example, against Flaubert. More subtly, in the
eyes of the same Marxist critic, the ideology redoubled in a case like
that of Balzac is an antidote to the author's own personal bias; the re-
sultant irony is the mechanism that would allow this author to describe a world realistically. Thus Balzac's writing subverts the author's own ideology, which in turn had subverted the processes of realist description. Doubly troped in that way, Balzac's writing becomes
the ironic double and completion of the project.

Yet I believe that even when we have understood the political unconscious or modes of counterdiscourse of a work, we have not fully
solved the crisis in the realist novel. For the ideology is not only an
argument but also a cover-up for an individual failure to fulfill a project that in the most fundamental sense cannot be realized. And the
two theoretical approaches of feminism and deconstruction have already made clear what the realists do not consciously know but un-
consciously compensate for.

To understand the resistance of realism from another angle, it
may be useful to think about realism after it is set against the coun-
terexample of romanticism. As opposed to its second flowering in the
France of the 1830's and 1840's, in the first phases of romanticism,
that of Wordsworth, Coleridge, Byron, Keats, and Shelley, the romanticism of Schlegel and Goethe's *Faust I*, self-reflexivity is endlessly shimmering as both goal and origin, neither knowable nor
complete. Irony, perhaps the master trope of German romanticism,
is itself undercut by this fragmentation and this incompletion. A picture is never finished; the act of construction reflected as memory is
always a partial one, even when its integral nature is necessary. In
other words, for the romantic aesthetic to take off, a whole must be

posited, a return to it must be possible—yet, at the same time, that whole is impossible. It is therefore no accident that the "rhetoric of romanticism"—to use Paul de Man's term—is one of the high points of literary deconstruction as practiced in the United States.

No such self-referential rhetoric exists for realism. The ideological interpretation of the realist text in its various forms, whether Marxist or feminist, still does not negotiate what seems to me to be the essential realist moment: not the underlying ideological contradictions of production, textual or contextual, but the breakdown of mimetic representation.[3] Now this may seem an outrageous statement, because it flies in the face of received knowledge about the verisimilitude of realist praxis. Again, it is not to say that realist writing is real or even that its verisimilitude is not skewed in various ideological fashions. It is to say that the acts of realist representation are predicated at their origin on the readability of the work and on the belief than an act of mimetic representation is occurring. Moreover, our concepts of verisimilar representation—indeed, storytelling—have not varied all that much from the means of writing fostered a century and a half ago. We are in a world that Balzac would not find alien; the flowering of talk shows is closer to the journalistic wars of *Illusions perdues* than we might otherwise think. To read Balzac critically today, we seem to be correcting some of the oversights in his representational pattern, his rhetoric, and his ideology. Yet even as we bring this correction to the realist work, we continue to accept the representational pattern as a readable one. Our reading and his reading intersect, whereas our ability to deconstruct a text by Shelley is enhanced by the fact that we no longer share the presuppositions of Shelleyan romanticism. The irony, of course, is that many of the presuppositions on which the American brand of deconstruction works do relate, as I have indicated, to the model of fragmentation with which romanticism is imbued.

For both feminism and deconstruction, realism is assumed to be readable: at a deep level of truth for feminism and at a classifiable superficial level for deconstruction. Hence the interest of one group of readers and the comparative lack of attention of the other. If, however, we posit the ambiguity and unreadability of the realist work as cardinal, if we let its radical nature shine, there is a seesaw effect. For the radical nature of realist representation, which is, I underline, as

much the problem of unrepresentability as it is the belief in representability, may skew a feminist reading that depends on a representational model of transparency, or at least ideologically biased readability. At the same time, the radical critique inscribed in this doubled position of representability and unrepresentability calls for,
indeed militates for, a deconstruction of the act of realist representation.

Simply put, my hypothesis is double: the assumption of readability is neither necessary nor true and the discourse of realism is as radically unreadable as any other literary work. The inscription of realist discourse depends not on an act of transcription but on an act of
repression that is the crisis of writing. The realist work is readable
only because the writer has willfully or strategically repressed the
radical difference in his or her work that is the difference between
writing and its absence. The hiding of the difference takes the forms
that one might expect from what has already been said: a knowledge
of the subject, the being of the object, and the theory of knowledge
itself. In textual terms, this amounts to asking who writes, how and
where, and of what.

In this view, realist writing is not the ideological act of representation but the radical questioning of the act of representation itself
in writing. If the world presents itself to be described, writing as
such, tainted by the world, is like language imbued with metaphysics,
the only available means of describing the world. On the one hand,
writing is radically different from the world and cannot represent
that which it is not; on the other hand, this radicalness is itself compromised by the participation of language in the world and the world
in language. The radical purity *of* language is endlessly refused *to* language by the banal taint of the world. So the crisis in realism that is
singularly invisible to institutionalized radical discourse and obviously nonexistent for less radical modes of literary criticism is the
subject of this study. The parallel should be clear: realism is as originally radical as feminism and Derridean deconstruction, and we
should not refuse that radicalness to any of them by accepting their
institutionalization.

A theorization of the crisis in realism is already possible but its
specific nature will become clearer after a schematic summary of the
realist models of writing. If we consider realism as a praxis including

the majority of nineteenth-century prose written after the first phase of romanticism, it is quickly said that realism is the attempt to capture in prose both the surface of the world as it appears as well as the underlying reasons for these surface phenomena. Despite some mystifications through ideological constraints, the realist model is the product of the Enlightenment and is therefore predicated on the rationality, logic, and continuity of the world. Considered not as a movement but as a set of literary praxes, realism can be defined in several meaningful ways. The simplest is by consensus: realist narrative would be fictional prose perceived as adequately and accurately describing its world. Realism then would be the writing that produces a verisimilar construct, a signified that corresponds to a class and organization of objects or to a type in the real world: it is the language whose *telos* is the production of the typical. Along with the reproduction of the objective goes the reproduction of the subjective translated into an object language describing psychology and consciousness. When used to describe an inner world, realist discourse has the objective strength of accreted opinions: it is both normative and predictive. In other words, realism can have an irrational fantasmatic posit, as long as that construct is translatable into the discourses of realism. This consciousness described by realist discourse is therefore one that can be understood by the reader, cast by the narrative in a position in which he or she can reconstruct this imaginary consciousness.

Certain corollaries follow from this first view of realism. First of all, the real is not only continuous in itself, but also continuous over the spectrum that leads from subject to object. Neither language nor consciousness produces a division, split, or fault. Seconding that concept of continuity is the idea that a neutral locus of discourse can be posited outside that spectrum from which reality can be described. Neither objective nor subjective, the neutral locus is the pure discourse of the other, the bank of language permanently invested with meaning. It is thus a language that reflects the language of scientific and philosophical inquiry, the discourse of positivism. This correspondence of discourses reflects yet another corollary of this first version of realism: the positivist discourse of inquiry, be it scientific, literary, or philosophical, is a normative and therefore conservative discourse. Concomitantly, along with the normalization of the perceived world comes what has been called the naturalizing of narrative form. Since the discourse in question necessarily entails a belief, as Françoise Gaillard notes, that "it is the nature of the real to be intelligible, thus narratable," narrative discourse and form become natural ("Innénarrable Histoire" 76). Thus realism posits an act of identity mediated by language: the object produced by language as a *terminus ad quem* is identical to the object that language produces as a *terminus ab quo*.

This model has its shortcomings, not the least of which is that realist discourse is neither neutral nor outside history. Like any other discursive modeling system, it is an invention that is neither natural nor all-inclusive. That this narrative practice is an invention can be seen in early examples of realism, where an author takes great pains to insert the natural correspondence between a world and narrative. Two well-known examples come to mind. The first is the first chapter of *Le Rouge et le Noir*, where it is precisely a question of inventing a world describable by narrative. The function of narrative is to dissolve the dichotomy between nature and culture. As the narrator begins to describe the little town of Verrières, he also is establishing the bonds he determines are appropriate between himself and the implied, idealized reader. Another example is an early novel of manners: *Pride and Prejudice*, in which some of the first stirrings of English realism can be seen. In the first chapter, Austen develops a moral system that is an effect of language, but is a system supposedly universally applicable. It arises in part as an oppositional discourse, opposed in praxis, if not necessarily in theory, to the discourse of romanticism.

No discourse is pure: a neutral locus is invented or produced by a negation or an exclusion. In addition, as an oppositional praxis, it contains encrypted or exhumed remains of previous discursive praxes. For example, even as its author refuses the mantle of what has preceded him, *Madame Bovary* is an inscribed monument to romantic discourse. As Henry James wisely notes in the Preface to *The American*: "It would be impossible to have a more romantic temper than Flaubert's Madame Bovary, and yet nothing less resembles a romance than the record of her adventures" (2:xvii). Even given abjectly, content influences form.

The neutral discourse of representation itself can be problematic; realism can be too realistic if it is not tempered with ideology or seemly behavior, what the French codified in the word *bienséance*. Think of the judgment on the trial of *Madame Bovary*:

Given that it is not permitted, under the pretext of painting personality or local color, to reproduce in all their differences, the facts, speech, and gestures of characters that a writer has undertaken to paint; that such a system applied to the works of the mind as well as to productions of the fine arts, would lead to a realism that would be the negation of the beautiful and the good . . . (1:683)

Though the court was undoubtedly wise not to condemn *Madame Bovary*, it still should not be construed as a literary arbiter; nevertheless, the presence of the key word "realism" in the judgment is significant. Realism must pick and choose, and in no way violate an idealist aesthetics or a received politically correct one. Because the court speaks by consensus, its judgment is most telling. Realism is not so much the correspondence of a literary discourse to a naturalized and continuous world as it is the correspondence with other discourses of verisimilitude, such as science, philosophy, and history. This correspondence entails a process of selection and exclusion; it is this double process taken along with the act of representation in discourse that describes realism. The process of selection means a choice; the process of selection or exclusion is the accomplishment of meaning.

To ensure that it is merely sufficient that the exclusions be agreed upon among the various discourses, the omission has to be considered a valid one. I am not suggesting that the various realist discourses have to omit or repress the same things; rather, they need to determine what each version of realism can treat neutrally. Thus, for example, science can determine a realm of inquiry into sexuality that may be an excluded possibility for narrative. And insofar as the excluded is concerned, realism necessitates that the unrepresented, and not the unrepresentable, not be another discourse. A censorious political discourse does not fit within the spectrum of intertranslatable realist discourses because it seems to exclude not the unrepresented but rather certain acts of representation.

My thesis is this: the point that defines realism is the point at which the processes of representation break down, a negative locus that simultaneously gathers and shreds, a black hole of textuality, a rent in the tissue, a rug covering a bald spot, a bare spot covering nothing, marking some abyss of undecidability. As the dictionary reminds us, a rug is *not* a text: it is related etymologically to "rupture," to "interruption," to "rob," to the archaic word "reave," which means to rob or despoil, and which found its way into a Faulkner title, *The Reivers*. Our notions of continuity, of readability, of representability, our ideas about unity and about ideological shift, and even—or especially—our notions of what is hidden, occulted, or absent all come from the realist model itself. And I for one am not convinced of the innocence of the model: it is as if we let a criminal make up the law as he or she ambles along, reaving right and left. Perhaps Vautrin the reaver and Stendhal's magic mirror are one and the same: neither an ideological epitome nor a mimetic reflection but a movement that signs itself as movement, instability, that marks realist detection as de-textion.

I am proposing then that we axiomatically reconsider our idea of the realist narrative, or indeed, the realist "text." My sense then is to look at what might be construed as interruptions in a realist work, interruptions that do not have the saving grace of ideological, ironic, or strategic explanations. Instead of assuming representability, let us see where the text does not continue the model, where there is a sudden falling off, where there is either an abyss or an insuperable mountain. And instead of reinscribing that unrepresentability as a circumscribed shortcoming, a hole in the fabric that is easily darned, let us look at that phenomenon as equal to the successes of representation. In other words, it is not that the reaving is a failure, an apology, or a tissue that is *tramé*, that is, both worked over a second time, and complicatedly intrigued. Let us consider the anomaly as being totally nonanomalous, part and parcel of the realist package.

My sense is that we need to move in this direction because ideological critiques of realism more often than not may seem to be explaining from the point of view of a reader who, if not imbued with a Hegelian or Lacanian absolute knowledge, certainly is in a superior position to the writer. If we are to understand realism, we must pull it out of its ghetto, after a fashion. It is perhaps time to stop wondering so much about the obvious limitations of one author's backward, even prehistoric or medieval, view of women or another author's apologies for capitalism. We know that such things are there;

realism is our ascendancy and these things are with us as well. It is perhaps time to read with other eyes, eyes that do not question the obvious, but eyes that wonder at the belief in a verisimilitude so complete and so fulfilled that it could, like Laplace's demon, predict every future textual position. It is time to read realism as the figure that produces the fiction of verisimilitude that still holds sway.

To that end, I have been writing and assembling a series of studies that are by and large devoted to some of the canonical works of nineteenth-century French realist literature. I start the next chapter at a moment just before realism, in a reading of Stendhal's *De l'amour* as symptomatic of the realism that is going to come into being in Stendhal's own work. After that, I look at what could be considered the moment of "reflection" of realism itself, the famous description of a mirror that Stendhal uses to discuss his theory of writing. The last part of the chapter is devoted to a reading of the signifying practices at work in *La Chartreuse de Parme*; it is my interest to see the signs by which and through which the realist enterprise is constantly stopping and starting. If one of the hallmarks of the received knowledge about the paradigms of realism is the sense of continuity, both in the act of representation and in the represented, along with the coterminality of the systems of signifiers and signifieds, the *Chartreuse* shows how the act of communication for Stendhal is always made of silences, gaps, and interruptions.

Following the chapter on Stendhal is a series of readings of some of Balzac's works, including *Le Père Goriot*, *La Muse du département*, and *La Cousine Bette*. In these readings I try to show how Balzac, while setting up the praxes of continuity on which his oeuvre depends, ruptures the works at various strategic points. In particular, in *Le Père Goriot*, Balzac disrupts the communicational model by putting the whole process of proper reading into perspective. And even more important, he shows how, in one scene of recognition (the discovery of Vautrin's true identity as Trompe-la-Mort), the models of reproduction and ideological dominance on which his works thrive rely on a context of marginalization, disruption, and even perversion. In keeping with my interest in the representation of the unrepresentable, I have included a section on Balzac's semiotics of mud, which corresponds in its own way to Stendhal's mirror and to the magmalike flows I discuss further on in the chapter on Flaubert. In

La Muse du département, Balzac in a comic vein disrupts the entire communication model, the roles of the writer and reader, and puts the authority of the "text" into permanent and immediate question. Finally, in *La Cousine Bette* and in *Modeste Mignon*, Balzac writes novels in which the plots themselves depend on series of disruptions, misreadings, misidentifications: these works are what I am calling novels of permanent dyslexia.

In the chapter entitled "Romantic Interruptions," I look at several works of Nerval and a forgotten novella by the younger Dumas. Both authors are part of a second wave of French romanticism and appear initially to have little to do with a realist project of verisimilar representation. I maintain, however, that the influence of realism is so pervasive that even those works are marked by the ideological, representational, and semiotic assumptions that produced both Balzac (for example) and the social construction of the individual as nineteenth-century paragons.

Like realist writing, that of Nerval and Dumas Fils negotiates the representation of the complex. For each, of course, the turn taken is a different one: for Nerval it is a question of defining originality; for Dumas, it is a question of maintaining the unity of a space of production. But in both cases, the game is the same: drawing and representing the complex, when the language offered can do one or the other, but seemingly not both at the same time. In the first part of the chapter, I concentrate on the mechanisms of intertextuality as a disruptive device. Through readings of Nerval's "Angélique" and *Aurélia*, I show how Nerval's work can never even reach the fictional status of being integrated with itself, of being conceived of as a whole, for at every turn, there is an intertextual interruption.

Little known, the Dumas novella *Diane de Lys* is not a great work but is certainly a fascinating one, in which the mechanisms of the myths of realist production are brought to light not as some reflection of continuities, but again, as a series of fragmentary interruptions. As so few people are familiar with the novella, in this part of the chapter I have broken with my usual pattern and told the story. As almost everything else I am examining is highly canonic, I have left reprises of the plot to one side, as I assume that readers are familiar with the ins and outs of the works at hand.

Finally, the last chapter on Flaubert starts with what I would consider to be the bookend to Stendhal's mirror: Flaubert's unfinished novel, *Bouvard et Pécuchet*, in which the very processes of writing come under an ever more acute critique by the author and his critics. The remainder of the chapter is a double interrogation, as befits the status of that author as the great high realist of French fiction, the first prose modernist, and the eternal critic of preceding praxes. It is my contention, as it was in the chapter I devoted to Proust in *The Shock of Men*, that the problematics found in the work of a watershed writer are often uncomfortably reflected in the work of his or her critics. So in this double interrogation I look both at how Flaubert incessantly makes things "unfit" and how critics, even the most perspicacious postmodern ones, are often wont to try to smooth over the permanent crisis of rupture that is the sign of Flaubert's writing.

Though I have begun these pages with a questioning of the word "text," I have not, for all that, considered it either as a model to be rejected or as a word to be eschewed. If I believe in its limitations, I believe ever more strongly in its usefulness. Roland Barthes's *Le Plaisir du texte* is a cry of freedom. The focus on texts and textuality in the sixties, seventies, and eighties saved many of us from a lifetime of slavish submission to a regally defined, unchallengeable canon. These pages may cause some to remember the magic textuality, the sorcery involved in weaving a textile hanging in space, a space that is there even when all the holes are covered up. And if my robbery, my reaving, my ruptured reading can help render—return, depict, melt—realism, I shall be grateful.

CHAPTER 2

Stendhal's Inventions

Pre-Realist Pathology

> I know of no word in Greek for saying a dis-
> course on the emotions as ideology indicates a
> discourse on ideas.
>
> Stendhal, *De l'amour*

Among Stendhal's early works, *De l'amour*, *Racine et Shakespeare*, and
Vie de Rossini, published in rapid succession between 1822 and 1824,
stand out as inaugurating a new phase in the author's writing. *De
l'amour* is the first of his books that breaks with the biographies and
histories that had previously occupied him and which had been
largely influenced by already published works of other writers. The
technique of adaptation was one that served Stendhal well and which
he continued to use as late as the *Chroniques italiennes*. Along with
Stendhal's original panegyric, *Vie de Rossini*, published at the height
of Rossini's renown, *De l'amour* and *Racine et Shakespeare* mark the
beginning of a period in Stendhal's writing that depends far more on
the author's own imagination and originality than it does on his tal-
ents as a scribe or adapter of what others had written.

Today, the best known of these three works is *Racine et Shakespeare*, which, along with the "Bataille d'Hernani," that raged around

Hugo's play, still figures as a touchstone of the nineteenth-century version of the battle of the ancients and moderns. The *Vie de Rossini* is seldom mentioned.[1] And of *De l'amour*, seemingly the work of a belated ideologue following eighteenth-century models, tradition has retained the commonplace of "crystallization." Crystallization is Stendhal's "shocking" neologism for "the operation of the mind, that makes the discovery from all presented to it that the beloved object has new perfections" (*De l'amour* 31). For Stendhal, "crystallization" is a phenomenon of nature: someone drops a bare branch of a tree in a salt mine in Salzburg. Several months later the branch is withdrawn and it is completely covered in crystals. This natural quality strengthens the metaphoric value of the figure and allows it to describe, and to analyze in a complementary fashion, the phenomena of human existence. The fact that this metaphor is natural, albeit motivated by certain human actions, allows the human to be brought back to the natural without resistance to metaphoricity. Thus the analytic and, ultimately, the narrative modes of describing phenomena are brought back to nature, facilitated in this passage by the metaphor of crystallization.[2]

By and large, the metaphor of crystallization is all that remains for us of *De l'amour*. Still, the book is revolutionary, for it is a break with the writing of the past in general and Stendhal's own previous writing in particular: it is his first independent, original essay and it is the spot in which he chooses to expound upon his theory of the novel. The exposition begins with the classic disclaimer of many novelists: "My goal was to indicate that, though it be called love, this was not a novel, and especially, that it was not entertaining like a novel" (35). What could Stendhal mean? If we know what defines the novel we can measure the import of Stendhal's denial. Though the novel is certainly the most elusive of literary genres, most critics could probably agree on a heuristic definition: it is a long narrative in prose with characters, organization, development, and plot.[3]

Despite the fact that this book does not even fit that most superficial definition, since it lacks all these features, I would still contend that *De l'amour* is Stendhal's first novel. As intrinsic to the novel as the phenomena just mentioned is one additional characteristic: *De l'amour* has a theory of the novel. And I would therefore contentiously propose a definition to replace the first: a novel is a sustained anecdotal narrative that has a theory of the novel in it. In the case of *De l'amour*, this theory is triple: the book denies its novelicity; it is a theory for a novel to be, but one that has not yet been written; it is both a straightforward and a dialectical critique of the genre. In fact, one could argue that the theory is even more radically essential than any of the contingent or accidental features of the novel as a genre, for it is theory that allows for the contradictory presence of plot, character, development, and the like. It is theory that permits the suppression of various negations and contradictions. As Julia Kristeva admirably shows in *Le Texte du roman*, theory reasons: in that organization, it establishes a hierarchy that suppresses the anarchistic elements of novelistic writing.

The familiar phrase "this is not a novel" winds up in many prefaces and expositions. A transparent means of excusing the depiction of shady morality, it simultaneously attempts to elevate the novel beyond simple diversion to a level of moral or metaphysical truth. And Stendhal, for one, claims to be interested in telling the truth in his writing: "I am making every possible effort to be dry. I want to silence my heart which believes it has a lot to say. I always tremble when I realize I have written only a sigh, when I think I have marked down a truth" (46). Stendhal couples this feint with another old trick: he pretends that the manuscript is not his, but simply something that has come into his hands. These means of avoiding the censor are the *mises-en-fiction* defining a framework or limit and serving as rhetorical devices marking the double movement of the writing both into fiction and into metaphysical truth. The denial of novelicity potentially marks the fiction as fiction and retains this mark even as it raises the fiction to a level of truth: "Each of us writes by chance what seems to be true to us, and each contradicts his neighbor. I see in our books just so many lottery tickets; they really have no more value than that" (72). At the same time, these feints protecting the author and putting him on a higher moral ground may help capture the reader's good will, and thereby induce the latter to accept the work as metaphysical truth, or at least as a neutral analysis of love.

It is an easy rhetorical feint for an author to write the phrase "this is not a novel"; it is just as easy for critics to ignore the phrase because of its ubiquity: the denial is entirely transparent. But here the denial of novelicity appears in a work where the remark seems out of place; moreover, the denial is found at the strategic discussion of crystallization. The denial of novelicity helps Stendhal defend his neologism as a useful means for analyzing love; certainly it is not his intention to shock the reader (35–36). The word, so he says, is a solution to an analytical problem; had he more literary talent, he would have avoided the neologism: "I admit that it would have taken literary talent to avoid [the word]; I attempted it, though without success" (35). Without literary talent, the author might still appear to be writing a bad novel. With literary talent, this book would not exist: Stendhal would have written a novel. Thus this is and is not a novel: it is a failed attempt and a poor substitute for a novel; on the other hand, it is an analysis substituted for the maudlin, the sentimental, and the merely amusing. Stendhal's denial is a way of going beyond potential accusations that he had written a bad novel, or used bad novelistic technique; it is the means of positing a field beyond the novels and their antitheses available to Stendhal at the time. Stendhal's "non-novel" is a means of attempting a new approach to novels, one that will substitute cogent analysis for the foolish and stereotypical excesses of sentimental fiction.

Stendhal even comments on the construction of the point of view. He defends his use of the first person, as he warns the reader not to understand it as a revelation of some personal subjectivity, and therefore of some analogy to sentimental fiction:

It is to be recalled that if the author sometimes uses the first person [*la tournure du je*], it is to try to vary the form of this essay somewhat. He has no pretense of offering his own feelings to the readers. He seeks to present, with the least amount of monotony possible for him, what he has observed in others. (111n)

Indeed, we may read the presence of the first person as the indication of a lack of alternatives. He has no other way to write. Successfully writing something cogent depends on the powers of observation and analysis of a perceptive writer, and Stendhal may indeed realize that the point of view he needs, the neutral third-person point of view nominally based on solid observation and analysis, as opposed to some godlike manipulative omniscience beyond textuality, has quite simply not yet been invented.

Along with the denial of novelicity at a critical point in his book and repeated in the first preface, comes another overt mark of novelicity in *De l'amour*: an intermittent complicated commentary on the novel as genre and praxis. *De l'amour* does not pretend to be a theory of the novel in the way *Racine et Shakespeare* is a theory of drama. Rather, like any strong novel that stakes out its own territory, *De l'amour* has an inherent theory proposing the novel's modes of representation, its hierarchies, its suppressions, and its semiotics. The theory organizes the material, refuses the anarchic, and sets up a rhetoric of comprehensibility. The inherent theory of any individual work is at least partly autoreferential, even if it can be extended to other works or if the facts themselves eventually upset the theory.[4] Here, however, there is no novel, in the traditional sense of the word, to be justified. *De l'amour* occupies a muddy middle ground: as an anecdotal narrative, it does not have the independence of theory from praxis that *Racine et Shakespeare* has; the latter is completely divorced from the theater on which it comments. *De l'amour* is only partially independent: there is always the possibility that its commentary relates to the organization of the anecdotes used for analysis.

In brief, *De l'amour* provides two kinds of commentary on the novel. The first set of comments relate to the existing genre. There are extensive remarks on the praxis of the novel, works by Stendhal's predecessors and contemporaries, works of which he by and large disapproves. The other set of comments is ultimately the more fascinating, for it is a sketch of a theory for a novel as yet unwritten and even unimagined, except as a theoretical construct. *De l'amour* is a novel in that it defines a locus in which a novel can occur. The work opens up a space of writing without being prescriptive in its theoretical judgments. It is not that, having written *De l'amour*, Stendhal will automatically be able to go on to write the masterpiece *Le Rouge et le Noir*, just as having written *Jean Santeuil* is not sufficient for Proust to be able to produce the *Recherche*. What it does mean is that through writing *De l'amour*, Stendhal has begun to address the theoretical problems for which *Le Rouge et le Noir* will be, to a great extent, his first successful answer: problems relating to the construction of a character, the interrelationship between the independent character and the narrative forces that tie or bind, the relation between the expression of desire and the expressions of language, and so forth. Thus a more sophisticated statement would be the following: in the theory of the novel proposed in *De l'amour*, Stendhal potentially hypothesizes the contradictions, ruptures, and interruptions that he will begin to render in his novel several years later.

In his mature works, Stendhal will engage a problematic of the double articulation of the subject of enunciation and the subject of action. Specifically, the greatest theoretical problem facing Stendhal is the following: Are the apparition of a protagonist and the development of a narrative contradictory or mutually supporting obligations in the realist novel? In *Le Rouge et le Noir*, Stendhal will struggle with letting Julien function as a subject independent of constraints, just as he, the author, simultaneously struggles with the creation of a world in which Julien fits and therefore by which he is consequently limited in his actions. At the level of the construction of the genre, and not merely at some level of a character's existential choice, freedom and the expression of desire are confronted with narrative conformity and analysis.

To follow Stendhal's radical critique of novelicity in *De l'amour*, we need to see the problematics of the genre he faced. To that end I am proposing a short recapitulation of some points of literary history so that the reader can appreciate what Stendhal's critique engages.[5] The novel is a comparatively recent genre whose social source is in the development of the bourgeoisie and the mercantile class. Its generic origin is found in the gradual development of a form out of an episodic, lay narrative that is courtly or picaresque. By the time the eighteenth-century novel reaches its maturity, the epistolary novel is in full swing. The novels of eighteenth-century France in general, along with the English epistolary novel, show a profound leaning toward the episodic: plots are often thin threads corresponding to only the most superficial matters in the work; weak, flaccid plots provide only the most mechanical of resolutions, and the interest in the works is found in the episodic treatment of material, the deployment of sentiment, and the construction of a power structure in narrative. Still, some contemporaneous English novels already begin to focus on the verisimilar development of a character grounded in real time. The crystallization of the genre that occurs in the novels of Daniel Defoe, for example, makes the hero or heroine a typical representative of his or her time, with few if any larger-than-life qualities. The hero(ine) is a protagonist who struggles in and against a system and whose strength of character is wholly consonant with an act of verisimilar portraiture. Indeed, the theory grounding the works— whether it be the possibility of constructing a world, as in *Robinson Crusoe*, or that of representing feminine independence, if not to say desire, as in *Moll Flanders*, makes possible the consistency and verisimilitude of a protagonist and the portrait of a society against which he or she stands.[6]

To say that the subject of action takes form is not to say that the eighteenth century lacks a problematic of narrative form. The problems posed by the epistolarity of Richardson or Rousseau or by the enunciative structures of Sterne are as central to the development of the novel as the solidification of the subject. As it develops, the novel searches for a form in which to cast the contents of a profane world and draw its portrait in prose. Thus the epistolary novel is one means of developing a profane form of writing in which there is no a priori authority system formally embodied in a narrative discourse. By providing multiple points of view, the author of the epistolary novel undercuts the possibility of establishing a definitive and authoritative point of view outside the action (the énoncé) of the various intercutting récits. At the same time, having posited a position of enunciation, the narrator of *Tristram Shandy* spends much of the novel undercutting that very position, either through a questioning, an act of reflexivity, or a vitiation of the énoncé. With nothing to tell, it matters little what the position of enunciation is. The eighteenth century posits both a set of fields in which the genre develops and a set of problems with which future practitioners of the genre have eventually to deal. In effect, then, the adequation of the nineteenth-century novel provides some common measure between the discourse of the subject of action and the totalizing discourse of the subject of enunciation translated into the omniscient narrator.

The road between both sentimental and epistolary novels and the novel that does not yet exist is certainly not straightforward. Indeed, there are at least two bodies of narrative fiction between the novel of the eighteenth century and the nineteenth-century realist novel: the romantic or confessional novel, like Goethe's *Werther* and Madame de Staël's *Corinne*, and the historical novel, epitomized by the work of Walter Scott. In some ways, what we come to think of as the nine-teenth-century novel, and especially Stendhal's own work, is a syn-thesis of these two strands. His works will show the priority of an in-dividual agent or actor, a subject of action faced with the necessity of historical truth and the verisimilitude of form and detail. On the one hand, as far as the construction of the individual character is con-cerned, the nascent nineteenth-century novel has the strength of the romantic invention of memory as *Erinnerung*, an act of rememora-tion that is the equivalent of the rhetorical inscription of the truth. On the other hand, the nineteenth-century novel will make use of the fictional construct of the verisimilar, based on a historical point of view, a purportedly objective frame of reference where authority is historical fact and not the prejudices or metaphysics of a sacred system determined to maintain itself whatever the cost. For the verisimilitude that develops in the nineteenth century, authority is the self-effacing transcription of a global truth in which essence is re-vealed. Thus the invention of this verisimilitude that is the praxis of realism gets its strength and momentum from this double-barreled inscription of the truth: the individual truth of the feeling subject able to narrate himself or herself combined with the global truth of objective history.

The dialectical point of view also seems the most appropriate for the novel because it is the writing of a society whose vision of its own development is eminently dialectical.[7] Stendhal would find this vision not "dialectical" but deeply novelistic; for him it would be the appro-priate picture of the constant ironization of a society that changes be-cause of its narratives: "One can say anything with a look, and yet, one can always deny a look, for it cannot be repeated textually" (87–88). Thus Stendhal is participating in constructing an idea of writing as he asks what can be represented in narrative and how the real is to be transcribed. These questions are not answered here, for Stendhal still must engage those who have written the world before him.

Stendhal has generalized from the look of love to the position of a general observer.[8] Just as the position of the lover is metamor-phosed into that of the observer producing writing, the theory of this narrative is already ironized by a constantly changing dialectic. The gaps appear even as the writing comes into being:

I have just reread one hundred pages of this essay; I have given rather a poor idea of true love, of love that concerns the whole soul, fills it with images that are sometimes the most felicitous and sometimes the most disheartening, but always sublime, and makes it completely unaware of everything else that exists. I do not know how to express what I see so well; I have never felt more painfully my lack of talent. (98)

But the truth needs always to have been there to be revealed as such. The dialectic does not engender a truth that was once fully absent and is now in the process of becoming absolute. By extension, then, the truth of the novel has always to have been there: realism is the sum or product of the dialectics that precede it. However neat it may be, this vision does not allow the novel the act of invention that it allows for all other aspects of the dialectic. Whereas the objectivity of history, the possibility of absolute knowledge, and the profanation of authority are all inventions, the realist novel is not perceived as such. It is seen rather as either the natural organic development of the novel or the natural dialectic of the novel.

Striking in this work that "is not a novel" are the extensive references to fictional narrative, with at least fifty references in the two analytical sections of the book preceding the fragments and accounting for well over two hundred pages in the Gallimard Folio edition. Sometimes the references are nothing more than allusions to a well-known novel like *Corinne* or *La Nouvelle Héloïse*. Though unworthy of being reference points, says Stendhal, these novels are sometimes all he has to serve as examples, be they negative or positive. Everyone has read and remembered them; everyone will know to what he is alluding. Indeed, the vacuity of the references serves him well; because of the novel's ability to represent typical situations, these commonplaces are more useful than the truth:

A man who has lived finds a whole host of examples of loves in his memory and has a wealth of choices. But if he wants to write, he no longer knows on what to rely. Tales from particular social groups in which he has lived are unknown to the public, and he would need an immense number of pages in order to relate them with the necessary nuances. It is for that reason that I quote well-known novels, but I do not make the ideas I am submitting to the reader depend on such empty fictions, most often calculated more for the picturesque effect than for the truth. (64–65n)

The truth itself is not transcribable through an act of alienation of this truth from oneself or through dogged perseverance. Stendhal already sees the truth as that which inherently resists the process of representation that is narrative. Thus narrative, be it fictional or analytical, is not a process of transcription of truth, but a means by which truth is merely represented in writing. Representation is not simply the opposite of truth, for that is the role assigned to the picturesque, the sentimental yet false inscription of the world in fiction. The role of representation—here as analysis and eventually as the novel—is to simulate the truth through the sleight-of-hand process of representation that is a calculation of the truth. Here, the inscription of empty fictions serves as an alibi for the very analysis that denies the support provided by the fictional exempla. Stendhal uses fictions as references and undercuts these references with a critique of the poverty of the novel.

Despite his critique of the novel, Stendhal still chooses to end his analysis with a chapter entitled "Werther et Don Juan." This concluding chapter is a long, detailed comparison of the two heroes; it serves concomitantly as a summation of the author's arguments on love. Instead of producing final arguments within the ideological and analytical frameworks that characterize *De l'amour*, Stendhal cheats for aesthetic reasons. Narrative, not philosophy or ideology, will provide the conclusion. At first glance, the chapter would appear to be merely a question of whether a man should act with women more like Mozart's Don Juan or like Goethe's Werther:

The role of [*des*] Saint-Preux is sweeter and fills all the moments of existence, but one must agree that Don Juan's role is more brilliant. . . . What makes me think all the Werthers happier is that Don Juan reduces love to being just an ordinary matter. Instead of having, as does Werther, realities modeled on his desires, he has desires that are imperfectly satisfied by cold reality, as in ambition, greed, and other passions. Instead of getting lost in the enchanting dreams of crystallization, he thinks like a general of the success of his maneuvers, and, in a word, kills love instead of enjoying it more than others do, as the vulgar believe. (237–38)

Now one would initially assume that Stendhal favors Werther or Rousseau's Saint-Preux over Don Juan because the first two are capable of the all-important crystallization of love, whereas Don Juan seems to reduce love to a function. Yet Stendhal criticizes Werther and Saint-Preux throughout *De l'amour*; they are hardly the figures he needs for a strong image of love and for a conclusion to his analyses. Most interesting in the comparison is not the contrast between the two characters drawn from the arts, but rather the insistence on novelicity. Not only does Stendhal use two fictional characters to exemplify his conclusions on love; he also substitutes within the realm of fiction: "The contrast would be more exact had I quoted Saint-Preux, but he is such a flat character that I would wrong tender souls if I offered him to them as being representative" (235).[9] Stendhal reaches the startling conclusion that to write it is necessary to separate truth and representation. Aesthetic value has as much importance, if not more, than the ideal incarnation of the truth. By separating truth and representation, Stendhal effects what he calls elsewhere "the first step."[10]

The argument about Werther, Saint-Preux, and Don Juan is thus triple. First, it is a concluding argument to his book, yet it is undercut by the very use of fictional figures as the vehicles for analyses. Second, it is a criticism of the novel that provides these figures as the only ones possible as vehicles of sentimental truth. And third, it is the ghost argument for the novel that does not yet exist. Still, even if only teleologically, the conclusion to *De l'amour* does forecast the development of an analytical aesthetic of love in Stendhal's mature novels, especially *Le Rouge et le Noir* and *La Chartreuse de Parme*. Now, the drawback to this third part of the argument is clear, for it implies that there is a possibility of theoretical resolution without praxis. It would imply that Stendhal's aesthetic of representation is already in place long before he gets around to writing *Le Rouge et le Noir* or even the earlier *Armance*, which would then be only fulfillments of an analytic. It does, however, open up a field in which Stendhal can eventually explore.

Stendhal has nowhere else to turn, because the possibility of Julien Sorel does not yet exist. Significantly, the chapter on "Werther et Don Juan" marks a stop, as it ends the continuously developed and rationally argued part of the work, almost as if what he needed to write—a novel with a Julien Sorel-like hero—could not be written. Instead of that novel, there is a break and a heterogeneous assemblage of diverse thoughts. The thoughts are bits and pieces, palimpsests on already drawn stereotyped images. Just as the book as a whole repeats and rewrites the stereotyped images of love in its constant references to novels, this part repeats the possibly valid fragmentary analyses to be found in the same genre. The observations are either to be considered well-worn and modest scrawls, wholly unoriginal because preceded by other writing, or they are to be considered fragments, not of a work that was, but of some work to be. So the passages in the section of "Fragments divers" are analyses for the novel that Stendhal has not yet written, sketches of characters and situations not yet written. In fragmenting an as yet unknown whole, Stendhal can rescue what he will from the past for the novel of the future.

The novel is a complex figure in *De l'amour*, formed of a denial, a critique, a rewriting, and a theoretical possibility. What can be said about the parts of this complex figure? First of all, the novel is, as we have seen with *Werther* or *La Nouvelle Héloïse*, a common reference point. Stendhal assumes the readers of *De l'amour*, who are not yet the hypothetical and belatedly apostrophized "happy few," will have read the novels of the eighteenth century as well as more recent works. These novels would include the list of books given in Fragment 165 (314), "the books from which Lisio [one of the narrator's alter egos] took his reflections and conclusions." Among these works are *Manon Lescaut*, *Tom Jones*, *Werther*, *Lettres d'une religieuse portugaise*, and novels of Auguste La Fontaine, along with various memoirs and letters.

As the reader may suspect, the list is not innocent, because it does not accurately reflect the references in the work. It tends to sin by omitting several of the constant references of *De l'amour*, including *La Princesse de Clèves*, *La Nouvelle Héloïse*, *Les Liaisons dangereuses*, the works of Madame de Staël, and most egregiously, the novels of Walter Scott.[11] In *De l'amour*, the largest number of literary references are to the works of Scott; their omission from this list is all the more notable because heretofore Stendhal has made reference to them more than obvious, as he often quotes at length from Scott in the original English. Thus Stendhal's writing neither covers the references nor covers up the blatant omissions. And with the exception of the presence of Werther on the list, the absences are more important for the essay than the books listed.

The presence and absence of certain references bring us to Stendhal's critique of novelicity, for the slippage in references reminds us of the very ambiguous nature of these references for Stendhal. At this point, one might ask what is so noxious about novels and specifically about the novelistic. Certainly Stendhal is not merely rehearsing the old Rousseauistic argument about the dangers of novel-reading, an argument joined to and issued from an even older debate on antitheatricality. The antitheatrical prejudice translated here into an antinovelistic prejudice relates fundamentally to the substitution of typicality, and thus of generalization and falsity, for the truth. Representation is a distortion both of mimesis and of the truth itself. Now to escape the vicissitudes and dangers of this act of false representation—though we have already seen to what extent this work is indeed founded on acts of representation—Stendhal merely has to produce the standard disclaimer already discussed about the book not being a novel. Why then go to such lengths in a critique of novelicity, in an insistence on novelicity, in a work where this seems to have no place?

Something in the traditional novel is profoundly unnerving, unsettling, and disruptive to Stendhal. The novelistic is not the locus of the falsified emotions that Rousseau sees in the theater, but of exaggerated emotions: "a tender, generous, ardent, or as the vulgar say, novelistic, soul" (36). The novelistic vulgarizes and stylizes emotion; it allows the group to provide a general conferral of meaning on fine nuances, something which Stendhal has indicated is contrary to true analysis. The vulgar seizes the word "novelistic" and all that the word truly or falsely represents in itself. Thus the validity of reference and representation in the novel becomes strictly undecidable, for the novelist has been joined or displaced by the plural voices of the vulgar. For Stendhal, the novel has already been debased so much as to cover a realm of stereotypicality in which the vulgar see the always unattainable idealized image of themselves. The novelistic has fallen into the hands of the unhappy many, who already exist in quite a banal fashion. To produce a novel, Stendhal must pin his hopes on the happy few, who do not yet exist.

Reflected anew in an audience that is always debasing the act of representation by turning it into a typicality, the novel becomes the index of what is low and false: "People blamed Mme de Struve for being novelistic, and only virtue, pushed to the novelistic, could touch L. B. She had him shot quite young" (79). The novelistic is both an exaggeration and a falsification that extends beyond the true and the real into an internalized distention that is not merely a phenomenon of reflection. The novelistic is inherently dangerous because it is both not true enough and too true at the same time. For if it falls into the typical, if it can be bartered and redefined by the vulgar, it also has the internal capacity of representing the extraordinary all too well. Beyond the apparent weaknesses of sentimentality and typicality, what is problematic in the novel is a lack of control.

The novel is the genre that exceeds its laws and upsets its own protocols. More and more, we realize that the errancy of love is a problem of the novel: "From the moment he loves, the wisest man no longer sees anything as it is. . . . Fears and hopes immediately become somewhat novelistic (wayward)" (50).[12] In *De l'amour*, the positions of reader, writer, and hero are not yet distinguished from one another and the novel is the wayward writing that makes them stray. The wayward adventure is the event in the novel whose meaning is only known or revealed once all the peripeteia have come to an end. The wayward son returns home and all is understood. But the wayward is equally the mark of the narrative which, because it is a form that represents through translation, wanders away from the truth of presence. The writing of the novel is wayward in that it does not freely or directly give the event it describes.

I have just indicated that the positions of the hero, writer, and reader are not yet separated in this nascent state of the novel. Their combined figure is the figure of the lover, who though blinded by love sees things in a new light. Untying these positions will eventually allow Stendhal to write a novel, *Le Rouge et le Noir* or *La Chartreuse de Parme*. When separated, the functions allow for the development of the hero as the protagonist, the establishment of the position of authoritative analysis, and the figuration of the rhetorically posited receptor of event analysis, récit, and discourse. An untying of these positions occurs as Stendhal is able to save what he will from the novel of the past by reducing its wayward state. His novel of the future will base its analyses and calculations on its own representational fictions, which have the allure of truth.

In *De l'amour*, the positions of event and analysis are still joined.

As it stands, the novel provides a locus for a clear remembering in an analytical sense, multiply written and always reinscribed: "As for the new viewpoints that a novel suggests for knowledge of the human heart, I still remember the old ones well; I even like to find them as annotations in the margins" (55). The problem with the traditional novel is that it substitutes analysis mixed with memory for the presence of the moment of love. A novel remembers for Stendhal, but he loses the essential, which is the "flight of fancy of love that cannot be written down [*qui ne peut se noter*]" (54). When love is written down in the novel it is deadened and transformed into philosophical analysis; it is this analysis, instead of the flight of fancy Stendhal wants but cannot enunciate, that is inscribed and remembered both now and in the future. Thus the fault of the novel is that memory is always internalized in the writing and in its reader. The writing of the novel or the reading of this writing voids the signified, the content, and the referent, and replaces them with the palimpsest that Stendhal has already remarked. The writing of the novel may freeze a moment and make it permanent, but there is an inescapable loss. Even though the flight of fancy "is the novel's true pleasure" (55), it is situated outside the writing, before the writing, or in an elsewhere that the writing of the novel does not or cannot yet inscribe. The reverie then can be produced in the reader as an afterthought or as a reaction, but it is at the expense of the writing itself.

The trouble with novels is that they have denatured humanity itself. As a result of the interminable pseudo-philosophical analyses in novels, the reader of these novels is caught in a trap of believing that he too must behave like a novel: "To express what one feels, in such a lively and detailed fashion, is a burden imposed on oneself because one has read novels; were one natural, one would never undertake such a painful thing" (75). We have, says Stendhal, all been transformed by the novel. It should be easy to write a novel based on nature, yet it is not at all easy, even for Stendhal, who, if deprived of literary talent (72), understands what is natural. Involuted upon itself and its reception and evolving dialectically according to its rhetoric, the novel is wholly cut off from nature. Nothing should be simpler for Stendhal than describing reality, but the pervasive ubiquity of the novel, the seeming typicality of its forms and functions, prevents him from doing so: in his world, writing is always substituted for the real thing.

This is not all bad, for Stendhal can get to know what is in his heart, and eventually, he will be able to surmise what is in the heart of his protagonist, for what is in his heart, be it reverie or memory, is readable, since it is already writing. Nature no longer exists, if it ever did, outside of writing: Stendhal ultimately concludes that writing has always replaced the natural. Indeed, the natural can only be considered, seen, or defined as "natural" if there is writing to say so. This is as much true in the world of ideas and ideals as it is in the objective world. Writing is always preceded by other writing; in fact, writing precedes imagination itself which is made possible only by writing. All writing is a palimpsest and everything else is an impossibility:

Imagine a rather complicated geometric figure, sketched with a white pencil on a slate. Well, I am going to explain this geometric figure, but there is a necessary condition: it must already exist on the slate. I cannot trace it myself. This impossibility is what makes it so difficult to write a book on love that is not a novel. (337)

Perhaps an impossibility can rhetorically produce a difficulty; logically, an impossibility can only continue to be an impossibility. Logically then it is impossible to produce a book on love that is not a novel. Yet it is this impossible figure that must found the new novel. What is necessary then is a reversal; since there has always been inscription Stendhal must write a novel that is not a novel: "I was writing in the French language, but not in French literature" (168). The white-on-black writing of the geometric figure has to be reversed into black on white, whereby it will seem there has been a transcription of the natural into writing.

To be sure, this reversal is not that of the opposition of "novelistic" and "prosaic," a flight from the effusiveness of the novel into the coldness of prose: "Prosaic is a new word, that I used to find ridiculous, because there is nothing colder than our poetry. If there has been some heat during the last fifty years in France, it is assuredly in prose" (248). Stendhal needs a different kind of warmth for his work, one that he has not yet invented. Still, in one sentence he does promise Monsieur de Rênal and Julien or even Charles Bovary and Léon: "one must have a prosaic husband and get a novelistic lover" (249).

With the figure proposed for the novel of the future, we can re-

turn to the famous image of crystallization, which is what many remember of *De l'amour*, and reconsider the hypothesis that crystallization is, for Stendhal, an image of the new novel. For Stendhal,
crystallization is not the solidification of the moment of love during
which love forms a solid core out of the vague set of unchanneled
emotional reactions and perceptions of the lover. Crystallization is
the process whereby the lover discovers new perfections in the beloved. This first crystallization is most often reinforced by a second
crystallization, which Stendhal does not fail to describe with a reference to the novel: "This second crystallization is missing in simple
women who are quite far from all these novelistic ideas."

To justify or to account for the word, Stendhal develops the metaphor of crystallization from an anecdote:

Let a lover's mind work for twenty-four hours and this is what you will find:
   In the Salzburg salt mines, one throws down into the abandoned depths
of the mine a tree branch that has lost its leaves in the winter; two or three
months later, the branch is retrieved and it is covered with brilliant crystal-
lizations . . . the primitive branch can no longer be recognized. (31)

Since Stendhal's book pretends to be one of applied analysis rather
than pure philosophy, we need not question the use of a foundational
metaphor as such. More important, the metaphor itself seems not to
fit. The mind of the lover is compared to the mysterious force of nature at work, yet it is ostensibly in the mind of the lover that the crystallization occurs. In the metaphor, the forces or agents are separate;
in the analysis or in reality, they are joined. In the metaphor, something living is killed: the branch of the tree could be reborn in the
spring. Burying it at the bottom of the mine effectively kills it and
though it becomes an object of beauty that joins timelessness, it is at
the expense of life itself. Patently, Stendhalian crystallization cannot
kill love. Moreover, the crystals are a replacement: the leaves, temporarily absent, are permanently replaced by the crystals. Again, if
the love is fixed it dies; if it is seen as a replacement it is factitious.
Stendhalian love cannot be a replacement but must always be born
anew. About the only thing that seems to work in the metaphor is its
correspondence to the discovery of new facts.

After all is said and done, the metaphor for crystallization just
does not work for Stendhal's conception of love. It does, however,

match Stendhal's inchoate conception of the novel of the future. The crystals replace the living, emotional, but uncapturable contents of love. They fix the vision which is a multiplicity of views that combine to form a whole that presents itself reflexively: the mysterious forces at work, the subjectivity of labor, is separate from the object upon which it effects its mysterious and invisible work. The novel comes out of the black box of the mine, dead and eternalized, with the critical facts of its prose having replaced and rewritten the fluttering leaves of the living object. In trying to write a book of love, in trying not to write a novel, Stendhal has certainly done both, but perhaps most important for us, he has laid the theoretical groundwork and written the inevitable palimpsest for the novels of the future, of which we, his readers, will most certainly be the happy few.

Stendhal's Mirror

In my library, French realism happens between two specific points: page 556 of the first volume of the Pléiade edition of Stendhal's novels and page 983 of the second volume of the Pléiade edition of Flaubert's works. A world happens between those two points that I am somewhat arbitrarily—and somewhat less than arbitrarily—calling the beginning and end of French narrative realism. Within that time period, whole textual worlds come into being, flourish, and perhaps most significantly, even compete with the real one. I will admit that the beginning and end points are not absolute and in fact are rather murky. Other candidates could be found, and one could certainly argue for multiple beginnings that would include a point of self-reflection in *Le Père Goriot* or even, though with greater difficulty, some moment in *Notre-Dame de Paris*. And as I have just shown in the preceding pages, there is a beginning before the beginning in Stendhal's own *De l'amour*.

At the other end, one could reasonably argue that Zola still is a realist. Zola continues Flaubert's struggles, and *L'Assommoir* is substantially contemporaneous with *Bouvard et Pécuchet*. Though Zola's writing takes an approach to the problem that depends on the fulfillment of realist promise, the *Rougon-Macquart*—which only became the naturalist novel with the publication of *L'Assommoir* and *Nana*—continues many of the problematics of realism by pushing the search for both detail and continuity to its ultimate limit. In subsequent works, the author fine-tunes the mechanism of naturalism, but for me, he does not really add anything else technically to the construction of the genre. Indeed, I would even argue that Zola's installation of the mechanism of scientific description, the rules of collecting data and of dispassionate observation, the fidelity to heredity, and the eschewing of psychology are for me the playing out of the death of realism that Flaubert has already predicted in *Bouvard et Pécuchet*. As much as I am interested, for other reasons, in the rest of Zola's oeuvre, I do not believe that after that point, for all his invention, Zola either adds or devises anything new for the realist repertoire. Still, one could argue in favor of Zola, even for a book like his *Lourdes*, as a death-knell for realism. And as I have already indicated, in many ways realism is prolonged into the early twentieth century through the age of high modernism in the *roman-fleuve* and in the writing of Gide and Proust, among others. Perhaps even more important, realism still in many ways determines how we read everything else.

So if I pick these two points, they are not as absolutes, but merely as very focused reference points that have helped critics delineate the major pathways of realism. The first point that I mentioned is the famous disquisition on the novel in *Le Rouge et le Noir*, not the passage in which the spurious quotation is used as an epigraph to chapter 13 of the first part (1:288), but the break from the plot in which the Stendhalian narrator tells the readers that a novel is a mirror (1:557). The passage can be read as a call to arms, a marking of difference, and it behooves the reader to consider the aesthetic changes that may or may not come into play. Without that passage, that novel might very well have been read as a late flowering of the first phase of French romanticism, though the argument would be hard to justify nowadays. Indeed, in my article "A Chronicle of Production," I have argued that the mechanisms of production Stendhal establishes at the beginning of *Le Rouge et le Noir* correspond to a means of production that reflects both the movements of an industrialized capitalist society and the economic structures necessary to the realist novel.

It is not that the phrase itself is essential to our understanding of Stendhal; rather, it is a focal moment for our reading, a moment that conveniently asks readers to consider a different approach to the art of writing a novel. That the moment may be spurious in its own way, that the aesthetic of mimetic representation that seems to be implied may in fact be neither Stendhal's aesthetic as demonstrated in the novel nor the nascent aesthetic of realism, is to my mind wholly beside the point. Even if the origin of realism is fantastic or fantasmatic, the convenience of the fiction is not to be ignored. So I would take the moment of that mirror as a watershed, after which we can no longer read nineteenth-century narrative in the same way.

The moment in Stendhal's work places the whole novel retrospectively in a new light, as it seems to demand and simultaneously forestall a new reading. Already, at the beginning of realism, there is cause for concern about how the new praxis may reflect the world, may render it, and what the cost will be. We are asked to read this novel, *Le Rouge et le Noir*, as if it were a narrative that holds a mirror, not up to nature as such, but up to the tamed Rousseauistic nature that is a sign of culture and civilization. And as we recall that for Stendhal this nature is always already inscribed in language, we remember too that Stendhal takes the matter one step further, beyond, so to speak, the famous "first step." For it is not merely what one sees of pure natural beauty that is reflected in the mirror, but the mud along the side of the road, nature having been channeled by engineers who build roads and bridges.

At the other end of this fictional canon I am constructing, I would not necessarily place a passage but an entire work, Flaubert's last, unfinished novel or metanovel, *Bouvard et Pécuchet*. Because of the ways in which the work can be read as a metanovel commenting on the structures and procedures of realist representation, I would propose the whole work as the endpoint for the praxis. Still, within the mass of that single work, one could point to a final moment, a point at which the work begins self-consciously to repeat itself: the pedagogical disaster in which Bouvard and Pécuchet take on the task of imparting their knowledge to others, in this case, the wayward Victor and Victorine (2:967–76). And there is certainly another moment, literally on the threshold between the novel and its nonexistence, the point in the notes for the continuation of the unfinished part of the work, in which the two feckless heroes are going to "copy as before" and to that end, will have a partners' desk (*bureau à double pupitre*) built (2:987).

What Stendhal's mirror and the whole of *Bouvard et Pécuchet* have in common is perhaps nothing more than a coincidence, but if so, it is a felicitous one: the novels are enmired. Stendhal's mirror reflects mud, muck, and mire; in almost every venture, the hapless title characters of Flaubert's work are overwhelmed by disorder, by entropy whose constant sign, it would seem, is the formless mud and muck of a universe gone awry.

What if, just for a moment, we considered that realism was not the attempt to represent the world accurately, but rather the attempt to represent the unrepresentable? This unrepresentable has many incarnations, but at the beginning and end, it is stuck in the midst of a generalized flow that is neither solid nor liquid, a slurry, a *flou*—an unsettled flow, a vagueness—of indeterminate physical state. It is in or with that *flou* that I would like to continue.

For Stendhal there are two ways of seeing the *flou*. Sometimes he conceives of it as a torrent of emotion, a flow or gush strictly subjugated to the language used to describe it. A Rousseauistic outpouring of emotion is channeled into the vehicles provided by an analytical ideology that separates, defines, and orders the flow by minimizing eddies, back-ups, and undercurrents. Yet, at the level of the represented, the *flou* is crystallized in the strict language of the laws of desire in a work like *De l'amour*, where the liquid of a precipitate vanishes to be fixed in a salt-encrusted object, the flow having been slowed down by analysis so that it can be made fast in time or space. In his novels, the flow seems subject to the laws of narration that determine motive, reason, and object. There is no open gap in the *flou* of Stendhal: Fabrice's various impassioned comings and goings or his disorder at Waterloo are overcome when subjected to the laws of space and time, the orders of reason, and the method of writing and reading.

In Stendhal's work, it is always a question of fixing the flow of desire by the imposition of the signifiers. The ardor of the person immediately cools without going through a liquid phase: in other words, there is sublimation without titration. At the end of *Le Rouge et le Noir*, the symptomatic undecidability of life and death is transformed into a marble block, and that marmoreal monument is the prelude to the systematic genocide of the last pages. No one lives happily ever after, because such a resolution would imply that the

flow goes on after the novel has closed, that, in fact, there is unchanneled, changing desire over which the narrative has no control.

In at least one strategic passage, where a psychoanalytic reading
might conveniently see both a denial and the return of the narrative
repressed, Stendhal frames the flow with his famous mirror. By having recourse to metalanguage, Stendhal spins the *flou* around to make
it reflect in a mirror that shows "the muck of the gutters." To be reflected is to be fixed in an image and to be harmlessly rendered; the
picture is set and is the structure that conquers the unchanneled free
flow of desire and of words. No matter how muddy reality is, the
route—*iter* in Latin—is caught in the mirror: a muddy, mucky, un-
crystallizable, and unchannelable reality is immediately reduced to
its own image, in a process that makes it, quite literally, repeatable:
reiterable. The true law of Stendhalian representation, opposed to the
represented on one hand and to the metatextual law enunciated on
the other, is far from being so simple.

Taken at face value, or at least looked at as a strategic starting
point, the passage on the mirror can be understood as a theory of
representation in which the task of the novel is to directly reflect the
world. This is most obvious in the first appearance of the idea, in the
epigraph to chapter 13 of the first part of the novel. The statement
is attributed to Saint-Réal: "A novel: it is a mirror that is taken along
a path [*Un roman: c'est un miroir qu'on promène le long d'un chemin*]"
(1:288). By all accounts, the reference to Saint-Réal is spurious, for
the quote has never been found in Saint-Réal's work; thus we can immediately consider the remark to be an ironic commentary on the
very process of verisimilitude.

Now the analysis of the situation of the remark will show that no
concept of *Wiederspiegelung*—that is to say, reflection as if in a mirror—will cover the very subtle deconstruction of verisimilitude performed by Stendhal. And even this ironic, telling absence has not
stopped critics from seeking the truth of Stendhal's image of the mirror. For, quite simply, the posited idea of realism, which after all was
perhaps Stendhal's "intention," is convenient for the framing of literature, literary period, and narrative technique. For example, in an
extensive archival study, *Un Maître oublié de Stendhal*, Josué Montello
notes a remark in the work of Saint-Réal like the one Stendhal in-

vents, for there is an allusion to a mirror: "There is no better way to avoid this inconvenience than to make them see the images of their faults in History, as in a mirror" (3:263, in Montello 111–12). But is it not the case that, by the elementary strength of the image, by the very use of the image of the mirror, one would naturally assume that there will be reflection on the ideas of verisimilitude, representation, and holistic images? And moreover, a difference from the truth, from a true quotation, should call into question the whole naive concept of the representation of the truth.

Grahame Jones's article about the epigraph merits special attention, not simply as a summary of the readings of the remark by previous critics but for its hypothesis about the reason, be it conscious or subconscious, for the spurious attribution of the remark. As Jones notes: "Saint-Réal literally means the 'holy real,' that is to say, the real treated with such reverence that it becomes sanctified" (242). If the real is holy, it is untouchable, sacred, or even taboo. So it is the name attached to the quote, rather than the quotation itself, that might merit attention. Just as one of the first spurious epigraphs from the novel points to Hobbes, and therefore to the idea of a Leviathan, to the idea of *homo homini lupus*, rather than to some detailed, accurate statement, so too the name of Saint-Réal may be more of a clue to the determination of meaning than the quotation itself. Here it is not even the author Saint-Réal but his name, as if the name might somehow, despite all telling indicators about the truth, be the sign of what is going on. In a sense, this is a double bind: the quotation about the truth is spurious and thus it is not the truth. The name of the truth, however, is real and true, yet that truth is untouchable and it too fails to be true. Yet, at the same time, that is the truth of the narrative: that it is not true. The truth of reality is, perhaps in the last instance, unmarkable, unrealizable, and finally, eternally absent from the novel. With or without its spurious origins in the works or name of Saint-Réal (which could also be read as Saint Royal, by using Spanish as the origin for "real"), the epigraph thus becomes an important literary *trouvaille* for Stendhal.

As Georges Blin (59) astutely points out: "He uses it again as an alibi, or as he said, a decoy or lightning rod [*paratonnerre*] in 'the second real preface' of the *Chasseur Vert*, then, more ingeniously developed, as an apology in the third preface." This lightning rod draws our attention and makes us focus, but it also may serve to draw our attention away from the fact that Stendhal is not producing *Wieder-spiegelung*. Even when we have dealt with the first, superficial levels of interpretation and seen them to be the decoys that they are, we are still drawn to the playing out of the remark. Stendhal chooses to re-call the epigraph during his long explanation (or digression) about the character of Mathilde de la Mole (1:559). These paragraphs form a defense of his painting of her character and a rationalization of her nature: "This character is entirely of the imagination . . . the per-sonality of Mathilde is impossible in our century" (1:557). In the space in which I have inserted an ellipsis, Stendhal embroiders on the fragment that he has supposedly taken from Saint-Réal:

Well, sir, a novel is a mirror walking along a main road. Sometimes it reflects the azure skies for your eyes, sometimes the mire of the puddles of the road. And the man who carries the mirror in his basket will be accused by you of being immoral! His mirror shows the mire, and you accuse the mirror! Ac-cuse instead the main road where the gutter is, and even more, the road in-spector who lets the water lie there and the puddles form. (1:557)

Let us take Stendhal at his word. Let us read this novel, at least this part of the novel, as if it reflected the world around it. And its immediate situation is one that is, by all accounts, both an exaggera-tion and a defense: the author's explanation of the character of Mathilde de la Mole. During a "night of madness," Mathilde comes to believe, albeit falsely, according to the rest of the novel, that she has conquered her love. This supposed turning point in the devel-opment of the character shows not her ardor but, as Stendhal says, her madness that is tinged with a streak of masochism, for she keeps singing: "Devo punirmi, devo punirmi, / Se troppo amai" (1:556). Now the explanation Stendhal offers of his character is an interrup-tion in more than one way. The narrator has brought Mathilde to the brink of madness, in an extreme ploy sanctioned by the excesses of the opera she has just attended. At that critical moment the narrator chooses to break away from his character. He immediately believes that the page he has just written will hurt him "in more than one way." It may be all right for his heroine to want to punish herself, but the narrator is not about to suffer along with her. Defending himself, the narrator says that Mathilde is a character who is "completely of the imagination" and he goes on to say that "it is agreed that the character of Mathilde is impossible in our century" (1:557). Between those two impossibilities comes the description of the novel as a mirror.

Mathilde does not fit into the world of exchange and order that Stendhal has developed heretofore in the novel, a world of tangible reality, a world of measure and knowledge. Her existence is of a different order, an imaginary, fantastic, or even fantasmatic one. Now here is the rub: Is the famous disquisition a defense of Mathilde, and therefore a defense of the imaginary, the impossible, or the unreal? Or is the disquisition a defense of the novel as a whole in which Mathilde herself is a dissonance? In either case it is a question of interruptions, of broken promises, of incomplete exchanges, a case in which the image reflects not at all what it is supposed to reflect. Arguably, Mathilde is an imaginary creation who is just like the images reflected in a mirror: they are virtual, intangible quasi objects with no palpable reality. Thus the discussion of Mathilde is consonant with the explicit theory of the mirror that follows. This interruption marks a movement from a classical mimetic theory of *ut pictura poesis* to a more sophisticated one that recognizes the nontangible nature of textual representation that is never three-dimensional, and which is at best an illusory depiction of reality. At first glance, Stendhal's mirror theory reflects the interruption of realism: not the direct *Wiederspiegelung* of simple reflection, but the images of incompletion, of disjunction, and of intermittence that are as much a part of the realist praxis as the acts of exact nomination we often associate with it.

The mirror prevents us from touching what is "in" it or "behind" it. The mirror is the locus of the imaginary but it is the locus of madness and of danger as well. Thus before the mirror reflects anything, it is installed to oppose illusory, transparent depictions of reality. It is situated in the midst of the mad, the dangerous, and the imaginary; the mirror is situated at the threshold of the fantasmatic. Before the mirror reflects anything, it is the hypostatization of the specular, and it opens onto something other and different: that which cannot be represented. Before the mirror reflects the same, and before it creates the simulacrum in which writing repeats the world, the mirror marks the unrepresentable.

In order to understand the ramifications of this problem we need to follow Stendhal quite literally. Where, for example, does the narrator stand to see what is reflected in the mirror, that is to say, in the space that is considered by him to be that of the novel? Given the constraints of the remark, he is not to observe the objects reflected. Instead he and we should concentrate on the reflection itself. In an ironic reversal of the allegory of Plato's cave, the narrator leads us to believe that the truth will not come of our own entry into the light, but of our looking at the images reflected in the mirror, akin to the shadows on the wall of the famous story. If the narrator stands behind the mirror to hold it, to move it up and down, or to reflect the blue skies and the mud on the side of the road, he sees the objects, that is, the sky and the mud, and not their reflections. If he stands in front of the mirror, he eclipses the reflection and all he sees is himself. He must therefore become invisible, so he can place himself in front of the mirror as a selective filter and yet be able to look into the mirror to see what is reflected there. Visible reality must therefore have its interruptions, not produced by the blindness of a reader, but by the invisibility of the narrator. At least for the implied reader there is an agreement on what to see and what not to see. And with that agreement comes the tacit acceptance of a narrative presence that is, to turn around an old expression, heard but not seen. Or, to be more precise, visibility is itself questioned: the narrator is read but not seen. The written word, reflection in the mirror of some amorphous reality, is not part of the visible the way the object it purportedly represents is.

Such a reading is admittedly an uncomfortable one to many critics who have tried in one way or another to make consonance from Stendhal's dissonance. Various clever solutions to the problem of the mirror have been offered; they amount, in essence, to turning the mirror a different way or to making it a different kind of mirror. For example, Epschtein (707) says that the mirror is not a harmonic mirror, that is to say, one that produces virtual images, but rather an analytical one. Blin (60) presents two alternatives that amount to a reinscription of the mirror as the emblem of a kind of realism that sees verisimilitude as *Wiederspiegelung*: "Whether it is a question of an immobile mirror in front of which the facts move or a mirror moved by the author through the cloaca of the universe, the meaning of this cliche stays the same: what it illustrates is untempered realism. It indicates first of all a passive novelist who does not interpret."

Yet no matter how clever these solutions are, they are misreadings of Stendhal's passage, which insists on being read literally. Depending on the critical stance one takes, Stendhal's mirror can be called a double bind, a paradox, a moment of deconstruction that is the one-sided, lopsided, unequal, partial presence of a mirror without silvering (*tain*), to use Rodolphe Gasché's shrewd expression from his excellent book, *The Tain of the Mirror*. If the frame of the figure is examined, the passage must be viewed as an interruption. And as an interruption, it accurately reflects Mathilde, herself an interruption in the novel, and therefore is an appropriate reflection of surroundings, and is in consequence not an interruption at all. On the other hand, if we read the contents and see the novel as a mirror reflecting the world of amorphous creations, it is as shapeless and as amorphous as the world it reflects. Moreover, it could not be viewed as the interruption we already know it is, an interruption in the seamlessness of the visible, proffered by the invisible hand of some imaginary creature called a narrator. And finally, if we read what is not there by seeing the mirror as some reflection of objects, we cannot for all that attribute that reading to Stendhal, but rather to our will to believe that the mirror image of which he speaks must be the comfortable one we want to see.

Unlike his depiction of Verrières, whose name echoes glass itself and whose schemes of production accurately parallel the incipient narrative ploys that will bring the representation of this world into our field of vision, Stendhal's mirror does not reflect the society, individuals, or historical events we might expect to see reflected in it. The mirror shows vague, dispersed, and undefined material: it reflects the azure of the sky, a phenomenon of refracted light; it also reflects the roadside muck and mire. Unformed and ill-defined images of shapeless and structureless material, the reflections can hardly be considered simulacra of the society that the author is trying to depict. Were the novel a mirror of that society, it would show crystal-clear images, better defined and more precisely contoured than the original referents in the real world; in fact, the mirror would become a selective filter that omits the tangential: it would become M. Epschtein's analytical mirror. The simulacra created in these virtual images would presumably be "more real" than their real referents because there is no place in these virtual images for accidental, contingent, and coincidental phenomena. These phenomena blur the edges of things in the real world but they could be eliminated in the novel. Stendhal's mirror shows the undifferentiated and the invisible; it is quite another mirror from the one that produces verisimilitude as a simple reflection.

Having rejected the apparent solution, we are still faced with the problem of what the novel as mirror actually reflects. The mirror is situated at the threshold of the fantasmatic, where danger, madness, and the imaginary intersect. These unrepresentable categories of excess go beyond narrative structures, and something must happen to contain them. Since the realist narrative cannot effectively represent madness but only contain or isolate it, Stendhal cannot risk an explosion of madness, for the whole realist enterprise would be called into question were that to occur. For these categories to remain within the realm of realist representation, they must be contained, overturned, and reversed in "this state of *reversed imagination*" (1:558). This is a state, for example, in which Julien Sorel finds himself to be "quite a flat being [*je suis au total un être bien plat*]" (1:558). Julien is now a virtual image, two- and not three-dimensional, a figure and not a representation. Thus, since we are no longer dealing with the madness or danger of a simulacrum, or with its realm of the imaginary, but simply with connotations attached to signifiers, the narrative can continue. Stendhal's or the narrator's control over the material remains intact. Ironically, then, the illusion of verisimilitude can continue from the point at which the destruction of verisimilitude occurs.

At this strategic point, the novel shows the impossible: the enunciator, seen and unseen, present and absent. This game of visibility and invisibility can be found from the very first lines of the novel: Danton, the headless revolutionary, speaks from an impossible position and he tells the truth in an equally impossible manner. The headless motif continues: Julien is deprived of speech by the narrator, and is already "beheaded" even before his trial (after which, like Danton, he will lose his head). Earlier, Stendhal uses Mathilde to indicate that Julien is not only like Danton but is a Danton, a representation of Danton and not merely an analogue (1:494 and 513). Julien is no longer either a subject or an object: he remarks, "I feel myself justly condemned" (1:676). And what follows this acquiescence to destruction are "headless" chapters without subtitles or epigraphs, but with Danton:

> Count Altamira used to say that the night before his death, Danton said, with his powerful voice, the verb "to guillotine" cannot be conjugated in all tenses; one can say "I shall be guillotined, you will be guillotined," but one does not say: "I was guillotined." (1:677)

Both Julien and the narrator are impossible figures of the equally impossible headless Danton. Danton speaks yet cannot speak; he is there, yet is not there; he gives the truth, yet he tells a fiction. If Julien is a Danton, he is also the narrator's alienated ideal self. All three come together in a "maybe" of authorial inscription of the act of writing: the sign of the theories of representation, the structures of enunciation, and the undoing of those structures. Presence and absence are combined with an ego that is affirmed grammatically but rejected as only a possibility:

> It is said that the memory of his wife moved Danton at the foot of the scaffold; but Danton had given force to a nation of whippersnappers [freluquets], and prevented the enemy from arriving in Paris . . . I alone know what I could have done . . . For the others, I am at best a MAYBE. (1:679)

What then is the novel as a mirror and how does it function within this overdetermined conjunction of elements? It is the trace of the constitution and subsequent disappearance of the enunciator of the narrative. The novel is a mirror and the path it reflects is the trace of the various presences and absences of the enunciator. The more secure the narrator is in having his story told, the less he is visible: there are fewer and fewer first-person interventions. The occultation of the first person is the means by which the narrator attempts to assimilate himself to the authorized locus of writing. The desired result is the assumption of the unique position of enunciation in order to produce a transparent narration: a chronicle. Having assumed this position as the giver of the law and of language, the first person assimilated to the Other can objectively tell the story.

There is never a complete assumption of the authorized position by the narrator, for all works bear the marks of an enunciative presence and all have been preceded by earlier ones. The novel is a reflection of this failure at complete absence: it is the system of conflicting representations and enunciations. In short, the trace of the narrator's presence is the same as the creation of the narrative. Stendhal's aesthetic of the mirror is the crystallization of the novel's theories and praxes of representation and enunciation. It now remains to see only how foreground and background coalesce as representation turns into self-enunciation.

The representation of Julien Sorel and his subsequent reinsertion into the figural or the discursive lead inevitably to the question of the foregrounding of textual elements. When certain elements come together as a whole to dominate a work, they are foregrounded as what Roman Jakobson and Iurii Tynianov called "the dominant." The assertion of Julien Sorel as a character against the rest of the novel foregrounds semiotic and semantic elements that permit him to stand out while the rest of the narrative recedes relative to him. And the assertion of a group of elements as this character corresponds to his assumption of a viable position of enunciation and action. There is a double narrative movement in the establishment of Julien Sorel and in his subsequent reduction to a textual figure.

In the first move, Julien Sorel can be seen as the ideal self of the narrator. In that guise he is set up against the Other, who takes the form and functions of the absolute law, crystallized in the form of the father or his surrogates and in the form of authorized writing. Here Julien struggles as an unauthorized voice whose manifest desire is to obtain a position as an enunciator. His attempts to assert himself are the representation of the narrator's own struggle to place himself in an authorized position. This dominant is thus the representation of the narrator's struggle as a writer to represent reality, even if this representation does not conform to the classical episteme or to the society's myths about itself.

The second move comes with the subsequent dissolution of this dominant back into the figural; this move corresponds to the insistence of the narrator's power over Julien Sorel. Here the dialogical textuality is no longer directed solely against the Other but also shows the struggle of the narrator with what he has allowed to become the dominant of the work. As the dominant, Julien takes over

the novel: the objective point of view that is the mark of verisimilitude finds an alternative point of view that vies for attention. By oc-
culting his own ego and assuming the role of the Other, the narrator
becomes the voice of authority in his narrative. But to perform this
coup, it is necessary for the narrator to prohibit Julien to be an enunciator in his own right. For the narrator to assume what he considers
his rightful place, he must be the sole dispenser of truth. He is now
the only one who has information: all that is in the narrative comes
from him.

The story of this novel illustrates the creation of the omniscient
narrator in nineteenth-century fiction. It represents a process
whereby the word is taken from the Other by a nonauthoritarian
enunciator, who in turn loses his position to a new Other, the omniscient narrator. The character that had been created as the dominant
recedes to become one element among others. Having revealed the
processes whereby the establishment of the omniscient narrator occurs, and the implications of this position, Stendhal can go on, in the
twin works of *La Chartreuse de Parme* and the *Chroniques italiennes*, to
discern the general implications of enunciation itself.

Fabrice the Semiotician

FINDING FABRICE

In this part of the chapter, I would like to consider the processes of
naming and giving meaning in the realist novel by examining a work
in which so much depends on those very processes, *La Chartreuse de
Parme*. Naming a character, creating an individual, separating action
from context are breaches that form Stendhal's fiction-writing process. Specifically, the *Chartreuse* enacts the difficulties in establishing
a realist aesthetic through the struggles of the protagonist to establish himself as a valid agent. Like Julien Sorel, Fabrice could be considered the alienated ideal self of the author, but here specifically in
his function as author; Fabrice's establishment of self is a direct reflection of the fiction-writing process. Indeed, the protagonist is a locus of narrative disruption: this process of defining his semioticity is
an interruption, not in some whole textuality, but taking shape as a
series of blanks that are simultaneous with the weaving of the narrative strands.

The process of naming a character should be an easy one and its results should be visible. Naming distinguishes the character from others, sets him or her up with an identity and legitimacy, and establishes a proper locus in which he or she can act. It is, of course, a convention that characters in a literary work usually have different names. When two characters have the same name, it is not a matter of coincidence, but a means of contrast, as is the case for the two Catherines in *Wuthering Heights*. That this is a convention can be seen in Eugène Ionesco's mockery of naming in *La Cantatrice chauve*, in which all the members of one family, including in-laws, are named Bobby Watson. In general, however, the process of naming establishes difference against a uniform background in which the name is considered to be proper.

In the realm of the literary, a change of name means a change of state, be it desired or real. Examples abound, including success stories like the various steps in the life of Maupassant's Georges Duroy in *Bel-Ami*, who becomes Georges du Roy de Cantel, and Vautrin's various incarnations in *La Comédie humaine* as Jacques Collin, Trompe-la-Mort, and Abbé Carlos Herrera. In contrast is a failed renaming: Lucien de Rubempré never quite escapes the ignominy associated with having been Lucien Chardon. Most realist female characters are powerless to change their own names, so it is an action performed on them by men. And the change means marriage, a change of state, a loss of virginity, a reconquest of virtue, the possibility of adultery, or the ability to create legitimate offspring: in other words, the total lack of freedom she has to be herself. When Emma Rouault becomes Emma Bovary, what has she truly gained?

Stendhal knows better than anyone what is entailed by naming, renaming, and misnaming. One can hide behind a pen name, and the pseudonymous Stendhal, as Jean Starobinski has pointed out, invented numerous names for various authorial situations. Naming and renaming are interruptions, not the uniformity that we have come to expect. Naming is quite a troublesome process, and is all the more so when, as is often the case in Stendhal's work, a name is somehow refused. To refuse one's name means to refuse one's rightful place in a hierarchy and chronology. For a male protagonist, the simple refusal is really a double refusal of legitimate filiation; it is a rejection of orthodox paternity. It is not only the refusal to bear the name of the father, which makes it a denial of filiality, but also, since it does not continue a rightful name, it is a refusal to be a father to another. The refusal of a name may in fact be the best way to avoid conflict: truth is buried in an unmarked grave, the name borne is a false clue, a misnomer that deflects the question of paternity.

In Stendhal's writing, this is certainly the position of Julien Sorel. His entry into the textual struggle implies a will to power, a desire to see the name of the father both overcome and retained, denied and assumed, read and reinscribed at the locus of identity. Still he must become a father. He is the Oedipal reader who finds it easy to deny the paternity of Sorel as a legitimate father. Julien is unlike his brothers and father, not a brute like they are; it is easy for him to leave the paternal household. Indeed, Julien will make his name by reading and internalizing the position of the authority, by assuming the mantle, at least in his secretarial duties, of Monsieur de la Mole. And he will eventually be rewarded for that internalization of another paternity as he becomes M. de la Vernaye. But it is a very different matter where Fabrice del Dongo is concerned. His struggles with his father would seem only to be the sterile pastimes of the idle rich.

Who is Fabrice del Dongo? How is his identity established? What relation does his formation as a character have to the narrative from which he emerges? Unlike the beginning of *Le Rouge et le Noir* in which Stendhal sets up a system of exchange and communication, no theory of representation opens *La Chartreuse de Parme*. In the *Chartreuse*, the narrator does not feel obligated to establish the right to tell the story to his rhetorical reader. Moreover, the reader can draw conclusions, because he or she has been brought into the game even before the rules have been understood. In other words, *La Chartreuse de Parme* is a realist novel for readers who have already read realist novels.

Let us consider, for example, the function of hating the father. This characteristic will come to be an essential part of realist narrative as it enacts distance between father and son, rejection of a son by a father, becoming an orphan, and such similar motifs: in realism, the male protagonist has to prove himself through independence.[13] In *Le Rouge et le Noir*, Stendhal feels obliged to establish this hatred twice. First, the description of M. de Rênal's physical reality is contrasted with his limited mind; as he will soon be a surrogate father to Julien, it is necessary for him to be hated as well as the biological father.

Second, Stendhal dramatizes paternal brutality in the odious behavior of Sorel toward his son. In the *Chartreuse*, the reader is assumed to hate the father just as Fabrice and the narrator do: the Marquis is quite identical to himself, ugly in body as well as in soul. Marking complicity with the reader, the use of "we" constantly re-marks the identity of the situation to itself and the characters to themselves. When Fabrice finally bothers to be born (2:33), he is already there with a title, born into a continuing history and hierarchy. Unlike Julien Sorel who has to accede in order to succeed, Fabrice is born identical to himself, a completed essence *avant la lettre*. As Jean-Paul Sartre notes in his *Carnets* (410), Fabrice, "even in the direst despair, is a perpetual source of happiness for his reader because he is *selbst-ständig*. He stands on his own two feet; he is viable; there is no disintegration in him."

The initial development of Fabrice does nothing to alter the state of sterile identity in which we find him. Fabrice belongs to a world where progress means stasis and where literacy is useless. He has no need to read the words of another if the position of the other, the position of power and authority, is already an internalized one: "We pass over ten years of progress and happiness, from 1800 to 1810; Fabrice spent the first few in the Chateau of Grianta, punching and getting punched among the village peasants, and learning nothing, not even how to read" (2:33). This is at least the second time that Stendhal has related the act of reading to an act of violence. In *Le Rouge et le Noir*, in the initial encounter with Julien Sorel, he is perched high above his father's sawmill and is reading instead of tending to his duty. Seeing this shirking behavior, Sorel jumps up, knocks the book from Julien's hand, and gives him a box on the ears (1:232). The punches given and received by Fabrice echo the box on the ears of the earlier novel, but in the *Rouge*, the hit goes only in one direction, from Sorel to his other-worldly son; there is a line of power and a mark of difference. Julien reads and is subsequently hit by a unidirectional force. On the other hand, Fabrice hits and is hit, yet does not learn to read. Nothing interrupts the exchange in which nothing is exchanged and in which the player remains identical to himself.

In the *Chartreuse* then, Stendhal starts from an uninterrupted position of identity in which the signs are part of a uniform, closed system and in which the radical excesses of difference are either turned into controlled, reciprocal acts, such as the case of violence here, or into an iterative, if not to say tautological act of self-repetition. In the beginning of the *Chartreuse*, reading is an act that is indifferent and unruptured. Literacy makes no difference in or to Fabrice; when he reads it is only the iteration of himself that is the Latin genealogy of the family published by Fabrice del Dongo, Archbishop of Paris.

Fabrice is of course misnamed, if we believe Lieutenant Robert to be his "real" (biological) father. There is more than a shadow of a doubt cast about his paternity in the beginning of the novel, with all fingers pointing toward the French soldier, Lieutenant Robert (André 23–30). The very name of the French soldier could be taken as a sign or clue of this uncertain paternity, offered to us by an Anglophile writer: the Frenchman is the "robber" who takes the place (*lieu-tenant*) of another. This robbery is always there, providing an identity as uncertain as the image in a mirror. At the same time, this robbery does not provide the rupture needed, because it is undecidable. There is a nondisjunction of events, as Kristeva would say: both the lieutenant and the marquis are Fabrice's father; the novel's genesis remains in that ambiguous position. And since the power of the iterative written word wins over some spurious deflected desire, Fabrice del Dongo remains identical to himself.

Although he has posited the possibility of illegitimacy and thus a variety of potential consequences, Stendhal does not seek his rupture there. In the first half of the book, Fabrice can read only self-identical signs that are part of a self-consistent system; his reading cannot interrupt and he must remain legitimate. The signs may be falsely ascribed in that there may be a point of difference—for instance, the legal versus "real" or mythic father—but the system is unimpeachable. Only when Fabrice is in prison does he first learn to capitalize on the difference between writing and reality. In the early chapters, Fabrice reads his own history in a family genealogy written by his namesake. What he assimilates, learns, internalizes, and quotes will be the useless supplement to what is already there. As far as Fabrice is concerned, writing simply reiterates being; Fabrice reads a book that was written by his ancestor, also named Fabrice del Dongo. In contrast, in the *Rouge*, when Julien reads what is already there within him, he is reduced to a state of reflection; he becomes a pale copy of what he once was (1:575). Writing is redundant and reading, for Fabrice, is nothing more than a means of feeding his narcissism: "This book quite pleased the young Fabrice" (2:34).[14] Fabrice always remains in the world of repetition, where no development is possible because everything is already there. In this world, writing is merely a sterile and useless supplement to being.

In this sterile semioticity, signs are useless supplements that repeat the past by reinscribing it. Nothing new is added, no information interrupts this world crafted to be as seamless as the imaginary "text" of realist fiction. This semioticity is soon confronted with an alternative sign system. Initially, it seems to be the continuation of the first system, since the Marquis asks Blanès to continue teaching Fabrice Latin, the language of the endlessly reinscribed genealogy. Yet instead of being the vehicle for the re-presentation of the past, Latin has no referents; it is devoid of content. In an amusing turn, Stendhal makes Latin a collection of empty signifiers, stale declensions, and meaningless paradigms: "It would have been necessary for the curate himself to know this language; but it was the object of his disdain; his knowledge in this domain [*genre*] was limited to reciting the prayers of his missal by heart, whose meaning he could more or less give to his flock" (2:38). On the one hand, Latin is useful for the sterile intoning of prayers, and as such has a linguistic usage akin to the sterile repetition of the adventures of dead ancestors. On the other hand, Latin represents a freedom from meaning: Latin is a means of not knowing and not meaning, for the system of written signs of a dead language has no tangible relation to the real world. And even though this is not essentially closer to the idea of rupture than we were before, at least the referential system has been unhooked from the semiotic one: with no knowledge of what the language means, Blanès, and *a fortiori* his pupil Fabrice, can move written language away from its parasitic and even parodic repetition of stultifying, iterative, and banal reality.

Returning the dead sign system upon itself, Stendhal replaces Latin in the realm of deception it already occupies in *Le Rouge et le Noir*, where Julien uses it for the parlor trick of reciting passages from the Bible. The sign system of this anti-Latin bias shows its own vacuity instead of being posited as the mere supplement of an eternal, unchanging reality. Written language, that is, "the study of languages" (2:39), quite literally represents both the absence of the past in the study of this meaningless Latin and, through the reference to the genealogy, the absence of a present that may be different from some historic past.

Blanès offers another possibility for semiosis. The sign-referent pattern is reversed; existing signs bring about the appearance of the object represented by the signs. Instead of representing, signs predict the future through astrology (2:38–39). The sign is supposed to bring about what is not yet and what will be. The event or object signified by the sign is ultimately the sign recalling the original sign. So the future event, rather than being some independent referent, is the sign of a sign, for the referent, instead of being the preexisting independent object that language comes to describe, itself refers to that original sign.

Stendhal puts Fabrice between the two competing sign systems, but belonging to both, he really belongs to neither: "Following their fathers' examples, they devoutly recited an *Ave Maria*. But at the beginning, right after the *Ave Maria*, Fabrice was often hit by an omen. This was the fruit borne by the astrological studies of his friend, the Abbé Blanès, whose predictions he did not believe" (2:40). Neither semiotic system puts Fabrice in a meaningful position, since he cannot interpret them. Thus if Fabrice has an excess of biological fathers, one legitimate, one illegitimate, he has a dearth of "father tongues": there is no struggle with the system of the past nor with that of the future. Fabrice has nowhere to go, for he has no means of signification. Neither the past nor the future is his: he can and must exist only in the present, undoubtedly identical to himself but incapable of assuming a difference, belonging to a situation, or entering into a relation that depends on difference.

Stendhal has created the possibility for semiosis; he has created the possibility of difference, since his hero has been inoculated with a belief in signs (2:40).[15] By proposing two theories of semiosis and by simultaneously foregoing any theorization about the possibility of representation, Stendhal has effectively displaced any question of representability in the novel. It is taken as received knowledge that his character is there and that the author has the readers' complicity in the establishment of that presence. Presented as a possible player in various sign systems, though in fact impervious to them, Fabrice exists from the first. By providing a multiple semiotic grid, Stendhal avoids the problem of grounding the work he had in the *Rouge*, but he foregoes the plot development that comes with such a *roman d'apprentissage*, both for him and his hero.

Stendhal seems to be writing, against received knowledge, the basic representational paradigm of realism he established in *Le Rouge et le Noir*, where the theory of representation and production are the means of establishing a ground to anchor the semiotic system to the referential world and of allowing for the manipulation of the system. The theory of representation permits the establishment of a transcendental position of enunciation, the observer who translates into language what he sees. Moreover, the existence of this transcendental position guarantees that the mode of production will appear natural; indeed, that referent, representational theory, and the means of giving them are a coherent whole appropriate for describing the world. The establishment of a paradigm of enunciation and the denial of its imposition, coupled with the use of a transcendental position as an operator of and within writing, is the mark of realist praxis.

In *La Chartreuse*, by foregoing the possibility of having his protagonist invest in and be invested by signs, Stendhal seems to be nostalgically recalling some sort of episodic adventure novel. If Fabrice does not learn, how can he be a realist hero or antihero? For realism, as we have seen, is bound up with the capitalization of the semiotic process. Still, Stendhal does not overtly appeal to a revisionist recapitulation of some earlier model of representation. No appeal is made to a more classical prose model like the model of painterly representation that Stendhal has already used at the beginning of *Le Rouge et le Noir*. Nor is there an appeal made to a true romantic model, formed around an inner absence or lack that the hero seeks to fill. In fact, Stendhal ironically undercuts the presuppositions of romanticism with his oft-repeated use of the phrase "our hero." Could realism already be in trouble?

For the novel to develop, this impasse must be overcome. In order to make this novel seem as if it really is a novel, Stendhal has to introduce difference, but to do so, he must abandon his position of absolute authority. The singular *mise-en-scène* has produced an unreal, utopian landscape, a world where characters exist fully formed and where there are no material impediments. It is not by accident that Stendhal reinvents Italy here, the country that does not exist, for in this world no adequation between word and thing need be made in a movement toward the establishment of realism; in fact no adequation can be made. In an excellent article on the novel, Leslie Rabine (123) points out the efficacy of the construct:

> Since it is at the same time *both* the sixteenth-century city of the Italian Chronicle after which Stendhal modelled his novel *and also* the nineteenth-century despotism of post-Napoleonic Austria, it is both in and out of history. . . . Life in Parma has a special temporal structure because the city-state has a special, and a very unusual, socio-economic structure. As opposed to the France of *Le Rouge et le Noir*, or any historically known society, Parma has no economic base, no system of productive relations underlying its political relations. Ideology creates the illusion of freeing ideas from an economic base, but Parma really is so liberated. (123)

Italy is a construct, a set of equipotential possibilities in which all difference is immediately negated. It matters little whether the sign system is identical to what is signified or if it brings about what it signifies, for in either case, the signified does not exist. And until difference is introduced, this Italy will remain a utopia equally amenable to every sort of representational, theoretical, enunciative, and productive system and schema. When difference is finally introduced, this utopian Italy assumes verisimilitude to the little principalities and city-states. This verisimilitude relies heavily on political discourse for its strength, easily seen in the novel's scenes with Gina, Mosca, and Ernest-Ranuce. In general, but especially for these three characters, the production of political discourse forms a corpus within the novel, and while it never is the sole means for one individual character to understand the semiotics into which he or she is thrust, it is a network of statements and remarks that seems, like the narrative as a whole, to cover the referent. Fabrice is different because, although subjected to that politics, he is by and large not a political agent. And Stendhal must find a means to action other than politics to suit his protagonist.

To establish the modes of production and representation, Fabrice must be put into a situation of difference. The project is dual: the utopia must be demythologized and the character must differentiate himself. In order "to be," he must do something; Fabrice takes the first step of difference: "And as for me, I told myself, as yet the un-known son of this unhappy mother, I shall leave, I shall die or con-quer with this man marked by destiny [*marqué par le destin*]" (2:49–50). Differentiation is not as simple as in *Le Rouge et le Noir*, where there is a theoretical support for action and difference. The passage just quoted recalls the mirror of the earlier novel that "shows the mire" (1:557); here it is a question of "this great image of Italy lifting itself up from the mire" (2:49). Still, the image remains bound to the realm of the undifferentiated. Though there are occasional soarings, they are due to the imposition of some divine breath of des-tiny; the world is still viewed from a sempiternal and immutable po-sition. There is no prop for Fabrice as a protagonist; unknown, he remains subservient, unable to enunciate himself, undifferentiable from the rest, and still bound by the chains of an unresolved Oedipal relation.

Italy is the zero point of the indistinguishable identity that cannot support Fabrice's development. Leaving Italy to follow Napoleon, Fabrice seeks to re-mark what is there, in the hope of inscribing him-self as marked by fate as well. Thus in his initial act of self-differen-tiation, Fabrice follows a pre-existing mark; he only begins to be dif-ferent when he follows this vague mark of writing that is itself a point of difference. Rather than being the reinscription of identity that Fabrice has absorbed through repetitive reading of the family tree authored by his namesake, this writing marks change. This mark of Cain inaugurates a difference for Napoleon and for Fabrice, who, like Julien Sorel, takes the Emperor as his model: it matters little whether Fabrice dies or conquers, since either would be a distin-guishing act of self-differentiation.[16] Fabrice is wrong in his predic-tion: he neither conquers nor dies with Napoleon. Yet even in this wrong prediction, for which he has misread signs, Fabrice finally takes the first step toward the development of a semioticity of differ-ence. And so Fabrice is off to war, and precisely to a war of words, a logomachy.

Passing through France, Fabrice arrives in Belgium for what will turn out to be the Battle of Waterloo. The entire section of the novel devoted to the Battle of Waterloo will be devoted to Fabrice's learn-ing to communicate for himself. Having established difference for his protagonist through a geographic change, Stendhal next must set up a code that will pierce through the noise that prevents communication. Confusing, out of focus, and as far as possible from being the absolute turning point and watershed of Napoleonic Europe, the battle perceived from the singular position of an individual soldier is anything but momentous. Rather, it is the locus of confusion, disorganization, and entropy, a babble of voices and bodies that do not become clear until they are absent.

The descriptions of the battle are rightly famous for showing both the confusion of the scene and Fabrice's inability to grasp the momentous nature of what is going on. The distance between us, who know that this is "Waterloo," and him, who naturally has no inkling of the importance of the moment, is measured and increased by irony. Depending on our own knowledge, which is presumed to be superior to that of Fabrice, Stendhal's ironic descriptions tend to increase the distance between us and him by underlining this inferiority. At the same time, Stendhal cannot risk losing his readers' sympathy for the character he is creating. Stendhal needs to develop Fabrice's knowledge, despite the fact that Waterloo is too confusing; there is too much information and too much noise. To lay the groundwork for Fabrice's possibility of communication, a position that will tend to reduce the irony, not only by making the reader more sympathetic to the wayward hero but also by making Fabrice's position more like that of the narrator, Stendhal transforms Fabrice into a storyteller in his own right.

Suddenly signs have meaning for Fabrice. Stendhal calls attention to the process of storytelling by a strategically placed shifter. He writes a sentence in Italian to launch an act of communication; he will repeat this technique in the signals from Gina to Fabrice in prison (2:340). Though the characters are presumably communicating in Italian throughout, French, the writer's own language, generally serves as the invisible translation of some nonexistent original. Thus it could be argued that much of the dialogue of the book is not identical to itself: when we read the word *cheval*, a word that Blanès would not wish translated, that *cheval* is itself the written translation of some imaginary spoken instance of the Italian word *cavallo*.[17] Here Stendhal's characters are presumably speaking Italian, which is almost always silently, invisibly translated as perfect French. At several strategic moments, however, Stendhal uses Italian when he wants to underline the artificial, yet radical, nature of representation itself: realist representation assigns itself the task of representing the world in its order and in its disorder.

In this instance, as a system is established, what is written is identical to what Fabrice would have said. At the point of origin of a sign system, Stendhal insists that the written sign be the absolute equivalent of the spoken sign:

> The cannon fire seemed even stronger to him; he could barely hear the general . . .
> —Where did you get this horse [*cheval*]?
> Fabrice was so confused that he answered in Italian:
> —*L'ho comprato poco fa.* (I just bought it a few moments ago [*Je viens de l'acheter à l'instant*].)
> —What did you say? yelled the general.
> But the noise became so strong at that moment that Fabrice could not answer him. We will admit that our hero was not very much the hero at that moment. (2:63)

This coalescence of written and spoken sign systems is the means by which Stendhal creates a fiction of representation for Fabrice: the written language that Stendhal is using feigns its own origin in a seamless, unruptured discourse. At the same time, however, the spurious origin is challenged: the written language projects gaps and inconsistencies just as the narrator is trying to hide them. In a careful reading of the passage, we realize that the translation that Stendhal gives is not absolutely accurate, for *poco fa* and *à l'instant* are not equivalent. Moreover, the "ghost" horse strategically reappears here, though there is still no *cavallo*: the *l'* that is the Italian direct object has no grammatical antecedent in Italian, but rather in French: *cheval*. Stendhal has set up the phatic structure necessary to a communicational model. The message is significant, since it establishes a general equivalent posited between signs and referents. Horses can be bought and sold; money is used as a transcendental signifier that can replace any object.

Fabrice begins to communicate, but it is a slow, tortuous process. First, just like Julien repeating the Bible or serving as a scribe, Fabrice begins to distinguish by following the indications of others: "At first Fabrice did not understand; finally he noticed that all the corpses were always dressed in red" (2:63). He begins to assess the field in which he is going to interpret and in which he will produce his own signs. Yet basic definitions escape him; he is still not sure if this is a veritable battle (2:65). In sum, the establishment of Fabrice as a valid semiotician is hit or miss; what is communicated is mis-communicated:

—And you, who are you?
   —I am the brother of the wife of a captain.
   —And what do you call this captain [*Et comment l'appelez-vous, ce capi-taine*]?
   Our hero was quite embarrassed; he hadn't foreseen this question at all . . .
   —Captain Meunier [Miller]! The other, hearing badly because of the cannon fire answered, "Oh! Captain Teulier? Well! he was killed." (2:65)

Here Stendhal is inscribing a primal scene of writing, one that serves as a competing origin for writing and which is different from the fictional one of identity of the spoken and written signs discussed above. This primal scene is a memorial process in which all writing, it would appear, is part of a process of mourning, a reinscription of death based on the need for having a body in a crypt, now present in the form of the dead Captain Teulier. But it is the wrong dead body; the process depends on a misnaming; there is no miller (*meunier*) providing grist for the *moulin à paroles*. Communication for Fabrice is still a hit or miss situation, for he continues to misread the signs. And if he cannot be related to the miller who produces flour for bread, perhaps others can do the work for him:

—Comrades, could you sell me a bit of bread?
   —This one thinks we're bakers!
   This harsh word and the general snickering that ensued wounded Fabrice. So war was no longer that noble and united trajectory for souls who love glory, that he had figured according to Napoleon's proclamations! (2:70)

Fabrice spoke wrong, thought wrong, and figured wrong. By taking signs as absolutes and as general equivalents of communication, he chooses the wrong model for his acts of communication. His money can no longer buy anything; Napoleon's proclamations were wrong. Although Fabrice is no better off than in Italy, for he is still nowhere, he has at least the potential to be somewhere.

Proper semioticity will begin only when the arbitrary ends and a point of origin is found, which occurs through the long-deferred enactment of an Oedipal crisis. The one who survives can be a valid participant in a semiotic schema; the one who does not overcome the threat is condemned to the world of the iterative and the undifferentiated. Fighting with a saber that is too heavy for him, Fabrice winds up being used as a scapegoat for the massacre of the previous day as he undergoes attacks by several assailants (2:86). Realizing that the victim was innocent, they begin to attack the sign and not what it covers: "The hussars soon saw with whom they were dealing; they then sought not to wound him but to cut his attire on his body. Fabrice got three or four little saber cuts on his arms that way" (2:87). The actual wound occurs as if by chance and the violence escalates:

Unluckily, one of those blows struck a hussar on his hand: rather angry with being hit by such a soldier, he returned with a deep thrust that got Fabrice at the top of his thigh. . . . Seeing Fabrice's blood flow down his right arm, [the assailants] feared that the game had gone on too long. . . . Furious, [another] hussar turns around and thrusts with all his might, cuts Fabrice's sleeve, and penetrates deep in his arm: our hero falls. (2:87–88)

Wounded like Tristram Shandy's Uncle Toby, Fabrice begins to bleed profusely and the little game stops, but not without a displacement. As if to hide what he has done to "our hero," Stendhal displaces the wound from a critical spot to an uncritical one. The earlier version of the work was more frank; it did not have the same act of self-censorship and the assailants see the blood flow "the length of his sky-blue pants" (2:1393). In the revised version, either the wound in his thigh causes bleeding in his arm or Fabrice bleeds before his arm is wounded. Stendhal has safely displaced the wound, which is covered with bandages and language. This hidden wound is now the suitable point on which to build a semiotic system that finds its elaboration in the suturing and encrypting of a trauma.

This absolute difference succeeds where the misnaming process did not. It is not enough merely to invent a story by writing it out of whole cloth. In other words, the scene of naming produces nothing that can leave that scene. In the naming process that relies on various shifters, language remains attached to the represented world. On the other hand, this double wound—the visible one on his arm and the occulted one on his thigh—is literally and figuratively a rupture. It separates, distinguishes, and displaces, and allows Fabrice to move away from the realm of the iterative. Fabrice is free to learn how to read and write in a mode of difference. The mark on his thigh remains as testimony to what preceded: "The cut on his thigh threatened to form a considerable abscess" (2:90). Drained of the humors of the past, both the blue blood that had been his and the pus from the abscess that remarks the actuality of the wound, Fabrice is left with only the mark of the wound. Fabrice is marked, just as Napoleon had been.

This act of difference leads first to reading and then finally to writing. He starts out totally alienated, the equivalent of a deaf-mute: "Soon a German officer entered his room: they were using a language he didn't understand to answer him; but he saw that they were talking about him; he pretended to be asleep" (2:90–91). And like Julien Sorel, who can recite from novels without ever having read any, Fabrice can understand without having to understand. Fabrice has begun to read without having any idea of what he is reading; he is mastering the sign system as a whole. Similarly, he can communicate with his hostesses in French, despite the fact that they hardly understand this language (2:91). But whether they understand or not is immaterial, since Fabrice has almost entirely forgotten his French. He speaks to his Flemish-speaking hostesses in Italian; he and they understand each other through signs that are unlimited by the restrictions of any code and which are thereby the means of ensuring instant and transparent communication. And the transcendental signifiers that at first could be used in an exchange (for a horse), and then could not be used at all (to buy bread), can now be used to produce absolutely anything: "When the girls, who were otherwise completely disinterested, saw the diamonds, their enthusiasm for him was endless; they believed him to be a prince in disguise" (2:91).

In point of fact they are not wrong. Fabrice is now perceived as being identical to what he is, since he is in fact a member of the nobility. Yet Fabrice's newfound identity is identity with a difference. He is no longer the sterile, iterative, blue-blooded son of a long line of marquesses. He now begins to occupy a position that is his alone. His position is now a statement of identity that *includes* difference: he is a prince disguised as a non-prince yet thought to be a prince; but the prince he is thought to be and the prince that he is are not identical. Having established himself at a position of difference, he can begin to separate signifiers from what they signify, by removing the immediacy that has characterized semiosis up to this point. He begins to write (2:90), but most important, he begins to read. Through the description of his reading, the readers are made aware of the gap that cannot be bridged between the event and the signs that signify the event:

Fabrice almost became another man, given all his deep reflections on the things that had just happened to him. He remained a child on only one point: what he had seen, was it a battle? And, in the second place, was this battle Waterloo? (2:93)

Since he is now "like another man" (*comme un autre homme*), the mark of difference is within him. And since he is the same yet other, Fabrice can begin to reflect on the meaning of events. More important, the distance produced by difference allows him to begin to ask metaquestions about meaning and definition: he wonders whether what he saw was in fact a "battle," and whether this battle, if it in fact was one, was "Waterloo." His Waterloo, so to speak, is a confusing flow of information taken from a single vantage point.

Having produced the necessary critical distance, Stendhal can now conflate the larger-than-life, mythic battle of Waterloo with the more banal and far more confusing historical version. For posterity, Waterloo is a turning point, the beginning of the return toward the restoration, as well as being the beginning of a certain modernity for Stendhal. In contrast, Fabrice's Waterloo is a confused mass of haphazard events. Between the general knowledge that Stendhal and his readers share and Fabrice's ignorance comes the mediation of objective prose. First of all, the sign is conceived of as a mediation between a relative truth and a generalized or universal perspective. The sign becomes the means for Fabrice to begin to understand his own position, different from the one he had, but still not fully comprehensible: "For the first time in his life he enjoyed reading; he always hoped to find some description in the newspapers or in the reports that would let him recognize where he had been after Marshal Ney and later with the other general" (2:93). Within the novel, reading becomes a generalized action that is the means of accession to a position of truth. Reading as a valid reader would read, Fabrice is now literate.

Yet reading is only half of a dynamic pair; alone, reading is at best a solitary, nonproductive pleasure. For reading to have weight, it must be transformable into writing. At the most fundamental level, the absence and difference that are realized when reading is successfully accomplished must be sutured over in the act of writing, as the writing writes over what is not there. With the act of correct and generalized writing comes the accretion of authority, and with it, a certain amount of power.[18] Within Stendhal's own work, Julien Sorel starts out as a reader. But he learns far more quickly what the game of reading and writing is about than Fabrice does, and Julien almost immediately puts writing into practice. By memorizing the Bible and using it to best advantage, or by appropriating Horace and Rousseau and reciting them, he re-marks what he has read, reinscribing it as his, and gains power from this transformation. Further on, having learned to write the word *cela* correctly, Julien enjoys success in the house of the Marquis de la Mole.

Writing must remark the difference that brings the writer out of the realm of sterile and repetitive identity. Just as the act of reading one's own family tree does nothing to further one's comprehension of the world of difference, the reinscription through writing of the relations of identity furthers no cause. Fabrice does not get very far here: his writing reinforces a preexisting relation of presence. Instead of being a remarking of absence, writing is seen as a sterile supplement to or mnemonic reminder of presence. For Fabrice, writing consists of letters to his good friends at the inn that he has just left. And the letters he receives from his mother and aunt are only a bundle of repeated urges to return to the position of identity (2:93). They reinforce the previously existing lines of communications and relations to a nondynamic, eternally repetitive model. His writing is subservient to that of another; in fact, his letters cannot be his: "Take care not to sign the letters you write" (2:93). He is recast into the realm of the anonymous and dutiful child; his letters reinscribe him at the point from which he started. He does now know how to read, and that in itself is something.

Reading without really writing recapitulates, though without a theory of representation, the eighteenth century's model of visual representation, which Stendhal already used and discarded in *Le Rouge et le Noir*. It associates imagination and the act of representation with the painting of a picture: "His imagination soon began to paint these misfortunes in most horrible detail" (2:93). Stendhal reintroduces the earlier model as a means of controlling his literary hero. Even though he has introduced difference as a means of moving the narrative forward, Stendhal needs to maintain his control by sending his hero on a peripateia—a wandering adventure. And since he is finally able to read signs, Fabrice can be successful in the realm of love: desire can be appropriated through its perception. Fabrice still cannot initiate the production of signs from his own individual position but at least he can read those who take his portrait to heart; he can react to others' reactions to him. No individual action comes to the fore, no development of the character occurs: Fabrice moves from situation to situation without becoming a better reader and without ever becoming a real writer.

The turning point is a rewriting and a reversal of a scene that has already occurred, the scene in which Fabrice is wounded, already discussed above:

Fabrice thought: given the pain in my face, he must have disfigured me. Enraged at that idea, he jumped on his enemy, with the point of his hunting knife in front. This point entered Giletti's right breast and came out toward the left shoulder; at the same time, Giletti's sword completely penetrated Fabrice's upper arm, but the sword slipped under the skin and it was an insignificant wound. (2:195–96)

This time, it is the adversary that has the outsized weapon; Fabrice has only a hunting knife, but it is a weapon that is legitimately his. Again, Fabrice is wounded in the arm, but this time the wound is insignificant and meaningless. And the critical wound is found in another: Giletti is the body that is finally to be buried in the crypt of the novel.

Fabrice still has nowhere to turn; he cannot yet look within himself to produce his own marks or writing. Having killed a man, he is condemned to disappear behind the document of another as he takes the passport of the very man he killed (2:199). Only then does Fabrice begin to realize both the alterity of the writing he is now claiming as his and that of the writing that is supposed to be his. Thus he can only lie against the truth of that second writing: "He was going to say that his name was Giletti and all his laundry was marked F. D." (2:199). Writing lies; when the lie is caught it is simply re-marked with an absence: the policeman who knows that Fabrice is not Giletti believes that discovering Fabrice's lie would in fact inculpate Giletti for having sold his passport. Therefore, caught in an aporia between two lies, the policeman conveniently allows another to stamp the passport in his stead. Though Fabrice is unaware of the cause of this lie that matches his own, it serves nevertheless to underline the movement away from the truth that writing holds for him. The movement is away from the truth of the Other or of authority that is given as a general, universal, and transcendental value. Moving away from this false hope, Fabrice can finally begin to invest his own truth in writing, which is both an individual and subjective truth and a ve-hicle for desire.

Fabrice's first individual act of writing is not solely his. More pre-cisely, it is his but the act is not identical to itself until it is re-marked. Fabrice writes two letters, but as they are in his own writing they could in fact betray him if they were intercepted. For his letters to get through, they should be copied by another. From having been the dutiful son who reads and re-marks the previously existing writ-ing of another, Fabrice is now the author of writing that pre-exists for another (2:207). Fabrice would have Ludovic copy the letters, but Fabrice's writing is not yet good enough to be re-marked by another. Fabrice must voice what he has written in order for the presence to come to the fore, a presence that, once there, is immediately sub-merged in the writing of another: "The letters will be done sooner, he said to Fabrice, if Your Excellency takes the trouble to dictate them to me" (2:208). Fabrice himself cannot write much more than the beginning of the alphabet, a beginning that will be repeated for effect when he is in jail: "When the letters were done, Fabrice wrote an 'A' and a 'B' on the last line, and, on a little scrap of paper he later crumpled, he wrote in French: *Believe A and B* [*Croyez A et B*]. The messenger was to hide this crumpled paper in his clothing" (2:208). Grafting his letters onto the writing of himself-as-other, Fabrice can muster no more than the first two letters of the alphabet. Their truth is the identity of the letters to themselves and is thus also the truth and presence contained in the letter. But this truth is only ascertainable through the double otherness of the supplementary message, which is written on a scrap of paper in another language.

Now launched on his own writing career, Fabrice begins to become an ever more subtle reader, rewriter, and writer. Sensitive to the possible importance of a few words written in Greek, Fabrice excises them from the letter the archbishop has written him (2:221). Though he has never studied Greek, Fabrice can instantly seize the meaning and importance of the Greek words, and he immediately knows that they must be destroyed. His subtlety in reading is matched by an ever increasing productivity in writing: "He answered immediately [*à l'instant*] with an eight-page letter" (2:210). Fabrice even knows how to make a letter reach the *destinataire* for whom it is intended, who is not the person to whom it is sent: "In order that his beautiful letter in Italian not get lost, Fabrice made a few necessary changes and addressed it to Count Mosca" (2:210).

By the end of the first part of the novel, Fabrice is fully ensconced in the subtlety and power of his newfound semioticity. He has power as a reader and as a writer, but the writing constantly reverts to a remarking of his own narcissism. The first part of the novel ends with Fabrice's own writing, but it seems strangely to echo the family network and sets of relations already in place at the beginning of the novel. He writes to his aunt again and tells her that he will not go to Paris for love or money; his aunt has nothing to fear; Fabrice will do what he is supposed to do (2:44). Semioticity eerily begins to repeat the realm of identity that had always been there. We have gotten nowhere quickly.

Semioticity must, however, be answered by semioticity; writing must be dealt with in writing. In fact, Stendhal cannot begin to write the second half of his novel without repeating part of the first part. More exactly, he cannot do so without misquoting himself proleptically, from a later chapter. This misquote now represents the nonidentity of writing both to itself and to what is said. While the misquotation is rather a different version of the same idea contained in the later chapter, it coincidentally sets the tone for the miswriting that is about to occur. It is clear that Fabrice cannot simply be caught through brute force. For Fabrice has entered a realm other than that of the pure self-identical presence implied in the first chapters: Fabrice has entered into the game of difference of writing. Fabrice must be caught in a web of words; he can be caught only in the absence formed by writing:

—His Highness [*Son Altesse*] would write me a gracious letter as he [*elle*] knows how to do so well; he would tell me that, unconvinced as he was of the guilt of Fabrice del Dongo, first vicar of the archbishop, he will not sign the sentencing papers when they are presented to him and that this unfair procedure will have no consequences in the future [*cette procédure injuste n'aura aucune suite à l'avenir*]. (2:254)

The semiotic level of this rather stilted request, with the third-person form of address in the feminine, as is grammatically correct, takes precedence over the reality and presence of the prince as an addressable, male, second person. Feminizing the prince also erases the threat that his sexuality poses to Gina. By erasing part of the erasure, Mosca restores the potency of the prince. Repeating the gesture of the absent writer, Stendhal once again has the letter written by another. And finally, the letter writer absent, the writing absent from the letter, the trap of written words is created, the parabolic prison into which Fabrice will soon be inserted:

Another few words were exchanged, but finally Count Mosca got the command to write the gracious note the Duchess had asked for. He omitted the phrase: this unfair procedure will have no consequences in the future [*cette procédure injuste n'aura aucune suite à l'avenir*]. It is enough, the Count said to himself, that the Prince promises not to sign the sentence presented to him. The Prince thanked him with a wink when signing it.

The Count was very wrong, the Prince was tired and would have signed anything . . . (2:255)

Finally Fabrice will be caught, and the decrees dictating that he be thrown into the Tour Farnèse for a twelve-year sentence will be faithfully reproduced by Rassi as they are dictated to him. The dictation bears no relation whatsoever to any "real" scene; writing is now pure invention, as a dialogue and tear-jerking scene are invented between the Prince and Gina (2:260–61). The writing of the Other has entered the realm of pure fiction, and in so doing lays down a challenge to Fabrice to continue to be a valid fictional character while in this prison of words. Up to now Fabrice has matched the movement from real presence into semioticity by a similar move of his own out of identity to a point of difference where he can read and begin to write. Now he too must write, not simply with a semiotics that symbolically relates an individual truth of representation, but a fiction as well. And, as everyone knows, in order to write fiction, whether the writer be Descartes in his little room, Marcel Proust in his cork-lined room, or Virginia Woolf with a room of her own, one must be in solitary confinement.[19] And thus will it be for Fabrice.

WRITING BEHIND BARS

Prison separates and stills: the law sees all and is silent, and in that silence it quiets the prisoner. But the law has a blind spot: having established itself as the law of silence, it cannot go beyond the walls it uses to separate. Only the repeated insistence of the law, be it verbal, physical, visual, or written, can in fact penetrate, thereby precluding all other thought: Poe's "The Pit and the Pendulum," Kafka's "In der Strafkolonie," and Stanley Kubrick's film *A Clockwork Orange* are among the more famous examples. A voiced law precludes dialogue, for it establishes itself as monologue; a silent law does not. As long as the law imposes itself silently, silent dialogue and monologue are not precluded.

Imprisoned within the walls of silence that define the power of the Other, Fabrice can think and dream, as Victor Brombert notes (*Prison* 62–87). Freedom to think means, at least potentially, the freedom to think of a message to send: "Fabrice's first thought, as he was glued to the iron bars of his window, was to give in to the childishness of banging on the bars with his hand, which would produce a little noise; then only the idea of this lack of propriety [*délicatesse*] horrified him" (2:316). Yet he cannot renew a childish system of communication that merely announces identity. Having passed through a communicational system that emphasizes the good reading of signs, the novel is now in a mode that emphasizes writing. Were Fabrice to use an "outdated" model, he would become the object of derision and scorn, to whom a fit response would be Clélia's absence: "I would deserve it if she sent her maid to take care of her birds for a week. This delicate idea would not have occurred to him in Naples or Novara" (2:316). Fabrice must establish a writing system appropriate to the situation in which he finds himself in the narrative, and appropriate to his own process of learning how to communicate. The first step maintaining an open channel: he must continue to be able

to see Clélia and have her see him (2:317). In order to establish even
the possibility for written communication, he must not simply open
a channel for communication, but must also see to it that the possibility of this channel is not blocked. In so doing, he reforms the
prison structure for his own benefit by taking the frame in which the
law of silence reigns to turn it into an effective channel of communication.

To establish a possible channel of communication *ab ovo* would be
tantamount to assuming an absolute origin for his own writing, a situation that is clearly not possible, given the fact that the law is already there, preceding him, surrounding him, and determining him:
Fabrice does not exist without its imposition. But in a sense, he has
never existed without some imposition, even if it is the imposition of
identity visited on him by his family, his name, his obligation to be
whom they want him to be. Thus he must set up his writing against
the writing that is already there. As one would expect from the structures of a realist writing that mirrors its context—a developing capitalist system—the writing is not made to depend on a transcendental signified that is figured in some ardent, immediate, or transcendental desire, be it a Rousseauist transparency or even the burning
youthful flame that motivates Julien Sorel to announce himself as a
man of action by taking the hand of Mme de Rênal.[20]

For Fabrice in prison, establishing a system of communication depends on a transcendental signifier. The moment of foundation must
be a means by which the writing of the Other is overcome. The transcendental signifier that signifies the system and the validity of communication is encrypted and overcome, yet is still preserved: "The
previous evening, before going to bed, he took the time to hide most
of the gold he had in several rat-holes that adorned his wooden
room" (2:317). The holes adorn the cell; thus they are suitable spots
for burying the transcendental signifier of the Other. Like the hiding place for Poe's purloined letter, they are the most obvious spot
and thus the least visible one. The signifier of the Other then lends
its aura of power without the insistence of its presence. In the cell
that is a metaphor for the impenetrable space of Fabrice's mind, the
signifier of the Other can be buried, neutralized in itself, yet giving
power to establish Fabrice's own writing.

For Stendhal, writing is established at the site of the neutralized writing of the Other. It is thus both a continuation of the process of writing and a break with it. No writing of the *arriviste* son can establish itself absolutely, but must come into being, somewhat like a palimpsest, at the neutralized locus of the writing of the Other. Thus Julien Sorel is instructed by Madame de Rênal to produce the anonymous letter by neutralizing another's writing (1:330). The channel of communication is given in the form of the book and the writing paper of Monsieur Valenod; this preexisting writing of authority is neutralized and overcome as it is put to use for a new writing project. In the *Chartreuse*, Stendhal uses a syllepsis to indicate a more subtle neutralization: "I have to hide my watch tonight. Haven't I heard that with patience and a jagged watch spring [*avec de la patience et un ressort de montre ébréché*], wood and even iron can be cut? I will be able to cut this shutter" (2:317).[21]

At the heart of the Stendhalian scheme for the establishment of writing, a figure unites the purely denotative to the literary or the figurative. And the troping movement of the figure is the same movement that covers up the inscribed signifier of the Other. The Other's word is eclipsed through the same action that deictically announces its own inscription at the point of poetic production. The figurability of the syllepsis guarantees the viability of the channel. The imposition of a figure of speech or writing already implies that, like Julien before him, Fabrice can also write. If, ironically, Julien ultimately cut along the dotted line—which he could not do at the saw-mill—as he assembles an "anonymous" letter according to Mme de Rênal's directions, Fabrice finally is going to go one step further than his predecessor: he is going to create the line to be cut along.

It is not enough to establish the channel of communication; the existence of the channel must be attested by the other, now co-opted in the new communicational schema. In this case it is Clélia, who must see that Fabrice sees her (2:317). As Stendhal has told us on the previous page, her act of sight is already an act of communication, for "she could not impose silence on her eyes" (2:316). Any interruption of the channel demands a strong countermeasure in order for the channel finally to be opened once and for all: "The evening of the day he had not seen his pretty neighbor, he had a great idea: with the iron cross of the rosary [*avec la croix de fer du chapelet*] given to all prisoners when they enter prison, he began, and with success,

to pierce the shutter [*il commença, et avec succès, à percer l'abat-jour*]"
(2:320). The power of gold can only buy a temporary stop to the closure of a channel of communication, just as bribes can delay the imposition of a punishment. But the cross, transcendental signifier
joined to its referent, can provide the necessary permanence in the
channel needed for effective communication. The cross is used ir-
reverently, yet its aura of power, the trace of the writing of the Other,
is precisely what allows the channel of communication to be opened
fully. Again Stendhal uses a syllepsis, but here the jagged watch
spring becomes the orthogonal cross and patience is turned into success; the figure is undone. By separating the syllepsis into two
phrases, Stendhal unyokes what had been yoked and allows the event
to be accomplished.

Opening the channel first permits an immediacy of reading: "He
had all the time to read the most tender signs of pity in her eyes"
(2:320). The situation of immediacy is bilateral and is less emotive
than it is phatic: Fabrice's signs mean only that he is there and that
he sees Clélia (2:321); the phatic element guarantees a "sign of presence." The system is not an adequate one, for it communicates nothing but the fact of its own existence: there is a message-sender, a
channel of communication, and a message-receiver. The message is
that there is no message other than the fact that there is a message-
sender. Writing must be invented, to be in the spot where there can
be no act of presence, no speech, and no sound: "He wanted to correspond with her by means of the characters he traced on his hand
with a bit of coal whose precious discovery he had made in his furnace; he would have formed the words letter by letter, in succession"
(2:324). The space of production of this writing is not one of
verisimilitude, for there is a divergence between the narrative, ultimately ambiguously conflated with its own self-reflexivity, and the
parameters of the verisimilar. If we take Fabrice's wish literally, we
have to imagine that his hand stays eternally clean and that somehow
it can be erased before the inscription of the subsequent letter. We
must therefore assume that as a prisoner Fabrice has unlimited quan-
tities of soap and water to help him in this endeavor. Such a rational
assumption is ridiculous, though Stendhal's irony is, even as we posit
such a possibility, very much in evidence.

Such writing is as impossible within the prison of verisimilitude as it is possible, and even necessary, within the prison of narrative self-reflexivity. In other words, the effect of verisimilitude depends on an absence of verisimilitude; there is a rupture in the representational process that needs narrative self-reflexivity as a guarantee for an approach to the verisimilar. For there to be writing that resembles verisimilar writing, the structuring of writing has to be anything but verisimilar. At the same time, the myth of writing must correspond to the nineteenth century's belief in concepts relating to verisimilitude: exchange, transcendental signifiers of meaning and grounding, the possibility of representation of a seamless whole through signs. The construct then shows that the seamless whole can be represented, if and only if there is one seam, flaw, gap, hole in the carpet, at the point at which the weaving of the threads occurs. The writing that Stendhal needs to posit is one of absolute presence, which stands by itself in front of the space on which it is grafted. As if a product of a magician, writing must float freely in front of its own space. Such a description befits the alchemical writing of a *grimoire*: the lowly base material, a lump of coal, will be turned into an absolute value fully present unto itself. The grimoire is not begrimed; it is rather the book of an immaculate conception, the product of a virgin thought such as the one proposed here. The writing proposed for this space is not accomplished; rather, it is palinodically countered by the impossibility of speech, which is too risky with the sentries below (2:324). This writing and this speech are both impossible because they are not grounded in any real or theoretical space of representation. Free speech is dangerous and free writing is impossible. In order for either one or both to come into being, there must be a space of representation, something more than the simple channel of communication that opens the theoretical possibility of communication.[22]

The epistemological space that provides the justification for good communication depends on the preexistence of other writing. Oral communication does not come to rest in the space of a previously existing oral communication. It is found instead at the locus of previously existing written communication. When the space is opened the potential becomes activated: Clélia communicates danger to Fabrice by singing new words to a recitative from a popular opera (2:331). Still, the space of production is not at all verisimilar. If Clélia is truly concerned about being understood, logic would dictate that she feign singing an aria—since recitatives are all too comprehensible—that is *not* popular or well-known. The recitative or an aria from a well-known opera would itself be well-known; someone overhearing her could detect the fact that she is not singing the right words. Changing the words of a less popular aria would not be as quickly remarked by a spy. Using a preexisting melody, Clélia performs an act of substitution, speaking, singing, or writing over what was previously written as she substitutes her own writing for it. The canceled libretto disappears leaving only the structure of a melody onto which Clélia can graft her new words. The original writing that stands in the space of communication—the libretto—is written over as the potential space for communication—the melody—remains ready to be reused for the production of a new piece of writing.

One palimpsest should call for another, but at this point Fabrice can only activate his dream. His message of the magic *grimoire* communicates two things, which are the emotive insistence on the channel of communication and the need for a means of communication:

Fabrice had kept the piece of coal he had found in his furnace as if it were a treasure; he rushed to take advantage of Clélia's emotion and to write a series of letters on his hand whose successive appearance formed these words:
   "I love you, and life is precious to me only because I see you; send me especially paper and a pencil." (2:331–32)

There is still too much real or imagined noise in the system, and the temporary means of communication, the palimpsestic recitative and the hand-writing, will not do: "Fabrice had the intelligence [*l'esprit*] to add: Because of the wind today, I hear the advice you give me by singing very imperfectly; the sound of the piano hides your voice. What, for example, is the poison of which you speak?" (2:332). Thus what is already written (like the melody, for example) is stronger than the means of communication. Instead of the temporary measures of the recitative and the hand-writing, there is a kind of indelible writing on the writing of the Other; to get there Fabrice uses "the little ruse" of noncomprehension. Fabrice now is wearing the mantle of the expert semiotician and the budding writer; with that guise, he establishes his own law of communication for the writing system.

The writing system is founded on a lie, whose announcement brings the reader recursively to question the establishment of previous systems of writing in the novel by which the process of fictional-ization is brought to the fore. This establishment occurs simultane-ously with the crossing out of the old system and with the concomi-tant denial that the new system is established through usurpation. The establishment of the new system is an act of writing over the old system, until the old system is canceled out by the overwriting. This overwriting often announces itself as such in a real, physical sense, as in Fabrice's hand-writing; in such a case, the novel enters into a sys-tem where all the parameters are based on considerations of writing and where there are no allowances for verisimilitude. The movement away from reality and truth is inherent in the establishment of a sys-tem grounded in a fabrication. The enunciation of the establishment of the system of writing as one based on Fabrice's fabrication is nec-essarily announced from a position of truth, relative to that lie.

Just at the moment that Fabrice begins to assert himself as the founder of a system of writing, the narrative strength of the author reappears. The truth told by the narrative about Fabrice's lie and his founding duplicity subjugates Fabrice to the exigencies of the law of the Other. The inexorable authoritative power of the narrator effects this act of subjugation and reasserts his own position as an absolute one. Just as Julien Sorel is returned by writing into writing that he has previously read, Fabrice is returned to the writing of the Other. The narrator reappears on the same page to give Fabrice a new epi-thet of "our prisoner" (2:332). Fabrice is now prisoner of the narra-tor and the readers; relative to his, ours is a position of truth and power. We know he has lied in order to found a system of writing. We have decided to agree to the narrator's scapegoating of Fabrice to guarantee the integrity of the narrative system as a whole.

The Other's writing reasserts itself, not as an impediment to com-munication but as a guarantee of communication. Whereas earlier in the novel the alphabet had been used as the guarantee of the writing of a new writer, as Fabrice writes "Croyez A et B," here the rein-scription of the writing of the other guarantees the lie. Writing given marginally announces the necessity of identifying the very substance of life itself. This is accomplished by inscribing the mark of the cross, a sign of the Other that has already been successfully used: Clélia will mark bread that is safe to eat with little crosses (2:333). Whereas the crosses, the signs of the truth of the other, mark the bread, both the writing of Fabrice and that of Clélia, surrogate of the surrogate, are consigned to the side. Beside the bread are a roll of paper to serve as second sheets and a prayer book in whose margins Clélia has already written. Writing is negligible as long as that of the self is not central and is marginalized to second sheets. As soon as the writing of the self begins to approach the Other's writing, it incurs risks. Hence, in an ironic act of annihilation, Fabrice, who now knows how to read very well and who now knows the power of writing, understands that writing entails obligation: "Fabrice rushed to removed the beloved characters that could compromise Clélia . . . " (2:334). Once again, the concerns are scriptorial rather than verisimilar; it is implausible that somehow Fabrice managed to produce an eraser or ink eradicator from the same lump of coal he had used before.

To fabricate his alphabets, Fabrice does not even use the second sheets that would have been the space of verisimilitude. Rather, he proceeds to annihilate the Other's writing. It little matters that a whole set of letters written in Fabrice's hand would be far more compromising than writing in the margin of the breviary or than the alphabet that Clélia eventually sends him (2:335). Fabrice's imposition of his own writing *must* take place *on* the Other's writing. He tears a number of pages from the book and makes several alphabets by writing with coal dissolved in wine (2:334). The verisimilar use of several alphabets is unclear, since he could only hold up to two letters at a time, and thus would need only two alphabets at the most. But it makes literary sense. Fabrice repeatedly writes over the previously existing writing, as if by sheer force of numbers his writing could vanquish that of the Other. Yet, at the same time, he must have good penmanship; he must write in a proper hand that is ultimately not his own. He cannot, for example, invent a whole new system of signs (Rabine 134–35). His writing must always be preceded: it can never stand completely on its own.

Clélia does not need to submit her writing to the writing of preexisting authority: she is not her father's rival and is outside the Oedipal model. She can write correctly, singly, and abundantly: "Far from objecting to using the alphabets, Clélia made a magnificent one in ink" (2:334–35). Since she is outside the system of Oedipal writing and since she writes to fulfill her own desire, Clélia can initiate magic tricks that Fabrice can only follow. Though Stendhal never has her make another alphabet, it seems that she has, or that she can magically turn one into many: "Fabrice had gotten her to send, along with water in the evening, one of the alphabets traced by her in ink, which could be more clearly seen" (2:335). And this act of magic brings about another: "He did not fail to write quite a long letter in which he took care not to put in tender things, at least in a way that might offend. This means was a success for him; his letter was accepted" (2:335). The magic lies not in the fact that Fabrice manages to write a letter without ink or paper, for he has the ersatz ink made of coal and wine and the second sheets that the narrator obviously saved for him for a greater purpose. It is rather that the letter can be accepted because of what it does or does not contain. In order to be refused it would already have to have been read and therefore already accepted. Magic writing persists and the chain of writing is now complete.

Fabrice's writing is now sealed with the inscription of his and Clélia's desire. Even though he, though not she, has to submit constantly to the constraints of Oedipal writing and to the eternal presence of the writing of the Other, Fabrice can finally escape them somewhat through the liberation afforded by desire. With desire in the writing model, writing is finally institutionalized in a fixed system: "Every morning, and often in the evening, there was a long conversation with the alphabets; every evening, at nine o'clock, Clélia accepted a long letter, and sometimes answered with a few words; she sent him the newspaper and some books" (2:335). Consecrated by Clélia's magical writing power and brokered by a state of mutual desire, Fabrice can become a reader again. Although he remains a prisoner, exiled from society, Clélia affords him reentrance into the system of social writing.

Having overcome the prison walls to establish a system of writing with Clélia, and having instituted this tentative system *as* a system, Fabrice has accomplished the founding act necessary for him to continue. With this act past, the walls of the prison no longer have the isolating function they once had. Able to write, Fabrice has for all intents and purposes been released from his prison. Communications can circulate unimpeded through his prison cell. In fact, communications even find their way to him as he perceives his own star of Bethlehem, there for all to see but only for him to read:

One night, toward one in the morning, Fabrice, lying by his window, stuck his head through the passage in the shutter, and looked at the stars on the immense horizon that could be seen from the Tour Farnèse. Looking toward the lower Po and Ferrara, his wandering eyes noticed by chance an excessively small light, but rather sharp, which seemed to come from a tower. (2:340)

His eyes guided toward the light, he figures out that it is blinking meaningfully. Even before he begins to decipher the message, he instantly realizes that it is a love letter from a girl to her lover. Intercepting a message meant for another, he acts as the child/interloper in the Oedipal triangle; only he himself is the Other in this case. Voyeurism notwithstanding, he begins to decipher the code and makes out the word "ina." The act of voyeurism turns into its own self-realization; Fabrice is spying on his own message:

Imagine his joy and astonishment, when the successive flashes separated by little rests, completed the following words:
GINA PENSA A TE
Obviously: *Gina is thinking of you.*
He immediately answered [*à l'instant*] with successive flashes of his lamp through the transom he used so well: FABRICE LOVES YOU.

This epiphanous enlightenment overcomes all constraints of verisimilitude. Apparently magnified into the wattage of an as yet uninvented klieg light, Fabrice's own lantern can communicate as well as that lantern of the message sender.

Stendhal goes beyond canceling his fealty to verisimilitude because the code itself begins to falter. Coming as it does at such a strategic point, this is hardly an accident or an oversight. Technically speaking, the Italian alphabet does not include the letters J and K (among others) and thus N is a twelfth and not the fourteenth letter of the alphabet, as Stendhal would have it for the message. Stendhal is familiar enough with Italian to know his ABC's in that language. The code is abandoned in favor of the absolute nature of the individual message.[23] The message that Gina sends is in Italian, though she verisimilarly uses the French or English alphabet, but it is immediately and obviously understandable to the French reader.

Writing has become individual instances of absolute messages, immediately understandable to the proper destinataire but invisible to everyone else. Fabrice can write however he wants to Clélia or to Gina and only Clélia and Gina will understand him. Stendhal underlines that these messages are writing; they are an exchange of letters: "The correspondence continued until daybreak" (2:341). As writing that is immediately understandable to those who use it, it must be made invisible to the others, even if it is already invisible in terms of verisimilitude. The writing must be written over scriptorially; the original discourse must be replaced by another writing, which is a false one that comes after:

> But everyone could see them and understand them; from the first night on, they began to use abbreviations: three rapid flashes meant the Duchess; four, the Prince; two, Count Mosca; two rapid flashes followed by two slow ones meant *escape* [*évasion*]. They agreed that in the future they would use the old alphabet *alla Monaca*, which, so as not to be deciphered by indiscreet people, changes the ordinary number of letters, and gives them an arbitrary one; A, for example, bears the number 10, B, number 3; that is to say, that three successive flashes of the lamp mean B, ten successive eclipses mean A, etc.; a moment of darkness separates words. (2:341)

In terms of verisimilitude, the passage has gone wrong in a number of ways, but in terms of writing it is on the mark, so to speak (Berg 173). This overwriting is only given in the wake of its own disappearance. The presence of naming is given by the blinking lights, and the absence [*évasion*], which is a return to presence with Gina, is also given as blinking lights. Yet everything else that has to be formed by writing is given by the eclipses of the light. Stendhal underlines the nature of writing, even as he tries to show its artifice. If Fabrice and Gina agree to use the alphabet *alla Monaca*, is it one that is already an agreed on substitution cipher or is it a new one that must be spelled out that night? If it is the former, the messages sent are still readable; if it is the latter, the system has to be developed and the metamessage sent, in which case it too can be read.

Even in his explanation, in which he unnecessarily repeats the mechanics of the communicational system, Stendhal points out the act of rewriting: the number 10, seemingly arbitrarily chosen to represent "A," is precisely the number at which the writing system went wrong in the earlier explanation. For in the straightforward system, 10 is precisely the number that has no letter corresponding to it:

there is no J in the Italian alphabet. In a way then, the substitution cipher is sanctified by the erroneous example. The original writing is given here as 10–3, the articulation of which is J.C. if the tenth and third letters of the alphabet respectively are taken. This J.C.—Jesus Christ—both can and cannot be written as such in Italian; it is all the auraed writing canceled and preserved up to now. This impossible message—like the gold, but especially like the rosary and like the series of crosses—is the material sign of the Other that continues to guarantee the ability of the system to function. It is the writing of authority and that of the father, but also the writing of salvation. The original writing is used in fact to signal to Fabrice and to all that "soon he would be freed, THANKS TO THE GOOODNESS OF THE PRINCE (these signals could be understood)" (2:341). Needless to say, the laws of verisimilitude would demand that those who read this transparent writing stick around to try to decipher the rest, but this is not the case. For no one else reads the writing: it is for us, who are rereading, that the writing must be distinguished.

Fabrice's escape from the physical prison is again determined by writing and not by the constraints of verisimilitude. As the critical moment of escape approaches, this writing is becoming both more dangerous and more daring: "Fabrice's head was almost broken by a large lead bullet that, thrown through the upper part of his shutter, broke the paper panes and fell into his room" (2:351). His paper is no longer useful and it gives way to the power of the writing of another; the bullet contains a letter from the duchess. This daring means of communication is a dangerous one that must be answered by a sign that confirms receipt. The sign is a renewal of the lamp signals. Stendhal takes the time both to remind the reader of the code being used and to change the code (2:352). Indeed, Stendhal seems to feel that it is necessary to remind Fabrice of four things. First, he needs to know that the code to be used is the one he has been using all along; second, he also needs to know that the specific substitutions are those already given. This is not entirely true, since the "B," already given, does not match the previous substitution cipher. Third, he must be aware that there will be an answer with a certain set of letters, and finally, he must know that the signals for those letters are those given. And all of this when any signal from Fabrice and any signal from Gina would have done as well.

The novel insists on the substitution of one writing system for another because verisimilitude has been eschewed and because the end
of Fabrice's writing is approaching. He himself is now returned to
the warp and woof of the work; he must concentrate on his reading,
which will soon become an obligation. Gina writes: "I hope to get
five or six letters to you through the same channels as this one. I shall
incessantly repeat the same things in other terms, so we are in full
agreement" (2:354). Gina dictates everything; even the irony of the
ultimate danger is to be signaled by the absence of writing, books
burned in a castle library:

I shall not hide the fact from you that we fear a most imminent danger that
might hasten the day of your flight. To announce this danger, the lamp will
say several times in a row:
   "*The castle has caught fire!*"
   You will answer:
   "*Have my books burnt?*" (2:354)

The act of writing has turned into a repetition of insistence. Moreover, writing will now masquerade as speech, as even the lamp has
the power of speech. This is no longer a correspondence by letters,
for when it is a question of burning writing, the lamp will speak.
   One act of repetition seems to bring about another. Fabrice is
about to receive a visit from three judges, whose very triplicity is a
reminder of the multiplication of the position of the Other. Now, as
Fabrice comes ever closer to freedom, this position of the Other,
given as the Law itself, is going to be constantly reinforced. Like
Julien before him, Fabrice has the ability to use the words of the
Other and turn them to his own advantage. If the position of the
Other is reinforced, the banal repetition of the words of the Other
diminishes its force:

Here are three judges coming up! They are going to interrogate you: think
before you speak; they come to trap you [*entortiller*].
   . . . Tell them you are suffering a lot and speak little; especially make
them repeat the questions so you can reflect. (2:355)

The critical word "reflect" (*réfléchir*) reappears here, and just as for
Julien Sorel, it signals the return of the semiotician or writer into the
general weave of writing as one who is subject to another. Specifically, Fabrice is going to be deprived of writing and even of the abil-

ity to read, as writing to him will be selectively edited and read. The judges announce the death of Fabrice's father, but since Fabrice's mother had added "inconvenient reflections" to her missive, he is not permitted to read the letter (2:355–56). Fabrice does catch a glimpse of his mother's words, but the truth of the letter is denied through the act of censorship: only the nullity of the censor's act of excision replaces the mother's words.

After nine months of gestation, the system of writing is fully destroyed and the escape begins:

> For nine months, extreme unhappiness had had a great influence on this ardent soul; it had strengthened him, and the Duchess was not carried away with sobs or complaints.
> The next evening she had the sign of great danger signaled to Fabrice.
> *The castle has caught fire.*
> He answered correctly.
> *Have my books burnt?* (2:362)

With that verbal conflagration ends the career of Fabrice as semiotician and writer, to be followed only by the writing of silence.

HOLLOW WRITING

In terms of writing, the last third of the novel is a catalogue of failed or travestied communicational schemes. Writing's new function is as a parody of itself; even the act of creating a poetic work is ridiculed: "Since he has a print shop at his command, said the Duchess to himself, we'll soon have a collection of sonnets, God knows what name he'll give me!" (2:420). The poet, Ferrante Palla, cannot write and the powers that be cannot read the words on the page or pronounce them well: "The Prince played rather badly; he could barely be heard and couldn't end his sentences" (2:420). Unable to read correctly, power is stripped of its force, and has to be guided through something written for schoolchildren, a fable of La Fontaine, "The Gardener and His Master" ("Le Jardinier et son seigneur"; 2:424–26). Writing is disseminated, misdirected, and most improperly used as a supplement to speech: Clélia makes a vow to the Virgin Mary and then repeats the act of faith by writing it on a small piece of paper which is then to be burnt on the altar of the church (2:455). Writing is annihilated in the action of sending a message to heaven; the writing is replaced by silence and absence.

Fabrice's writing also turns into an iterative parody of what it once was, as it remarks the lines of power. Even Stendhal's narrator asserts the vain nature of Fabrice's writing:

Barely arrived in a safe spot, Fabrice first took care to write to General Fabio Conti a perfectly polite letter that was rather ridiculous in a way; he asked forgiveness for having escaped. . . . It little mattered what he wrote; Fabrice hoped that Clélia's eyes would see this letter; his face was bathed in tears while writing it. He ended it with a rather pleasant sentence: he dared say that, finding himself free, he often missed his little room in the Tour Farnèse. That was the main thought of his letter; he hoped Clélia would understand it. (2:392)

Fabrice's writing remarks an absence, and it is no longer contained by a channel of communication as it had been through much of the novel. Both the channel between him and Clélia and the one between Fabrice and Gina had been absolute, noise-free, optimum modes of communication. Now, however, it is only by chance that a message will reach its destinataire. Moreover, in this iterative mode, it little matters who the destinataire is: "Hoping to be read by someone, Fabrice addressed his thanks to Don Cesare, the good chaplain who had lent him theology books" (2:392). Aside from marking an absence and aside from being disseminated rather impotently, Fabrice's own writing will now be used to re-mark the lines of authority. Fabrice creates a palimpsest with an erasure; his writing is a marginal error. The error can easily be rectified by reimposing money as the transcendental signifier:

Several days later, Fabrice had the little bookseller of Locarno travel to Milan, where this bookseller, a friend of the celebrated book-lover [*bibliomane*] Reina, bought the most magnificent editions he could find of the works lent by Don Cesare. The good chaplain received these books and a beautiful letter that told him that, in moments of impatience that could perhaps be forgiven a poor prisoner, the margins of Don Cesare's books had been filled with ridiculous notes. He was thus being entreated to replace them in his library by the volumes that deepest gratitude [*reconnaissance*] allowed [Fabrice] to send Don Cesare. (2:392–93)

Fabrice denies the originality of his own act of writing, which is so remarkable that it is infinite: there are the "infinite scribblings with which he had filled the margins of a folio edition of the works of Saint Jerome" (2:393). Written when his writing was strong, it can be read only by select eyes, Clélia's for example, but not those of the owner of the book, Don Cesare (2:393). Returning to prison, Fabrice is a pale copy of the strong semiotician and writer he once was. His opening act of communication parodies Clélia's communication by recitative, as he sings that he came back to prison to see her (2:434). He rewrites his marginalia with pristine margins, and allows Saint Jerome to reign supreme.

Within the framework of the novel, writing is now no more powerful than a blank page. Whereas Fabrice had originally been condemned to prison by an act of willful omission of writing, all that is necessary to provoke his final release is a blank piece of paper signed by the prince (2:445). The narrator removes power in writing from *two* loci. Fabrice is rendered impotent as his writing is reflected back onto him. But the writing of those who have stood for power itself is also stripped of its validity. Both the alienated ideal self and what might be called the alienated ideal Other lose all value and strength. What remains is the power of the novel's writing itself, which is the structuring function that this narrative has to shape the representations given.

It is not without final ironies that Stendhal re-marks the sterility anew, even as he gives Fabrice the bewitching power of speech. Since Fabrice is now a "speaker" rather than a writer, his writing suffers:

The simple letter he wrote every day to the Count or Countess seemed an almost unbearable burden to him. He will be forgiven when it is known that a whole year passed thus without his being able to say a word to the Marquise. All his attempts to establish a correspondence had been rejected in horror. (2:472)

Clearly, the readers are still in the narrator's lofty sphere: like the chaplain who is to forgive Fabrice for having written in the margins, we are to forgive Fabrice his written trespasses. Given as a sermon and thus made the full equivalent of speech, as speech is made the full equivalent of writing, Fabrice's writing launches him fully into another realm. Since writing and speech have both foundered, failed, and been resurrected, there is no longer any difference between them. The disappearance of this difference is the transfiguration of the narrative: "While reading the written paper, Fabrice found two or three ideas on the unhappy state of mankind for which he had come to ask for the prayers of the faithful. Soon thoughts came to him in bunches [*en foule*]" (2:487). Clélia's writing to him is also a mark of the divine; when she finally writes Fabrice (2:487) after she has spent fourteen months without seeing him, Fabrice recognizes "those divine characters." The system of communication is now established for the novel's dénouement. It is a divine system with the narrator, seconded by the rhetorical readers, serving as an inexorable god of judgment. Now a discursive system founded on a lie will not be considered valid:

It was in vain that the most well-known casuists, consulted on obeying a vow, when fulfilling it would be harmful, had answered that the vow could not be considered to be broken criminally, insofar that the person bound by a promise to the Divinity withheld action, not for a vain sensual pleasure, but to avoid causing an obvious ill. (2:492)

All other discourse founders, as all is reduced to silence. The creations that have stood out withdraw to their crypts: Sandrino dies, as does Clélia. Fabrice retires to "The Charterhouse of Parma": that is to say, both the Charterhouse and the novel itself reach their conclusions. He dies and Gina dies as well. Even the loci where writing was once produced are endlessly and eternally silent: "The prisons of Parma were empty" (2:493). And it is only Stendhal and we, the happy few, who are left to read and write.

CHAPTER 3

Balzac's Improprieties

In the studies of Balzac that follow in this chapter, I focus on what I perceive as some of the improprieties in Balzac's work. What I mean by "impropriety" is exactly what has been the subject of this book so far: the glossed-over holes and gaps in the writing, the pits of realism, and the means, tricks, and techniques by which the author seeks to overcome them. A large number of tricks figure in *La Comédie humaine*, not the least of which is Balzac's use of an omniscient third-person narrator. This was seen as artifice even when he was writing: *La Canne de M. de Balzac*, by Mme de Girardin, is the tale of Balzac's trickery. Like Gyges with his ring, the Balzac that Madame de Girardin creates has a magic cane that allows him to penetrate into the darkest areas, the most recondite, out-of-the-way places, and the most unknown corners of space and the human mind; Lucien Dällenbach has recently made much of this image in *La Canne de Balzac*. In this chapter, I should like to look at several of these improprieties in detail. The first is the meeting of public and private spaces and the use of violence to negotiate that meeting; the study is essentially a meditation on one scene in *Le Père Goriot*. After that initial reading, I propose a short wade through Balzacian mud. From that I turn to the improprieties of gender and genre in *La Muse du département*. After that, I turn to a long study of misreading in a theoretical sense, which is bolstered by references to *La Cousine Bette*, in a dramatic vein, and *Modeste Mignon*, in a comic vein. And finally, I turn to one of the figures endlessly hinted at in *Modeste Mignon*, the figure of the sublime, as Balzac's candidate for washing away impropriety.

Violence and Recognition (Vautrin)

How does Balzac relate a tale of violence? More specifically, how does Balzac use violence as a narrative mechanism to create possibilities, futures, actions, and events in his writing? Scenes of brutal violence are rare in Balzac's writing of the thirties and the forties. He punctiliously observes *bienséances*, for which violence is to be eschewed. Moreover, he takes into consideration his readership, ostensibly composed of bourgeois readers of indeterminate gender, seeking diversion in their reading and holding their books "with a white hand" (3:50); this is the last group he would risk offending.[1] And he knows he does not need a violent solution to wreck a character: more often than not, Balzac lets society ruins characters with whispered, noninvasive processes of rumor, abrasion, comeuppance, and degradation. Instead of acts of violent destruction, there is a wearing away of virtue, an abrasion through debt, a derogation through an accumulation of language, stories, and rumors. For every melodramatic and bloody ending like that of "La Fille aux yeux d'or," in which we see the aftereffect of violence, there are a dozen acts of degradation, misdirection, and ruin though rumor. If, for example, Bette's role in *La Cousine Bette* is so manipulative as to ruin the relations among an entire group of people, she accomplishes it by and large through a channeling of energy and acts of misdirection instead of through overt acts of violence.

Among the acts of violence, those that happen to women are inevitably off stage. We come upon the death of Paquita, the girl with the golden eyes, as she is expiring, "drowned in blood" (5:1106), but we do not see the act of violence itself. Certainly, Balzac gives us the clue earlier in the story of "La Fille aux yeux d'or," when, having given the reader a description of Paris that resembles Dante's Hell (1046) and that expressly refers to the figures of the Terror (1048), the narrator concludes: "This view of moral Paris proves that physical Paris could not be other than it is" (1051). There is thus no rea-

son to paint the degradation of the physical event, when it is necessarily the consequence of a moral or ethical situation. If characters
behave according to a certain code of ethics, the physical presence
and actions of the characters go without saying. Adduced in a rhetoric of language both at the level of the narration and at that of the
characters, moral and ethical violence replace the physical act (without, however, completely erasing it). Moral violence, which might be
otherwise termed the degradation of a character, whether it be the
experiences of Lucien de Rubempré in Paris or the fall of Goriot,
signals the violence to the individual at every level; there is no need
to depict it.

This substitution is not always at work in Balzac's writing. The
earlier *Etudes philosophiques* frequently rely on a much more visible set
of references to physical violence than does the remainder of *La
Comédie humaine*. In works such as *Louis Lambert* and "Le Chef-
d'oeuvre inconnu," the excesses associated with immoderate cere-
bration acquire an incontrovertible and unforgiving violence, as do
excesses associated with an abuse of power in *La Peau de chagrin*. This
violence is not an acquisitive violence of mimetic rivalry, for the
Balzacian vision of violence in his romantic pieces (in the *Etudes
philosophiques*) is associated with the impossibility of attaining an
ideal. In such works, the mimetic rivalry, if that be the term for it, is
with God.

There is a sea-change in Balzac's work, and when Balzac begins to
shape the general idea of the *Comédie humaine*, beginning with *Le
Père Goriot*, the ideas relating to violence and its representation
change as well. In the *Etudes philosophiques*, violence often relates to
metaphysics of power and scenes of emasculation.[2] On the other
hand, with *Le Père Goriot*, there is a shift from the act of emasculation to a marginalization of the violence of power. That marginalization is a powerful displacement of violence to a safe, controlled
environment, where it nevertheless remains useable or invocable for
the narrator, the successful, and the powers that be. Ordering society by banishing the other to its margins is one of Balzac's first rhetorical moves as he develops the realist aesthetic of the entire oeuvre.
At the same time, the knowledge of that displacement is what will
help Vautrin and Rastignac, to name only two, succeed where others
fail.

That change can best be seen in one episode of *Le Père Goriot*, the critical moment at which Vautrin is unmasked as the most heinous and powerful criminal in all of Paris. Though the recognition scene of discovering Vautrin's identity as Jacques Collin or Trompe-la-Mort is brief, it is a compact and complicated collapsing of various strands of narrative that extend along two time lines. For the sake of simplicity, I would like simply to repeat the *fable* of the scene, from some imaginary point outside the *Comédie humaine*. At some moment before a fictional 1819, when the novel is set, a certain Jacques Collin, also known in various societies and times as Vautrin, Trompe-la-Mort, and the Abbé Carlos Herrera, was found guilty of crimes and condemned to hard labor. Along with that punishment came a permanent and supposedly indelible mark of the condemnation: his back was branded with the letters "T.F.," which stood for *travaux forcés*, that is, "forced labor." Some time after that initial moment, but still during the Bourbon Restoration, the police suspect he is living under the name of Vautrin in a Parisian boarding house named the Pension Vauquer. To confirm his identity, the police ask Mlle Michonneau, an old maid of dubious background, to drug Vautrin, undress him, and slap his back to make the faded letters appear. This having been accomplished, the police arrest Vautrin. About a decade after that, in the real world (1832), the practice of branding is stopped in France; again, in the real world, shortly thereafter (1834–35), Balzac writes *Le Père Goriot*. Back in the fictional world, some time after Vautrin's arrest, he escapes from prison, and, having done so, scars and disfigures his back to make the letters disappear for all time. He then resurfaces in disguise as the Abbé Carlos Herrera; helps, though ultimately unsuccessfully, Lucien de Rubempré make his way through Parisian society; and finally becomes the chief of the secret police.

This having been said, it is clear that the Vautrin narrative forms one of the major arteries of *La Comédie humaine*. Vautrin is the metonym of the changing public space in which and on which narrative occurs, a space that moves from a physical insistence, in which he and the Maison Vauquer are equally readable in their own fashion, to a world of misreading and palinodic unreading, to the ironic apotheosis of the scarcely read, barely perceivable traces of an act. Vautrin is endlessly about to become the purloined letter as well as all its possessors and readers. Be that as it may, I want to focus on the heart of the scene, which is the kernel of recognition that comes with the identification of the branding.

In the scene, Vautrin is definitely identified as Jacques Collin, mastermind of the underworld. Here it is in French, followed by a literal translation: "Vautrin retourné, mademoiselle Michonneau appliqua sur l'épaule du malade une forte claque, et les deux fatales lettres reparurent en blanc au milieu de la place rouge" (3:213). In English, this becomes: "With Vautrin turned over, Mademoiselle Michonneau gave a hard slap to the ill man's shoulder, and the two fatal letters reappeared in white in the middle of the red area." The most powerful man in Paris has been laid low by a slap from an old maid, who, to get to that position, has had to undress the man in question.

As I have already indicated, the replacement of physical violence with rhetoric and moral analysis is Balzac's stock in trade. It is in *Le Père Goriot* where that exchange is first successful. Instead of action, there is narrative implying violent images; instead of an execution, there is a set of rhetorical signs of violence. One need go no further than the second sentence of the novel, where an act of violence is reduced to an allusion to violence in language. That violence, moreover, has not taken place: "This boarding-house, known under the name of the Maison Vauquer, admits both men and women, young people and old, without slander [*médisance*] ever having *attacked* the mores of this respectable establishment" (3:49; my emphasis). A few sentences further, Balzac displaces the language of physical violence onto others: "Despite the discredit into which the word 'drama' has fallen through the *abusive* and *twisted* manner in which it has been *brandished* during these times of *painful* literature, it is necessary to use it here" (49; my emphasis). And again, toward the end of the paragraph, right before we discover the imaginary reader ensconced in her or his soft armchair, we find civilization itself described in a language of violence: "The chariot of civilization, like that of the idol of Juggernaut, barely held back by a heart less easy to crush than others and which slows down the wheel, broke it and continues its glorious march" (50). Here, however, Balzac uses an abstract concept of civilization and the rather exotic image of Juggernaut to distance the violence from his writing, and concomitantly, to keep his writing safe from that violence's infection.

Thus in the very first lines of the novel, Balzac sets the tone for the translation or replacement of violence by language, as if he knew that the act of violence itself would not be productive. As both René Girard, in *La Violence et le sacré*, and Jacques Derrida, in *De la grammatologie* (164–65), have pointed out, there is a translation of an original violence (Girard) or an archiviolence (Derrida) into language. Through that symbolic transfer comes the possibility of productivity instead of an all-out war of mimetic rivalry (Girard) or the impossibility of developing difference (Derrida). Thus Balzac's translation of violence into a vocabulary of "attack," "abuse," and "brandish," for example, or his reference to Juggernaut, is the means by which he will create a world in which violence is subdued while being incorporated into the very heart of the system. Indeed, the interrelation of nascent capitalism, and specifically speculation, with violence is one of the origins of the story: Goriot makes his fortune as a war profiteer.

And there is a realist imperative as well in this case: though the *supplice* itself—the torturing of a convicted criminal—had been abolished through the modernization of the penal code in France in 1791, An IV, 1808 and 1810, as Michel Foucault notes in *Surveiller et punir* (13–16), criminals were still branded, a practice that was not abolished in France until 1832. So although at the time Balzac was writing *Le Père Goriot* (1834–35), the mark had itself disappeared, prisoners were still branded during the Bourbon Restoration in which the novel is set. And while it is tempting to see the disappearance of writing from one register—the real branding of prisoners—and its appearance in another—that of the novel as some sort of magical shifter that moves from reality to writing, it is not at all necessary. Suffice it to say that the mark becomes in and of itself the verisimilar sign guaranteeing the realism of the scene as it is described. Moreover, as the recognition scene is in part based on the memoirs of Vidocq, used by Balzac as a model for Vautrin, this scene can be found in those memoirs as well.

All in all, Balzac's inscription of the scene seems therefore to be motivated by nothing more than a faithful rendering of some historical accident that is the continued marking of the criminal with a brand through the period of the Restoration. Thus there is sufficient reason to see the episode as one in which nothing of the novelistic is added. Moreover, the scene itself is almost unnecessary: the novel could survive without this *coup de théâtre* taking place on stage. The violence itself is supplementary to the language used to describe it. The violence, represented as violence, is a rhetorical translation of the language of the moral code and the narrative model. Violence has become supplementary to a system that has inscribed its effects without needing the act itself.

The scene is overdetermined in its supplementarity, and it is precisely because of that overdetermination that I shall concentrate on it. My thesis is simple: the scene's rhetoric, its theatricality, and its depiction of violence are emblematic of the book as a whole. As befits a *coup de théâtre*, it is the spot in which the various strands of the work come together in a very visible figure of violence and rhetoric. Though the scene itself is not necessary to our understanding, it is a convenient mise-en-abîme of the novel, as well as being the illustration of the taming of violence, the marginalization of the other, and the moral rhetoric that supplants violence itself. Iconically, therefore, this scene illustrates Balzac at work. In short, given the relative disappearance of violence from Balzac's writing, the appearance on stage of violence at this very point is of paramount importance in our understanding of the relation of violence to writing and to the development of realism in Balzac's work. Thus the very singularity of the event makes it all the more fascinating, as if it were demanding to be read.

Let us anatomize the scene. The element of violence as such, the *claque*—the slap on the back—is itself a double repetition. On one level, it repeats the words of the narrative that predict it. The police officer, Gondureau, tells Mlle Michonneau to slip Vautrin a mickey, undress him, and slap him when she is alone with him. Given the teleological force with which this narrative is constructed, that is to say, the lack of red herrings along the main narrative line, this motivation is tantamount to a speech act with a perlocutionary force at a distance. When Gondureau says "you will slap him," Vautrin is already slapped, already read, and already recaptured. The violence is in the language, a language certifying that future by predicting it. The disorder we habitually associate with violence as such, the entropy of the action, is transmuted into dead certainty. As any reader of Balzac will know, this certainty is guaranteed by a reference to chance at that very point, which assures that the event will take place, as David Bell has shown (111–93).

What of that chance? Gondureau offers Mlle Michonneau a 2,000-franc finders' fee if the letters are on Vautrin's back, and 500 francs if they are not. As a good Balzacian character, Mlle Michonneau knows that one does not take such odds. Chance is a sign of a sure thing: Balzac sends Raphaël de Valentin to the gambling house so he will lose everything and has Eugène de Rastignac make a roulette bet for Delphine de Nucingen that is 36 times his age, followed by a neat double for red, so he will win. There is no hedging of the bet. Mlle Michonneau thus wisely asks for a martingale, double or nothing. She bets on a sure thing: 3,000 francs if Vautrin is Trompe-la-Mort, nothing if he is "un bourgeois" (3:193). Clearly, she cannot lose: the supposed game of chance underlines the redundancy of the act of violence, just as it underlines the redundancy of the chance itself. Vautrin must be Trompe-la-Mort and must have been marked with the fatal letters. Nothing is left to chance.

In the novel, the scene is prepared by a narrative that tells us what will occur; the dramatic effect of the unveiling is itself invalidated because we know what will happen. It is always already written, prematurely obsolete; the narrative of the drama is dead writing that marks Vautrin even before his body is present to be read. The preview of the scene of recognition undermines the double act of reading: Mlle Michonneau's reading of Vautrin's back and our reading of the scene itself. Reading becomes rereading, a repetition of what we know has already been written, even if we have not yet seen that writing. We read what is there as a secondary effect of a writing that always imposes itself as having been read. And the violence of the slap, the brutality of a scene that is almost a rape, is linked to the act of reading—that is, really reading—as both excessive and unessential. Both violence and this reading—her reading, our reading in fact—are unessential and redundant for Balzac because they are always an aftereffect moving us away from the pure being of the body and the pure act of writing.

Yet this is only half the story. For the scene between Gondureau and his two stool pigeons repeats a previous act of violence. That act is the branding, marking, or tattooing of Jacques Collin with the "two fatal letters." And just as Gondureau's official words ensure the act of violence to come, they certify the official branding of the prisoner that has occurred at some previous date in some world outside the narrative, a world where official violence occurs without mediation, where the body of the other is the property of the state, public property for all to cross and read. Language is the medium or the mediator placed between the Balzacian reader, with her white hand unsullied by any act, and the brutality of force. Thus the voice of authority, even in its most perverse form (Gondureau), doubled and purified in the Balzacian narrative as such, takes on the *tache* or *marque* (spot, task, mark, or marking) of violence, to allow the reader to maintain her purity and her peace.

Still, the novel is impregnated with aspects of a code of violence This structure continues the system of transmitting worldly goods while repressing the concomitant violence as such. This transmission is effected through the reproduction of the structures of the system: the alliances, the organization of the family, and the assurance of legitimacy. What perpetuates the system is not some periodic expulsion of a scapegoat, innocent victim of society's collective view of a mimetic crisis. The expulsion of Michonneau and Poiret from the Maison Vauquer is a repetition of the real violence and real expulsion of Vautrin. And in this expulsion, the system breaks down, as almost everyone leaves the boarding-house.

The victim, as much Mlle Michonneau as Vautrin the outlaw, is consciously chosen as the negation of society's values: Mlle Michonneau is guilty of not being married, Vautrin is as guilty of being queer as he is of being a criminal. Neither one nor the other fits the paradigm of reproduction. Or, more exactly, they make the paradigm by determining its limits. Hence there is a raison d'être for the act of violence, albeit a grotesque one, which amounts to the symbolic rape of a gay man by a non-woman, a *vieille fille*, an old maid. Whereas the importance of reproduction is valued in having the nursemaid Eurykleia recognize Odysseus, in the most well-known of all anagnoroses, here the value of reproduction is removed from the female character to reduce its value. Mlle Michonneau is one of the first of these Balzacian *vieilles filles* of whom Bette will be, like "la dernière incarnation de Vautrin," the apotheosis.

In Balzac's late novels, a woman like Bette who does not fulfill her metaphysical destiny of becoming wife and mother, that is to say, of perpetuating the system to which she is subjected, manipulates elements of the system in order to reformulate the structures and/or recenter her own marginality. But that is late Balzac, as is Vautrin's last incarnation as the chief of the secret police. Incarnations of the contradictions of capitalism itself, as Lukács would have it, Balzac's last writings are the ironizations of the familial, social, ideological, and economic structures of the state, of which everyone—and not only the "woman"—is a victim. In these works, Balzac will understand that the center of the structure is truly just as marginalized as the legally defined margins.

Here in *Le Père Goriot*, however, we are at a different point: Eugène's teleologically determined success ensures the stability of the structure, and thus the relative disposition of the figures at the centers or at least within the structure; the margins thereby remain stable. Mlle Michonneau and Vautrin are both operating at the margins of the structures of the narrative. What law governs them? What marks them, one might wonder? Sitting at the margins of the Balzacian structure and incapable here and now of operating an inversion or perversion of the structure *à la Bette*, the two are an unholy couple whose defining features do not match those of the central majority in any way. Each member of the majority is double: Eugène, Goriot, and Mme Vauquer are each both an individual and a part of an ongoing social structure: son, father, or widow. Being double means participating in displacement, hypocrisy, and a renegotiation of the meaning of violence in language. Being double means having that individual nature perceived as being as redundant as the redundant act of reading.

Now Vautrin and Michonneau are not double. They remain their individual intact selves, unrelated to the system. Unity is dangerous unless backed by a double, a hypocritical position, a redundancy of reading. This becomes obvious if we compare Mlle Michonneau to Mme de Restaud or Mme de Beauséant—the latter most aptly named, as she epitomizes upper-class behavior—who are characterized by an illusion, a seemliness of behavior. The latter is named "Mme de Beauséant," but she signs "C" for "Claire de Bourgogne." Each of them has a social role to play that is different from a self-defined egocentric position. On the other hand, neither Mlle Michonneau nor Vautrin has a social role involved in the perpetuation of the system.

Yet this doubling of positions is the essential structure of the system. The forces of power cannot accept Vautrin as self-identical, individual, and unhypocritical. The law seeks to double or anatomize him by repeating criminal jargon:

> *Sorbonne* and *tronche* are two energetic expressions of the language of thieves who before other people felt the need to consider the human head in two aspects. The *sorbonne* is the head of the living man, his advice, his thought. The *tronche* is a word of disdain intended to express how the head becomes so little when it is cut off. (3:209)

The law ultimately fails, even if it captures him this time. Although marked by the tattoo, Vautrin escapes this dangerous doubling through his multiple incarnations. He will never be beheaded and there will be no autopsy.

This little fact of anatomization is a lesson that Flaubert will learn well from Balzac. The endless anatomizations in *Madame Bovary* or *Bouvard et Pécuchet* owe as much to this idea of divisibility as they do to the mere absence of beautiful metaphors, as Proust would have it. For if Flaubert's descriptions seem to Proust more like anatomy lessons than poetry, it is equally true that they arise from Flaubert's belief that every character is somehow in this anatomical no man's land. On the other hand, the profusion of metaphoric description of characters in Balzac elides the violence, insists on the structure, and ultimately underlines the dual nature of a character while rationalizing it: character X is both himself and a lion, a basilisk, a typical provincial; or both herself and a wife, mother, or widow.[3] The character is thus both himself or herself as a material being and some representative or symbolic Other, be it ideological, repetitive, or reproductive. And violence can fall by the wayside in such cases.

When there is unity, the possibility of unleashed power is too strong; it is no wonder Louis Lambert wants to castrate himself. As I have already indicated, in the *Etudes philosophiques* violence is negotiated through a rhetorical movement, a displacement of brute force onto a grid of power and impotence, matched or shadowed, often as not, by a teratological sexuality: Louis Lambert's threatened self-castration, Séraphîta's angelic bisexuality, la Zambinella's shadowy figure walking from room to room in "Sarrasine."[4]

If we return once again to the grotesque scene of anagnorisis, we see that it is simple in construction yet far-reaching in its implications. Mlle Michonneau undresses Vautrin, unwraps him, rapes him, as it must be, as it has been predicted, as it has been written. And because the violence of that action has been a violence twice foretold, the action itself lacks impact. Rightfully so: the scene cannot happen in its brute force. The woman who has officially touched no man uncovers the man who has been touched by no woman. In this novel, the third sexuality, which in Balzac's work includes bisexuals, castratos, and male and female homosexuals, is pushed to the margins, so that the structure can unviolently reproduce. With that marginalization comes the simultaneous displacement of violence to a safe point outside the system. Thus no one but Mlle Michonneau could hit Vautrin, for no one functioning inside the system of production could reintroduce violence. And Vautrin's own violence, specifically the arranged death of Taillefer, has no consequences in the novel. That is to say, Rastignac does not immediately capitulate, does not marry Mlle Taillefer, and does not assume the role of Vautrin's liege, indebted to the latter for his success. Rather, Rastignac, in a "first challenge to Society" (3:290), will find other ways of making his way through the structure. Not for him is the proposed feudal system of murder for money, abuse for power, itself doubled in Vautrin's dream of being Monsieur Quatre Millions, a plantation owner with slaves in the American South.

There are thus two economies, two structures of appropriation, as well as two ways of dealing with the *part maudite*, to use Georges Bataille's phrase for the excess or accursed share that remains. There are two ways as well of dealing with a troubling sexuality that is not easily arranged in a binary structure. But there is only one way of dealing with violence. Either violence remains at the point of reversal or it is just not there: reversal is violence and violence is reversal. Forced out, ejected to the margins of the work where it can do no damage to the structure, violence seemingly has no import for the ongoing structure. After all, Vautrin and Michonneau are secondary and tertiary characters, respectively, in the novel, though Vautrin is obviously compelling. And Michonneau has no function but helping to produce a dénouement or *dénuement*—a disrobing. Again, in the next work, "La Fille aux yeux d'or," Balzac saves the simultaneous revelation of violence and third sexuality for an offstage *coup de théâtre* at the end of the story.

In the recognition scene as an economy of reading, writing, and exchange, we see how Balzac astutely negotiates the ruptures of his writing that had been and will continue to be the marks of the *Etudes philosophiques*. To avoid rupture and to foster reproduction, Balzac defines his system of reproduction by what is placed in the margins. So it is not that violence and perverse sexuality are excluded, it is that the marginal position allotted to these specific things guarantees the stability of the system from without. When Michonneau hits Vautrin, it shows the validity of a system whose margins they form. The recognition scene is the crystallization of Balzac's developing concepts of power and identity in the mature production of *La Comédie humaine*. This power frame develops in the shift from a physically based structuring of *supplice*, and punishment in general, to a mechanism of vision and perception. In a perfect illustration of Foucault, Vautrin already proves the system, not at its heart but from without. He is not beheaded in the public square, punished through *supplice* at some center. Rather he is marked before the work begins, beheaded in language, and marginalized. By relegating the physicality of the action to the margins, Balzac effectively makes the system work by exchanging the barterable object of the body for a visible, movable commodity. Vautrin becomes a commodity to be seen by all who have the right to possess him, a right accorded by their status as law-abiding citizens.

At the same time, the shift from the physical to the visible is evidence of the need in developing realism to create a mise-en-abîme of its own signifying practices. Rather than being the simple index of material representation, realism in some ways sets itself up as a mirror of production, and in so doing gives weight to the visible as the primary means by which phenomena are understood. That this shift from the analytical to the phenomenological occurs is no surprise, as all can trace a line from Locke and Berkeley through the *philosophes* and Hegel to the nineteenth century's insistence on giving primacy to the visible. Balzac's singular approach to the process is to make a subtle shift between understanding the visible as the means of access to phenomena and understanding the readable as that means of access. Thus Balzac translates the visible, which marks, for example, *Le Rouge et le Noir*, into the readable, the means of communication of *Le Père Goriot*, and a fortiori of works like *Illusions perdues*. Stendhal too will recognize this, especially in *La Chartreuse de Parme*, where, as we have seen in Chapter 2, he has Fabrice invent an alphabet and a means of communication.

Now Balzac goes one step further: it is not merely the readable that is the primary means of communication, it is Balzac's construction of the misreadable that shows both the construction of nineteenth-century French society and its ironic contradictions. So Vautrin can be read, rewritten, and ultimately erased in his final incarnation as he becomes the best reader of all. The entire structure of *La Cousine Bette*, as will be clear later in this chapter, depends on a series of misreadings and misdirections; the structures of *Illusions perdues* and of *Modeste Mignon* also depend on a similar series of misreadings.

When Balzac sets into motion a mechanism that depends on observation and the power of reading instead of physical contact— though retaining the supplementary signs of that physicality—it becomes one of the supreme motifs of Balzacian irony. As has already been noted, Vautrin will go on to become chief of the secret police. Balzac already seems to be laying the plans for this final reincarnation of Vautrin as the supreme reader. The marginalization here already relates to the panoptical position. The development of *La Comédie humaine* eventually comes to focus on the coalescence of the various panoptical positions: that of the narrator, always already present; that of the rhetorical reader; and that of the marginalized figure who will become the power broker through reading, and through directed misreading in some of the final books. In terms of the reader, there is a shift away from the rhetorical construct of the improper reader, posited as both male and female in a work like *Le Père Goriot*, to a position that assimilates the reader to the greater panopticon.

The triple panoptic position includes the attributes that bring us to that point. It includes the position of the omniscient narrator, which takes shape in *Le Père Goriot*. It is here, precisely, that the master idea takes the place of repeating characters. *Le Père Goriot* is the beginning of *La Comédie humaine*, and its techniques are protocols, paradigms, and rules of order. In the case of Vautrin, it must necessarily include his marginality, his violence, and his sexuality. In the case of the reader, it must include the ambiguity and misdirection of the rhetorical cues that settle on a zero-degree reader who is both male and female.

For me, then, *La Comédie humaine* starts with that slap, a picturesque repetition of Michelangelo's finger of God creating Adam, or a doctor slapping a baby. Balzac's genius, like that of Michelangelo, for whom the hands precisely do not touch, was to have figured out how to ironize that creation by putting the scene center stage, making this melodramatic moment in the novel completely dedramatized. In a different way, he will dedramatize Goriot's pathetic death by the discussions of money. This is to say that such a *part maudite*—that even melodrama and romanticism themselves—is what guarantees the integrity of the realist process. Perhaps, in the end, the homosexual Vautrin has his wish to be a plantation owner fulfilled: where else but in Balzac's Paris could Vautrin find 3,000 heterosexual slaves who dance according to the strings he pulls from his eccentric, panoptical prison control booth, *pignon sur rue*?

Balzac's Disorder

I have already discussed the function of the unformed, of muck and mire, in the critical episode of Stendhal's mirror, and below I shall look at the role of flow in the work of Flaubert. But what of the unformed between those two fictional endpoints? Should we take the nineteenth century's fascination with the unformed literally, narratively, psychologically? Into what tubes shall it be forced? It is tempting to liken mud, wherever it appears, to the unformed. The most famous flow in all of nineteenth-century literature can be found in the sewers of Paris in Victor Hugo's *Les Misérables*. In his work, however, the *flou* is controlled twice: in a mechanical fashion by the system of pipes and in a metaphysical fashion by the coincidence that allows characters to meet, find one another, and lose sight of one another. The law of Hugo's metatextuality submits the real not to a realistic, romantic, or clairvoyantly Freudian psychology, but rather to a metaphysics of divine intervention that comes from coincidence. To arrive metatextually at his goal, Hugo gives a role to coincidence, and thereby to determinism and to a rigged game, that goes beyond the opening up to the unconscious proposed by Rosalina de la Carrera, who views the chapters on the sewers of Paris as a novelistic topography, as an "allegory *avant la lettre* of the psychoanalytic process" (843). In other words, the sewers of Paris can be a symbol or allegory of the unconscious except when Hugo has some novelistic accounts to balance. At every moment, letting oneself go with the stream does not mean getting lost, but being found: there will be another coincidence, another meeting that occurs, as if by chance, but in reality never "by chance" and always for reasons of textual economy, between Jean Valjean and Javert or Thénardier or Marius.

Balzac's extraordinary semiotics of mud is quite another story, and he puts a twist on the unrepresentable quite different from Stendhal, Hugo, and Flaubert. Mud is quite meaningful for Balzac. Whereas Hugo uses the flow as a narrative device, in Balzac, flow is submitted to the semiotic system and is thus always in the process of becoming a metaphor. As Allan Pasco (363) has noted of nineteenth-century novels in general, mud is the "most common image of living in the depths of society." Thus, in *Le Père Goriot*, mud is a sign of poverty: the spot on Rastignac's boots turns into a synecdoche of his generalized economic distress. Rastignac gets splattered because he cannot afford to take a cab:

Eugène walked, taking a thousand precautions so as to avoid getting dirty, but he walked while thinking of what he would say to Mme de Restaud. . . . The student got dirty; he was forced to have his boots polished and his pants brushed off at the Palais-Royal.

—If I were rich, he said, getting change from a thirty-sou coin he had taken "just in case," I would have gone by car, I would have been able to think at my leisure. (2:234)

And, as Balzac notes in *La Peau de chagrin*, the mud is the point of difference in an economic system that is itself a translation of a system of emotions and meanings: "My happiness, my love, depended on a fly-speck of mud on my only white vest! Give up seeing her if I got dirty, if I got wet? Not to have five sous to have the slightest spot of mud removed by a cleaner [*décrotteur*] if I got dirty!" (6:469).

Elsewhere the *flou* is the sign of other semiotic orders, whether it be human psychology, economics, or ethics. In *La Rabouilleuse*, for example, *flou* is the product of human mischief, opposed to the divine order of the universe. Thus, "The Knights of Idleness" [*désoeuvrance*], a group of young men in Issoudun, smoke out an apartment and create a false volcano: "they put three bundles of sulfured straw and greasy paper in the fireplace [...] she thought she had lit a volcano" (3:127). Balzacian semiotics is inevitable, and far from letting order be perturbed by the *flou*, Balzac uses it as a part of the semiotic system.

As Corbin notes, there are "numerous references to kitchen odors" in Balzac, as well as to "the odor of the sink, and the smell of badly cleaned rooms," "the characteristic effluvia of unaired bedrooms," "the smells of a nauseating bed," and so forth (196). He remarks the relations made by Balzac between odors, effluvia, or the *flou* and psychology, character, or semiotics of the person or spot: "Attached to the coincidence of beings and spots, Balzac makes a parallel between the specific odor of the rooms and the character of their denizens." For Balzac, then, the *flou* is a metonym of a world, as in the Pension Vauquer, where "tout suinte le malheur," and where the enormity of the flow sometimes daunts even the Balzacian narrator:

Maybe it [the smell of a boarding house] could be described if a process were invented to evaluate the elementary, nauseating qualities of the catarrhal and *sui generis* airs thrown there by each roomer, be he young or old. (3:53)

It is a world waiting to become the slough of despond that Balzac already knows it is: "If there is no muck yet, there are spots; if it has neither holes nor tatters, it is going to fall into a state of rot" (3:54).

For Balzac, there is something beyond all that muck, which is the truly unrepresentable. And he will treat the unrepresentable in a different way, as a disruption or a forced detour in the interpretive system. Though he can organize the flow to give it meaning, he does not always negotiate the unrepresentable, the monstrous, or the mixed that interfere with that meaning. With Balzac, the question of the mixed or the unrepresentable becomes more generalized. In his works, there is a conflict between, for example, word as printed text and word as authorial meaning or writerly afflatus. No amount of adequation can make the two coincide: the materiality of the sign and its aesthetic cannot be compossible, yet they do coexist just as right and wrong readings coexist, even though they too are not possible. This is Balzac's real mud, the meeting of sign and referent, material and spiritual, interpretive and disruptive.

Musing on Literary Values

All readers of Balzac are familiar with his disquisitions on the printing industry in *Illusions perdues*. The discussions of printing, the explanations of paper production, the strategies of marketing, and the machinations of the printing and publishing industries are essential to the plot of the novel. On the mechanical side, David Séchard is a printer looking for a new sort of paper to manufacture; at the corporate level, the plot involves a hostile takeover by the Cointet brothers. And in Paris, as Lucien de Rubempré tries to sell his novel and poetry, he meets various sorts of booksellers and publishers and learns how "books were merchandise to be sold high and bought low" (5:303). In the Paris of burgeoning capitalism, it matters little what Lucien's creative works contain, how good his novel might be, or how well-wrought his poems. For the booksellers of Paris, his works have no essential or intrinsic value but only an exchange value. Balzac uses printing to show how his two poets, David and Lucien, are victimized by a means of production that swallows up creativity.

Balzac peppers his writing with overdetermined details when he makes a mise-en-abîme, as if the process of creating such a reflection necessitated filling in the gaps. Thus just as Lucien's real name (Chardon, French for "nettle") has echoes in the production of pulp for paper, and David's family name of Séchard implies the drying necessary for the pulp to become paper, the name Cointet also contains the word *coin*, which means "quoin," a printers' term for a block used to lock forms within a chase. In this part of the chapter, I would like to explore how similar overdetermination operates in a work less well-known than *Illusions perdues*, *La Muse du département*. I would hypothesize that Balzac seeks to overdetermine his mises-en-abîme, precisely because he knows what we have often forgotten in our readings of the nineteenth-century narratives on which I focus here. To wit: they are made up of many more gaps and interruptions than we have seen fit to remark, more holes than we have cared to admit.

So the processes of overdetermination of a mise-en-abîme are compensations for those gaps and artifices of the writing process. Their raison d'être is the regularization of what amounts to an over- and undervaluation of the writing process through an act of misprision common to the writerly project and to the readers for which it is intended. In both cases, writing is overvalued as the means by which the world is purportedly, although fictionally and falsely, represented; it is overvalued by being seen as uninterrupted, as unbroken as the world itself. It is undervalued because it is nothing but writing, a copy, an imitation. Neither action nor event, writing assumes its value only when it can be detoured into event and action.

In the rather heterogeneously constructed work that is *La Muse du département*, Balzac posits a means of evaluating textuality without erecting this means into an extratextual law of production. He does not do this by focusing on the value of writing, but by seeing what is judiciously added to or subtracted from it: it is a novel about the printer's quoin, meaningless in itself, but capable of imparting meaning by locking the form in the chase and allowing printing to occur. Specifically, the determining functions for "writing" will be found between those functions seen in its mechanical fulfillment in printing and the total free play of reading as understood in and against a value system.[5]

La Muse du département is a singular novel that weaves together the familiar Balzacian themes of unequal marriages, ill-fated love affairs, and worldly success with a story about reading and writing. The standard Balzacian systems of social and monetary exchanges, changes of fortune, ideological biases, and gender politics remain intact. The work is an odd hybrid, composed in part of some earlier writings that Balzac put together to form this novel in rather short order.[6] At times the novel may seem heterogeneous or badly stitched together: William Paulson calls it "bricolé"; in his article "Reading as Suture," Lucien Dällenbach uses the word "suture" in describing the work. Faced with that heterogeneity, readers have tended toward reading one part of the novel or the other. Patrick Berthier, who calls the novel "un drame d'amour," concentrates on the Balzacian novel of social and monetary matters, as he examines the three "typically Balzacian choices" in the novel: "The husband is greedy, the lover is a journalist, the *fable* is political." As Berthier rhetorically asks:

"Balzac and money: how can something new be said about this enormous subject?" (119). On the other hand, looking at a singular and fundamental scene, Dällenbach, following Wolfgang Iser, relates reading the gaps in writing to a process whereby these gaps interrupt the process of reading and thereby help the reader "re-member" the writing. Dällenbach contrasts the distanced reading performed by Lousteau and Bianchon and the identifying reading performed by Dinah. Dällenbach (201) also points out that every work by Balzac has its own gaps, and thus that *Olympia* is a mise-en-abîme of the novel; for him, Balzacian completeness is a myth used to camouflage these blanks.

The central scene of *La Muse*, a comedy of manners, concerns the speculative reading of some papers used as wrapping paper for a manuscript by one of the characters, Lousteau, who, not coincidentally, is Lucien de Rubempré's guide through the Parisian world of publishing in the second part of *Illusions perdues*. In this scene, there is a discussion of the uses of spoilage and make-ready sheets. Problems of mechanical and authorial production are intertwined with Lousteau's explanation of the printing process. The characters also speculate on how to read the romance novel *Olympia, ou les vengeances romaines*, whose thrown-away spoilage (*maculature*) and make-ready sheets (*mise en train*) are used as the wrapping paper for Lousteau's proofs. Working with the fragments of *Olympia*, of which there are about a score out of a presumed thousand, the characters attempt to reconstruct the story from the scattered pages. So in this case, as opposed to the rather separate stories of David and Lucien linked thematically in *Illusions perdues*, the motif of printing is linked to a set of speculative protocols about reading. This double motif signals the range of possibilities for the roles discerned for reading and writing.

When we know where Balzac places printing, we will be able better to read the work. Four possibilities come to mind. First, Balzac needs to tread, coast, or glide for a while: writing on something he knows effectively may delay "the conclusion in the next issue" (4:703) may get him more money, or may speed up the writing to help him meet his deadline, as the case may be. Yet arguments of intentionality, penury, authorial need, or anecdotal writer's block should not cloud the issue of the writing per se. Even if Balzac's method of "bricolage" uses readymade chunks of writing, it is oddly enough a

mise-en-abîme: the motifs of the scene of reading continue throughout the novel, as readymades are transformed into make-readies.
Second, the printing process relates to the industrialization of the
creative act. Clear from *Illusions perdues* is the fact that the author
only becomes an author when he learns how to market himself by
selling odes and palinodes to the highest bidder.[7] The author who
thinks he has a corner on the truth will not get his wares to market.

The third possibility is that printing is a metaphor for the creative
process; after all, in the first part of *Illusions perdues*, Balzac gives
equal billing to Lucien and David as "the two poets" (*les deux poètes*).
But there is a down side: using the mechanics of printing as a metaphor for writing means that the process of writing has been fully absorbed in the mechanics of its own production. In fact, Balzac sup-
ports this conclusion, for both in *Illusions perdues* and *La Muse du département*, the supposedly pure writing that serves as a counterweight
to mechanization always has rather a "retro" tinge to it: Lucien's *Les
Marguerites* and his historical novel, *L'Archer de Charles IX*, and Dinah's two poems, "Paquita la Sévillane" and "Chêne de la messe," as
well as *Olympia*, all seem to participate in an older aesthetic that contrasts sharply with the ironies of Balzac's realism. Treating Lucien's
production cynically and Dinah's rather condescendingly, Balzac
does little to rescue their works from the realm of scribblers of
Schwärmerei.

The fourth possibility is the most seductive because it points to a
figure of writing: printing is the opposite of writing. Printing is precisely *not* the metaphor for writing because this writing—Balzac's—
is not guided by metaphor, but by its ironization. Writing is defined
apodictically as the absence of all other metaphors that might liken
writing to anything else; what metaphors there are must be re-troped
as homologies: metaphoric relations are classified in the "zoography"
of the human condition. I am not proposing a total demetaphoriza-
tion of *La Comédie humaine*. Rather, Balzac is showing how writing
itself may be demetaphorized: he is excluding the possibility of saying that writing is *like* something else.

As Lucienne Frappier-Mazur and Bernard Vannier have shown,
there are subtle, complicated networks of metaphors, often relating
to characterization, that are at work in *La Comédie humaine*. Writing
seems to escape that metaphoric system. Neither a system of ex-

change, nor a repetition of the industrial structure, nor even a variety of production, writing remains what it is by refusing submission to the metaphors of the world. Balzac maintains a privileged realm for writing by detaching this unique activity from the global process of metaphorization on which much of the armature of *La Comédie humaine* depends. Thus he exempts his own work from this act of metaphoric relation that would debase the writing by turning it into something other than itself. If the writing of *La Comédie humaine*, especially from 1834 onward, is supposed to reproduce the world, writing cannot be anything else but this act of representation as reproduction. This process of abstraction clearly does not escape from the metaphorics and metaphysics that doubly structure discourse, but ironically places Balzac's writing in a relation to an idealistic metaphysics of representation.

The complementary figure of reading is found in the reconstructive approach to reading as a society game. *La Muse du département* casts the act of reading as the construction of what we would, in all good conscience, call a "text" nowadays. Indeed, as we have noted, the central piece of the novel is a discussion of how to read, which is integrated into the discussion of printing. Lousteau receives proofs for a story he is writing. While Lousteau's story is tangential to Balzac's novel, the papers in which the proofs are enveloped become the focus of the remainder of the scene. As we have already noted, this wrapping paper is spoilage from a novel entitled *Olympia ou les vengeances romaines*, ostensibly written during the Napoleonic era, and characterized by Lousteau as "the prettiest novel in the world" (4:703).[8] The society game that ensues is a literary jigsaw puzzle that pieces these fragments together. It is an activity not unlike Balzac's own. In this case, the result is the constitution of an integral piece of *Olympia*, whose logic and order are clear when the breaks and ruptures are written over, bridged, erased, or sutured. The readers succeed by depending on their own knowledge as competent readers of the rather stereotypical works of which *Olympia* is a more or less predictable example. The characters in Balzac's novel know how one of those overblown romances is supposed to go, and they certainly know how to read the semantic units of Italy, tales of Gothic keys and locks, young love, and masquerading nobles.

Still, the skills of Balzac's group of competent readers can never fully restore the writing, no matter how predictable it may seem. The last page (216 of *Olympia*) of the spoilage ends midsentence; the next page of spoilage (217 of *Olympia*) starts with a non sequitur. The story of Rinaldo and Olympia thus reads as follows: "Suspecting that only considerable treasure could oblige a duchess always to wear at her side [*à sa ceinture*] . . . corridor; but, feeling pursued by the Duchess's men, Rinaldo" (4:707, 709). Even the reading of the page, or the announcement of the reading of the page—"Shall we read and decipher this enigma?" (4:709)—is interrupted by comments from several characters before the sentence about Rinaldo can continue. The information given is enough for the readers to know that 217 does in fact belong to the same volume, of which there are at least four, of *Olympia*, but it is never enough to constitute the whole novel. The process of reading repeats the fragmentation of the world and can only approximate a whole through a series of ellipses. The complete, reconstituted whole *always* remains an illusion.

This simple, predictable novel, which is understandable despite the fact that the readers have only twenty out of a thousand pages (4:718), contrasts quite strikingly with the current writing scene. Additionally, as Paulson (34) rightly points out, there is also the absence "of everything that has been added to novelistic writing since that era." Despite the thousand pages of *Olympia*, this Empire novel takes an utterly straightforward approach to tale-telling. Lousteau remarks that the literature of that era "had ideas, but did not express them." So the thousand pages of this stereotypical novel must be bereft of ideas; the novel relies merely on "interest" to propel it along. In contrast, the contemporary novel depends on art: "Formerly, people asked only that there be interest in the novel; as for style, no one cared, not even the author; as for ideas, zero; as for local color, nothing" (4:714). We seem to have a paradox here: the Empire novel has no style, ideas, or local color, and depends on the reader's interest or the story's inherent interest to propel it. But the more or less successful reading of this spoilage depends precisely on the predictability of the writing, on the stereotypical quality of the local color, and ultimately on the lack of interest in the plot, for the reader's interest cannot be maintained if he or she knows what is going to happen. On the other hand, style and local color would seem to have a predictive value and ideas would seem to follow a logic or an ideology.

Where then does the novel sit? What does Balzac really tell us through this mise-en-scène of his own conception of the act of writing? The contrast between the current and older forms of narrative is an unresolvable paradox. What is fruitful is a reassessment of the combined acts of reading and writing that depend on no preexisting totality or closure to give them meaning. Along with the competent readers within *La Muse du département*, we agree that the prose of *Olympia* is drawn from a closed universe of positive markers whose combination, even at the length of a thousand pages, maintains the readers' interest. The markers thus come from a set, each of whose parts is simple and understandable. No better analogy exists for that than an alphabet of movable type: twenty-six letters, all knowable, can be endlessly repeated while their comprehensibility as units is preserved. On the one hand is "printing": an alphabet of twenty-six letters, a limited set of possibilities that Balzac can ably combine— keys and prisons, Gothic settings, elements of romance novels, clichés of old-fashioned literature. On the other hand, there is a set whose elements are themselves unlimited, a world where the parts are never wholly knowable but where there is an *illusion* of a potential whole. In this world, there are as many unknowns as there are aspects to the human condition and no set ever gives a complete picture of the whole. The world is a collection of fragments that do not form a whole, but which continue endlessly to exist as fragments: in short, it is *La Comédie humaine*, where the semantic, semiotic, or narrative units are never completely defined on an individual basis.

Balzac never makes the scheme so easily oppositional, for the world of fragments defined by Dinah, the title character of *La Muse du département*, is not guaranteed by an ideology of the illusory whole but ironically by the very same old-fashioned ideology that makes her an ideal reader of *Olympia*. A Madame Bovary before the fact, Dinah keeps an autograph album and writes poetry. For Dinah herself, this poetry, some of which is published and some not, even becomes a metaphor for her own existence: Dinah "down in her province led a life of struggles, of repressed revolts, of unpublished poems" (4:673). She also collects fragments of language that she then reemploys at the optimum moment as a *bricoleuse*, though bereft of Balzac's "genius" or Lousteau's cleverness:

She gathered quite a lovely collection of phrases and ideas, through her reading, or by assimilating the ideas of her coterie. She thus became a sort of mechanical singer [*serinette*] whose songs started as soon as a chance event in the conversation hit the right note. (4:644)

Dinah's imagination is novelistic in the worst sense of the word: "For three days Dinah's vivid imagination was busy with the most insidious novels, and the conversation of the two Parisians had acted on this woman like the most dangerous books" (4:723). Her fragments merely parrot her own misconstruing of the reading and writing processes. In fact, the provincial woman herself is like "one of those novels," as Balzac might say, where characters over- and undervalue various forms of textuality.

As far as Dinah is concerned, a good poet, observer, or philosopher—a good reader—should be able to read the provincial woman well, because what is "natural" is readable though not predictable: "A poet like you or a philosopher, an observer like Dr. Bianchon could guess the marvelous unprinted poetry, I mean all the pages of this beautiful novel" (4:671). For Dinah then, both the provincial woman and the pure, natural writing with which she is coterminous should be an endless source of readable pleasure to its reader or her lover: "The dénouement profits some felicitous lieutenant, some great provincial man" (4:671). But in fact her stories are no better than the fragments she collects; she is not made whole by her reading process of identification, and, on the level of the plot, she falls into the most banal arrangement in her private life when she leaves her husband for Lousteau. Dinah becomes a prisoner of her own misreading of the world, for she believes she is thinking, while all she is doing is moving words around: "Loving to talk about discoveries in science or in art, newly developed works in the theater, in poetry, she seemed to stir thoughts as she stirred 'in' words [*les mots à la mode*]" (4:641). She gets caught up in her own poorly plotted novel and writes endless love letters to Lousteau, follows him to Paris, and lives through a stereotypically novelistic love affair with him, only to end up in a banal dénouement.

From one end of the novel to the other, Dinah is a misreader. For example, misreading the contents of religion, she converts from Calvinism to Catholicism for social reasons (4:635). And in the last part of the novel, Lousteau even says to her that her reading, weakened by a process of identification and sympathy—to use Dällenbach's terms—is faulty:

You have read Benjamin Constant's book profoundly, and you have even studied the last article about it; but you have read it with only a woman's eyes. Although you have one of those beautiful minds that would be wealth to a poet, you have not dared to put yourself in a man's point of view. This book, my dear, has both sexes. (4:780)

By insisting on a process of defamiliarization, by making writing something different, and by providing a correction for misreading, Balzac forces us to come to a better understanding of the singular nature of writing. One technique that Balzac uses is to mix genres by inserting some of Dinah's poetry: "Although the marriage of verse and prose is monstrous in French literature, there are, nevertheless, exceptions to this rule" (4:657). Referring to *Illusions perdues*, Balzac continues, "This story will thus offer one of the two infractions in these Studies committed against the Count's charter; for, to show the intimate struggles that can excuse Dinah without absolving her, it is necessary to analyze a poem, the fruit of her deep despair."[9] Still, he further complicates the "monstrosity" by giving only fragments of the first poem, which, like *Olympia*, remains both fragmentary and readable in its predictable banality. So what is monstrous for Balzac is the stereotypical predictability of so much writing, which contrasts with his singular writing that corresponds to the singularity of the world.

In a sweeping generalization, Balzac lumps together all such writing and ironically reverses aesthetic polarities: what is bizarre or monstrous is stereotypical; what is real is both central and singular. For Balzac, the writing of women is generally far more bizarre than that of men: "As far as bizarre concepts are concerned, women's imaginations go much further than men's, as Mrs. Shelley's *Frankenstein*, *Leone Leoni*, the works of Ann Radcliffe, and *The New Prometheus* of Camille Maupin show" (4:718). And writing *for* women, be it by men or by women, is monstrous as well, forming a Sade-like cautionary tale: "'I know,' continued the journalist addressing Gatien, 'a newspaper director who, to avoid a sad fate, allows only stories where the lovers are burnt, chopped up, pounded, dissected:

where the women are boiled, fried, cooked'" (4:677). For Balzac, the excesses of women's writing are no better than spoilage. Just as the predictable writing of *Olympia* serves to wrap Lousteau's pages, Dinah's own writing acts as nothing more than a wrapping for a metonymic *odor di femmina* and nothing more: "Toward the end of December, Lousteau was no longer reading Dinah's letters, which he allowed to accumulate in an always open dresser drawer, as they lay under his shirts they scented" (4:737).

Contrasting with the bizarre excesses of women's writing, but equally off the mark, is the absence of writing. The blank page is a repository of fragments: "She had an oblong volume that was even more worthy of its name, since two-thirds of the sheets were blank" (4:673). If Balzac relies on the etymology of the word "album" (from the Latin for "white"), the statement is even more true when we think about the contents of the album. For there is nothing but page after page of clichés and fragments: "a line of Rossini . . . the four verses that Victor Hugo puts on every album." The album overvalues the presence of the author and his residing genius in whatever fragment he chooses to put in such a collection. Yet these scattered occasional pieces are little more than self-authenticating bourgeois conventions: this writing has no meaning; it is simply what Hugo, Nodier, or George Sand writes in an album. The writing itself has little if any intrinsic worth; its value comes from its attribution or signature. Thus the album is the provincial bourgeois equivalent of the mechanization of written language: there is no value other than use value, as a means of showing off one's conquests, the literary materialization of the French expression for "show-off," a *m'as-tu vu*. The use value of the album comes from its being shown to others: "This beginning was ever more valuable to Dinah in that she was the only one to have an album for ten leagues in any direction" (4:674).

Occupying *le juste milieu*, though not without irony, Lousteau turns out to be the vicar of Balzac in the novel. If not wholly admirable in his approach to life, Lousteau understands how to manipulate writing, how to make it work for him, how to imbue the fragment with the fiction of originality, how, in short, to create the fiction of completeness. For with Lousteau we see that this completeness is not so much the totalization of the world that Dällenbach seems to imply, but rather the rhetorical marriage of the disparate fragments with the appropriate signature necessary to create the illusion of the whole in the mind of the reader. It is an illusory whole that mimics the world that it is supposed to describe. Though Lousteau does the same thing as Dinah with preexisting writing, he does it with a complete awareness of its value. Where Dinah merely has a "collection," Lousteau has a "fund" of stories to tell that together form his "narrative bank account [*fonds de narration*]" (4:688).

Lousteau's story fund works at the level of his own theater, as he orchestrates a whole scene between Bixiou and himself in which he professes his love for Dinah to overhear so that she will eventually give him up. Again, it is a question of over- and undervaluing signatures and that to which they are attached. Within this scene, Bixiou says: "What's a brat without our name? The last chapter of a novel!" (4:748). So to avoid being part of a bad novel, Lousteau performs a theatrical coup to turn away from the stereotyped romances of the time and toward real life. But real life means precisely "this novel," where signatures are neither over- nor undervalued, where fragments are sutured when appropriate, and where things are given their proper names.

As a writer, Lousteau aims to reject the mediocre in literature even if he does not do so as a character. He is concerned about legitimacy in writing, which, oddly enough, parallels legitimacy in children. And it is with the game of the *faire-part*, or announcement (4:762), that this is made most clear. Lousteau sends out a birth announcement in which he announces that he is the father of Dinah's child; a second, palinodic birth announcement goes out in which Dinah's husband, the Baron de La Baudraye, is said to be the father. The proofs of the first announcement are destroyed and all copies but one recuperated; finally the last is obtained as Nathan, Balzac's successful fictional publisher, remarks: "I wanted you to feel the complete cost of my sacrifice" (4:764).

This, then, is the price of true writing for Balzac: neither under- nor overvalued, circulating and retained at market price, writing knows when to unite truth and reality and when to separate them. With judicious blanks, writing is truly, for Balzac, the quoin of the realm.

Balzac's Dyslexia

> There is no theory, there is only practice in this
> profession, Lisbeth had said maliciously
>
> (Balzac, *La Cousine Bette*)

HOW TO MISREAD A NOVEL

Who among us would say willingly "Monsieur Bovary, c'est moi"?
No one would admit to being the doltish Charles, who spends much
of his fictional life not knowing what is going on. Starting as the
noisy self-enunciation of a shivaree as he pathetically garbles his
name when he enters the classroom, and left in the dark most of the
time, Charles belatedly learns the truth about his wife's behavior only
after the major events of the book are over. And how does he accomplish this? For a while after Emma's death, he leaves a secret
drawer in her desk untouched. But not even the letter of Rodolphe
he finds by chance prompts him to seek the truth of his wife's past
(1:604). This drawer contains Emma's letters; in other words, it holds
the plot of the book "in other words." This unrealized writing clues
him in to the story that the readers already know. But it is only after
a slow ripening period in which understanding dawns that Charles finally breaks open the drawer in Emma's writing desk and finds both
the love letters from Léon and Rodolphe's portrait.

Charles is hardly a likely candidate for the reader's sympathy or
his identification. Now I have said "*his*" identification for a reason.
The process of identifying the reader or critic as male is a fiction, but
is part of the process of misreading that has been taken as a necessary
figure in the inscription of realist literature. Although I shall address
this fiction of masculinity below, for now I would just schematically
say that in realist narrative the female reader is posited wrongly but
necessarily as being no more than a variant of the male reader, even
when, at first glance, she seems to be the rhetorical or implied reader.
Still, despite his doltishness, and with all questions of gender brack-
eted for the moment, Charles's reading skill closely resembles what
occurs during the real reader's actual process of reading a work.
Starting from a point of absolute ignorance relative to the local
knowledge invoked by the author for the world being signified, the
reader gradually finds out information by looking over people's

shoulders, reading their mail, listening in on conversations, and generally being a parasite on a communicational model. If the process is the same, the time line is different: the reader learns and understands things far earlier than Charles does. Thus Charles can seem to be the belated figure of knowledge only from the point of view of a reader who already knows. This knowledgeable reader, future Baudelairean hypocrite, can thus distance himself from this pathetic and unknowing figure whose position is, as far as the reader is concerned, never his own.

We need to consider the hypothesis that the position of the reader relates more to that of Charles than to that of the ideal reader normally posited for a realist narrative. The reader who refuses to see that the position of nonknowledge is his own both denies the process of reading that he has undertaken and refuses to see the implications of this denial. It could be, one might counter, that the position of Charles Bovary is an extreme one. For Flaubert, in the founding movement of a literature of modernity, might willingly be breaking the reader's bonds with the writing, as Tony Tanner has duly noted. The position of the ideal reader, the implicit reader, or the narratee, would thus be a position of nonknowledge in this agonistic writing that Flaubert seeks to place before us.

The reader is negatively apostrophized as the one to whom this work is *not* written; he thus refuses to take cognizance of the fact that the work is formally excluding his position as one of knowledge and as a locus joined in a linguistic contract to the interlinked positions of the writer, narrator, and implied author. So there is a difference between Charles and the reader that goes beyond the temporal difference between the two scenes of reading. And this difference cannot be subsumed in the process of the reader's internalization of the writing. Rather, the process of reading makes this absolute difference clear: in reading we wrongly internalize the position that is not ours and should never be. The reader reads writing that is absolutely closed off to Charles; in fact, Charles himself is part of what the reader reads. On the other hand, what Charles reads is only relatively closed off to the reader. One can imagine a situation where this relative closure barely exists, as in the epistolary novel. But in a nineteenth-century narrative, the absolute closure is certainly always operative. Thus the event of misreading that occurs depends on the absence of identification with any act of reading in the novel, even the one that seems most likely to offer itself as the model of identification. The reader must (yet cannot) identify with Charles because this identification is neither symmetric nor reciprocal.

Despite this absolute difference in the act of identification, Flaubert's writing is a convenient means of positing, at a zero degree of complexity, the position of the implied nonreader or nonnarratee of a narrative, either within the story or external to it, what is known in strict narratological terms as intradiegetically or extradiegetically. But are the processes of identification even possible? Are the positions so easily defined that we can say with some assurance that there is an implied nonreader or nonnarratee? And if so, are they unique, discrete, and distinct? In his influential and far-reaching study of the narratee, "Introduction à l'étude du narrataire," Gerald Prince distinguishes between the narratee, the implied or virtual reader, and the ideal reader (180). As distinct from the narratee, whose position is a pure narratological function, the implied reader is the one conceived of as belonging to a group of certain kinds of readers with distinct qualities, abilities, and tastes. The ideal reader is of course a construct that relates to an ideal communicational system.

Prince posits a zero-degree narrator as a pure, implied textual function without person or gender, the creation or the production of the act of narration itself. So the zero-degree narrator is ostensibly a position that excludes any difference; it is an idealization of a figure of the writing that may or may not be subject to that idealization. In a later article, "The Narratee Revisited," Prince (300) returns to his seminal theory of the narratee but dispenses with the concept of the zero-degree narratee, though he still believes "that it can be a useful *garde-fou*." Now, just as I am concerned about the ambiguous relation among the categories of narratee, implied reader, and the ideal reader, and even more so about the perception that the female reader may only be a variant of the male reader, I am concerned about that expression *garde-fou*, the French word for guardrail, literally "protect-mad." In all of these cases there is the implied hypothesis that there can be a neutral foundational act, that there can be an ideal spot in which to read or narrate, one free of any influence whatsoever. But what *folie*—madness—does this railing keep out, and can this exclusion be itself a foundational act? Is there ever a neutral position that does not depend either on some preexisting definition of two or more polarized gendered positions? Is that neutrality not always a forced neutralization or a castration?

I would hypothesize that there is always a difference from the zero degree of the neutral position, a difference that manifests itself on the one hand as the impossibility of identity, and on the other in the fact that this neutral voiceless voice cannot be. To have a neutral voice, some *folie* must be kept out; for reason and dispassion to be defined there must be exclusion. Neutrality in writing is always an aftereffect, a perceived coalescence based on one sort of exclusion or another, whether it is the appurtenances of gender, the decision that the female narratee is a variant of the alternately defined male and neutral positions, or the madness excluded from the text so that reason can operate and organize the material of logic and order on which the text's propulsion is based.

This very difference from the zero degree is included in the function, be it rhetorical or narratological, of the ideal reader, the implied reader, and even the narratee. We recall that one of the main thrusts of Jacques Derrida's critique in "Le Facteur de la vérité" of Jacques Lacan's "Séminaire sur 'La Lettre volée'" is that Lacan excludes that difference. In his study of Poe's "The Purloined Letter," Lacan had stated that "a letter always arrives at its destination" (41). Thus within the very act of transmission of writing for Lacan, an ideal point of acceptance is always reached. Derrida's criticism is clear. Commenting on Lacan's final line Derrida says, quite simply, "a letter can always not arrive at its destination. Its 'materiality,' its 'topology' relate to its divisibility, to the partition that is always possible" (*Carte* 472). Derrida adds that the professed integral nature of the writing that includes the ideal destination depends on a presumed materiality of the signifier; thus, this "'materiality,' deduced from an indivisibility nowhere to be found, corresponds in fact to an idealization" (492).

Thus we have three points of difference from any zero-degree narratee and thus from any ideal of reading. First, there is the absolute impossibility of mutual identification. We know what Charles Bovary does not know; if we identify with him we espouse his ignorance; if we refuse the possibility of being or having been the wrong, late, or bad reader, we are refusing an important part of the narrative process. Second, there is the problem of irreducibility. There are certain characteristics inherent in the reader—real reader, ideal reader, or narratee—not all of which can be explained in order to extrapolate or hypothesize a zero-degree reader. These characteristics are ultimately not arranged as singularities, but rather in oppositional pairs in a hierarchy for which there is no zero point. Third, the very act of communication and reception depends on the false idealization of the system and the concomitant idealization of the message into a material presence resisting dissemination.

Thus if Charles Bovary's position cannot be classified as one even approaching a zero degree of nonreceptivity for the same reasons that the position of Poe's Dupin in "The Purloined Letter" or Lacan or Derrida cannot be that of the ideal receiver of a message, we need to reconsider Charles's position. Commenting on the Lacan-Derrida debate, Barbara Johnson remarks, "Everyone who has held the letter—or even beheld it—including the narrator, has ended up having the letter addressed to him as its destination" (144). One would have to add the counterpart of the argument: everyone who has beheld the letter is simultaneously *not* the addressee; the beholder of the letter is always reading someone else's mail. To borrow terms from Michael Fried's study of the art criticism of Diderot, one could add that the reader's absorption in the message or object is necessarily accompanied by a degree of theatricality given to us as the necessary falseness of which Diderot writes in his "Paradoxe sur le comédien."

Call it theatricality, falseness, or nonabsorption for the eighteenth century; call it a double focus or dyslexia in the nineteenth. Whatever it is called, it does not start with Flaubert (or, I would add, Manet); it is merely, though exquisitely, that Flaubert and Manet, in the justly famous *Déjeuner sur l'herbe*, remove the last vestiges of the fictions of intentionality along with the similar traces of the artist's supposed good will in seeking to seduce his readers. The position of absolute ignorance or nonreceptivity is not the product of the famous birth of modernity, the rift that occurs with Flaubert's writing that distinguishes it absolutely from a straw-man version of Balzac. The break is only radical if we have forgotten how to read Balzac. In fact, Charles Bovary's negative position only becomes what it is in a gradual moving away or modification of the Balzacian position, itself more modern than we have cared to admit in recent years. As Franc

Schuerewegen correctly notes, "The famous historic split between Balzac and Flaubert . . . risks being part and parcel of the interpretative *doxa*" ("Muséum" 41). It thus behooves us to consider that the Flaubertian break of which Charles's stupidity and belatedness are overt signs may not be a break at all. The figure of the bad reader in Flaubert is not so much a disruption as it is the gradual elimination of motivation from a function of the bad reader already extensively present in the works of Balzac. Flaubert would therefore have simply removed the accidents of bad reading, the most fundamental of which is motivation, and thereby reduced the figure of the bad reader to its essence. Charles Bovary may simply be the last Balzacian.

The bad reader is a fundamental, unavoidable figure of narrative prose, at least from foundations of the modern novel—both Sancho Panza and Don Quixote come to mind—but he, she, or it is absolutely central to nineteenth-century narrative. In a general sense, realism's tropes depend on a misreading by which the narrative corrects the misperception of writing it has set up. Second, the figure of the bad reader casts doubt on the possibility of inventing an ideal act of reading, even at the level of theory, because there is always an act of parasitism, always a position that is determined by dyslexia. In my reading of realism, I am positing neither an implicit yet mappable misreading, as Harold Bloom does for romanticism, nor an allegory of reading, as is the case for the postrealist Proust of Paul de Man. Rather, I would offer the following hypothesis: each form of literature—each genre, movement, or style—has critical figures that must themselves be subject to the "law of genre" for that form. Thus realism, in its search for verisimilar representation and in its insistence on the literal, must posit its figure of misreading as a verisimilarly represented figure (character) misreading writing.

Let us now turn back to Balzac after having seen where we were led by the implications of Charles Bovary's belated, tongue-tied literacy. Much attention has been paid to the figure of the implied, apostrophized reader in Balzac's work. The most complete examination of the subject has been done by Jean Rousset, whose study of the inscription of the reader proposes a schematic of choices for the qualities attributed to this reader. Selection or exclusion is based on worldly qualities such as Paris/provinces or masculine/feminine. As an example of femininity, by the way, Rousset (245) points out the apostrophe to the reader in *Le Père Goriot* (2:217); he sees this reader as feminine, elegant, aristocratic, and qualified to read and to judge.[10] Furthermore, the reader is variously qualified as active or passive, knowledgeable or ignorant, and finally as someone who can identify (or not) with this function of narration. Rousset notes that "the novelist counts on similarities of existence, memory, knowledge, for the agreement to be reached, one necessary, according to him, between what he tells and the one or the ones to whom he tells it" (253). Even if it is clear that Balzac is always addressing the reader who must be included, the contrary remains a possibility. There is always the hypothesis of a reader who is reading despite the lack of similarities of existence, memory, and knowledge. The ghost in the machine, for the Balzacian narrative, is the fact that even the implied reader is paired off with a phantom double, a bad reader who is always lurking in the wings.

Why do we need to consider this bad reader at all, if Balzac restricts entrée to his story to those who can agree to read it? First of all, as Nicole Mozet shows in her reading of *Illusions perdues*, there may be an another ideal reader at the antipodes from the ideal one who is created to conspire with the narrator (24). She wonders if "the ideal reader" is not actually "the one who does not know how to read." Mozet proffers the following explanation: one of the reasons Balzac allows for a non-reader is his nostalgia for an aural means of perception. For Mozet's Balzac, the privileged position is that of the listener. This idea of the alternate ideal reader, the antimatter version of the ideal implied reader, has merit. Invoking it shows why we cannot just assume that there is a unique point at which the ideal occurs.

Yet even within the model of the antireader, there are things that do not fit. On the one hand, no one actually fits the position of being 100 percent passively aural; there is always interaction, a process that means memory and inscription, which depends on performativity and perlocutionary acts. And moreover, for every postulation of a "pure" illiterate like Séchard—and I do wonder if that purity is ever demonstrably there in Balzac or if it is just another way of beguiling the reader into establishing false oppositions between readers and listeners—there are cases of bad listeners or bad storytelling practices. The frame tale of "Sarrasine" is a case in which telling

leads to loss and disruption; good listening does not necessarily produce good results. And there is no guarantee, other than the spurious one of immediacy involved in a listening model, that the listener
can understand any more or less than an absent reader. Still, this
true zero degree of readership, that of the absent reader, reminds us
that any position other than that point is fraught with difference and
rupture.

The ideal reader who is actually active in his or her reading is the
mirror image of that absent reader. In both cases the position is complete and ideal, but whereas in the first no reading takes place, in the
second all reading has always already occurred. This ideal Balzacian
reader may be the model reader proposed by semiotics. Eco defines
"a Model Reader whose intellectual profile is determined only by the
sort of interpretive operations he is supposed to perform" (*Role* 11).
Yet this restriction seems part of the idealization of the system of
communication, the very same idealization that Derrida criticizes in
Lacan. Moreover, the position of the model reader is restricted, one
might add, by some fealty to the results of an intentional fallacy: the
model reader is "supposed" to perform certain interpretive operations. This supposition must be seated somewhere. That site is found
within the domain of the implied and/or real author. This supposition or obligation is an important part of the semiotic method as Eco
uses it, even despite his inclusion of an clinamen at the position of
the reader. He sets out what he calls a slogan: "the competence of the
destinataire is not necessarily that of the sender" (*Lector* 53). Still, the
obligation is there: "Naturally, the empirical reader to figure himself
[*realizzarsi*] as the Model Reader, has 'philological' obligations: that
is to say, he has the obligation of recuperating, with the greatest approximation possible, the codes of the sender" (*Lector*, 63).

Despite the convenience and scientificity offered by the ideal
model, there are two possible reasons for criticizing this restriction
to the codes of the sender; one is *extra muros*, so to speak, and the
other *intra muros*. In *Le Père Goriot*, Balzac writes:

However discredited the word "drama" has become due to the twisted, abusive manner in which it has been used in these sad literary times, it is necessary to use it here: not that this story is dramatic in the true sense of the
word; but, perhaps, having finished the work, one might have shed a few
tears *intra muros* and *extra*. (3:49)

In a number of works, Balzac presents us with figures who misappropriate reading; outside the contents of the work, the apostrophe of the narratee is not as simple or direct as it might seem if we question the possibility of a zero-degree narratee. I am hypothesizing here that the two differences from the norm are in fact figures of the same lack of identity that informs misreading, and that they are varying versions of the same process and position.

The *extra muros* reason is clear enough from the example most often used to talk about the Balzacian narratee, the apostrophized reader from *Le Père Goriot*. I have already noted that Rousset posits this example as a possible variant within the scheme of the range of narratees. In his earlier article, Prince uses the very same example to define his concept of the narratee ("Introduction" 179–80). While he does not posit a paradigmatic framework in the same way that Rousset does, he does offer the possibility of a zero-degree narratee from which all variants may derive. For Prince, the zero-degree narratee "lacks all personality, all social characteristics. He is neither good nor evil, neither a pessimist nor an optimist, neither a revolutionary nor a bourgeois . . . " (181).[11] Yet the zero-degree narratee, even beyond grammatical constraints, is most resolutely a "he." And the "white hand" of the apostrophized reader may belong to a man or to a woman, to a bourgeois or an aristocrat. Thus we are faced with an unsolvable situation: if there is a zero-degree narratee, the female reader (narratee) must be a variant of the male, the bourgeois a variant of the aristocrat, or vice versa; these are unacceptable possibilities. If there is not a zero-degree narratee, then the schematic system falls apart: an equally unacceptable possibility, if only for heuristic reasons.

If we have learned one lesson from the combined programs of deconstruction and feminism, it is the law of gender/genre: we cannot consider the narratee in one case or the other to be a variant of the other sex.[12] Nor can we consider one class merely to be a variant of another. Queer theory, which I shall not enter into here except in passing, adequately shows that the homosexual position is not merely a variant of the heterosexual one.[13] Thus the position of the narratee is never in fact a proper one, because it cannot be appropriately submitted to the law of the proper. Any such act "feminizes" the narratee by submitting him or her to the discourse of the Other, which in turn violates the law of the proper. Yet this so-called feminization is only such in a phallocentric world: it is feminization in contrast to masculine dominance, male discourse, the model of power necessarily but not properly invoked and in vogue. Thus, to import a term from psychoanalysis, there is a hierarchic opposition in the model, but it is not even between masculine and feminine or male and female; it is between male and castrated. The position of the narratee-as-female, though clearly possible according to a gamut of possibilities, is excluded when we consider the possibility of there being an ideal system. As Robert Scholes puts it, "Can Mary actually read *as* a woman or only *like* a woman? If neither John nor Mary can really read *as* a woman, and either one can read *like* a woman, then what's the difference between John and Mary? My own feeling is that until no one notices or cares about the difference we had better not pretend it isn't there" (217). There is another implication to Scholes's point: no matter how necessary or useful a distinction is among the categories of real reader, rhetorical reader, ideal reader, and narratee, the differences are not clear, the distinctions are not discrete, and there is certainly an overlapping, if not to say a scrambling, of the categories—if not at the narratological level, where the distinctions are necessary, then at the rhetorical level. So there is never any proper female reader, because she is always improperly submitted or subjected to the ideal male reader. But there is never any proper male reader because he is always subjected to and castrated by the coercive narrative authority.

The problem then is that the implied reader or narratee is constantly called on to agree with the marks of discourse given by a phallocentric writer, yet cannot independently come to the desired conclusions. The writing is polarized along a line that excludes any real possibility for a neutral, zero-degree position for the narratee, however desirable this may be. There is nonetheless the figure of this neutrality, a figure that shows itself ultimately to be a product of the fictions of narration. That is, of course, the figure that is neither one nor the other, neither male nor female, be it the castrato or his specular image in the character of Sarrasine in the story of the same name or the apostrophized mysterious third in *Le Père Goriot*: not the white-handed reader, but Vautrin. Emblem for all to read, the sign at the Pension Vauquer calls to a mysterious third, who may properly read it improperly: "Pension des deux sexes et autres," that is, "Boardinghouse for both sexes and others." This third category is variously specified as homosexual (*Le Père Goriot*, "La Fille aux yeux d'or"), castrated ("Sarrasine," *Louis Lambert*), unmarried (*Pierrette*, *La Cousine Bette*), or completely disengaged (*La Peau de chagrin*). This third category seems to be the most appropriate model for the position of the narratee in Balzac. It too is always wrong, but in wonderfully right, narrative ways.

The castrated one, as Lacan and Barthes (*S/Z*) would note, is the one who cannot identify himself with the Other. In a specular fashion, it is he who is incapable of representation of self or other; it is he who cannot be read; it is he, ultimately, who cannot read. The castrated figure, actually present in "Sarrasine" and potentially so in *Louis Lambert*, is the powerless figure who cannot identify or iterate; more important, he cannot be iterated or inscribed since he is always a mark of difference. He is, then, emblematically, the figure of the bad reader in the narrative. The zero degree of the narratee is not then the figure deprived of all specific worldly qualities, but rather the figure who so deprived is always in a state of difference. The system of the narratee is built on an absolute difference from zero, a difference always present and usually elided.

What then happens at this point of difference where there is a textual blank that somehow must be filled? If the difference marks a position of undecidability that is neither one nor the other, neutral, neuter, or neutralized, it is the discursive variant of what Wolfgang Iser has called *Leerstellen*, points at which the active participation of the reader determines the reading and comprehension of the work. Iser sees the blank (*Leerstelle*) as a paradigmatic structure in a fiction: "The shifting blank is responsible for a sequence of colliding images which condition each other in the time-flow of reading. The discarded image imprints itself on its successor, even though the latter is meant to resolve the deficiencies of the former" (203).

The clue as to how to formulate improper writing comes from Iser himself, who relates his concept of the implied reader to the work of Erwin Wolff who, like Iser, is an Anglicist studying the eighteenth-century English novel. Wolff offers a sociological reading of the implied reader in the context of the horizon of expectations. Not coincidentally, Wolff's examples come from literature of the English eighteenth century and most notably from the didacticism of Pope and the dedicatory epistle of Fielding's "benevolent" novel, *Tom Jones* (150). In both cases, the example does not test the theory because it can very well provide for the possibility of an ideal implied reader, since the channel of communication is not closed. Following Wolff, Iser says that "the intended reader, as a sort of fictional inhabitant of the text, can embody not only the concepts and conventions of the contemporary public but also the desire of the author both to link up with these concepts and to work on them—sometimes just portraying them, sometimes acting upon them" (33). That the Iser-Wolff model is idealistic and dependent on a transcendental validity is clear from Iser's remark that "the concept of the implied reader is a transcendental model which makes it possible for the structured effects of literary texts to be described" (38).

Yet it is not my purpose to underline a facile contrast between the English eighteenth century and the French nineteenth century, but rather to suggest two possible ways of viewing the contrast. The first would be to see the French nineteenth century as a perversion of the ideal model of the eighteenth century, be it French or English. The narrative would have proceeded from a zero degree of neutrality along a clinamen that leads us first to the ambiguity of Balzac and then to the rupture of Flaubert. A second view would assume, more radically, that the very difference of the narrative, along with its figures of *Leerstellen*, improper neutrality, and a priori dyslexia, is the "proper" figure of reading the novel as genre. Such a proposal would not change our concept of continuity of reading and writing between Balzac and Flaubert, but it would cast the genre into ever more radical terms. From the foregoing, it should be clear that I am inclined toward the second version of literary history, as it accounts for the aporias of reading in a way not allowed in the first version.

By eschewing benevolence we are also excluding as a priori considerations the valuations of the work imposed by an implicit or explicit transcendental meaning toward which the reader—in this case, of the Balzacian narrative—is coerced by various processes of *captatio benevolentiae*. Thus since these processes seek to include the reader through an effect of rhetorical language, we can begin to understand how the process of reading works in Balzac without the additional layer of rhetoric that would otherwise accomplish what the narratological layer itself cannot do. Indeed, it is the function of these rhetorical figures to coerce, urge, or otherwise engage the reader at exactly those points, be they *Leerstellen* or clear-cut invocations of the narratee, where the dyslexia operating in the work would normally disrupt the communicational model.

FOUR VARIETIES OF MISREADING

I would like to propose four varieties of misreading in Balzac, and start with what I perceive as an alternative to the zero-degree narratee that Prince formulates in his earlier article. Now to do this I am hypothesizing that within the Balzacian narrative, just as is the case for the narrative of Flaubert, the model that Balzac himself gives us of misreading is one with which we are asked both to identify and to misidentify. The zero degree of Balzacian dyslexia would thus not be a pure communicational system but rather the complete illiteracy of the model: the spot at which reading does not occur despite the positing of a communicational model. Two emblematic examples of this new zero degree can be found at two generic extremes of *La Comédie humaine*. The early example is in one of the *Etudes philosophiques*, *La Peau de chagrin*, where there is a command equivalent to a double bind: a written sign that says "do not read me." The other end of the spectrum is found in *Illusions perdues*, where an author finds solutions in the unreadability of his works. Between the two are two hybrid works in which the zero degree of unreadability has been transformed into an operant. The dyslexia is no longer at a zero-degree level but rather functions as an intrinsic part of the ongoing plot: *La Cousine Bette* and *Modeste Mignon*. As will be seen from the argument that follows, I will consider *Modeste Mignon* as the ultimate version of the figure, both in terms of chronology and in terms of sophistication. But here, in an overview, *Modeste Mignon* seems to be a hybrid along the dyslexic scale. Needless to say, it is an appropriate irony that the range of misreadings must itself, as an ideal metafiction, be read dyslexically.

Any reader of the *peau de chagrin* is the figure of the dyslexic reader. Whoever reads the skin is diminished by it, castrated by it, and ultimately killed by it.[14] Whoever reads the skin shrinks the writing and thereby disfigures it as well. Whoever does not read the skin is also most obviously the bad reader, for such a person is willfully illiterate. No clearer model stands for us to read or to ignore than the imprinted inscription of the skin which as good readers we are not expected to read, for we are not assumed to be able to read Arab script. Yet we are no longer good readers since we are ignoring part of the writing; also, we are relying on the narrator's translation, and thereby submitting ourselves to his power.

Raphaël is exhorted by the antique dealer to behold the skin. But to look is to be absorbed in it, even without understanding it, even if this skin is supposedly in Sanskrit but is really in Arabic. To behold it is to misread it, for it is already to be included in the skin that compels: "your life will belong to me" (6:441). Fascinated by the skin, Raphaël is caught by the Medusa-like writing and is always the wrong reader of it. No matter what one does, one is always the wrong reader of this writing, for there is no right reader. The act of communication is subject to the double bind that compels and kills with one movement. The skin compels us to misread, but what is most disturbing is the fact that it compels us to misread ourselves, and specifically our own desire. As Samuel Weber remarks:

This *textual reader* reads his "own" desire, yet not merely expressed, represented in a work waiting to be repossessed by an interpretation that strives to fix its price and to define its value; the textual reader discovers his own desire as reader inscribed in the text, in a repetition which is irreducible because it precedes what it seems (only) to repeat. (126)

The problem of reflexivity in the narrative is one to which Balzac will return in *Illusions perdues*, where he tries to make sense of a system based upon dyslexia yet requiring a position of nonreflexivity. Far from *La Peau de chagrin* is the realist version of zero-degree dyslexia that corresponds to the philosophical quest for nonreflexivity in the early novel. Ostensibly the case of zero-degree misreading in *Illusions perdues* is due to the consideration of writing by booksellers as merchandise. Regardless of its contents, as I have already noted in the beginning of this chapter, a book is considered to be something bought cheap and sold at a high price (5:303). The idea of selling books includes reading in a process that insists on repetition and exchange instead of content or meaning: "You will agree to produce two novels a year for six years. If the first goes out of print in six months, I will pay you six hundred francs for the others" (5:306). This is a world where reading the system is a talent that pays off and where reading the contents does not. Thus, the closer to ephemeral prose a bit of writing is, the more journalistic and journeyman it is, the more likely it is to be read. The further from such prosaic language a piece of writing is the more likely it is to be the object of extreme Balzacian dyslexia:

Your *Marguerites* will remain chastely folded as you are holding them; they will never bloom with the sunlight from publicity in the field of great margins, enameled with the buds that the illustrious Dauriat uses, the bookstore for celebrities, the king of the *Galeries de Bois*. (5:342)

The reason for this sliding scale of readability is clear: the closer the writing is to reproducing a fictional presence filled with deictic references to current events, the more likely it is to be read. Thus readable writing is the writing that is confusable with the rumors of discourse. No matter how much lying goes into the production of journalistic prose, there is a relation to a known presence that confirms the work as merely a variant of the voice. Thus a piece of writing is read within the plot of *Illusions perdues* in direct proportion to its lack of validity as pure textuality. The pure textuality, the flowers of Lucien's rhetoric that form his collection of sonnets, remains unread or unreadable because it does not depend on some factitious presence for confirmation of its textuality. His novel occupies a hybrid middle ground: it is read to the extent that it recapitulates a middle ground between these fictions of presence and the purity of a bit of writing that does not seek representation as its goal. Hence fictional representation that consists of the verisimilar reproduction of reality is considered exchangeable. To the extent that it is exchangeable, it is readable. Again, contents are less readable than the system of exchange that allows them to circulate.

Balzac's irony is his insistence on the double model of zero-degree reading. The more readable a piece of writing is, the less it is really profoundly read, for its readability derives from its exchangeability. The more theoretically readable a work is, the less it is read; a pure literary work is maintained in its purity by its never being read and thus remaining untouched by the deformations of dyslexia. Balzac provides us with a figure of this unreadability as well; the zero-degree of readability, doubled into two poles of unreadability, is seen in the emblematic figure of reflection in the *Galeries de Bois*, in a scene that

Christopher Prendergast (92) sees as an important part of the novel's representational system: "Here man sees what God cannot see. Cost: two cents" (5:359). What "man" sees, of course, is his own reflection. To the extent that "man" can read, he winds up reading a fictional representation of himself, solipsistic in nature and tautological as well; this readability functions as an exchange and as a dehumanization, for "you went away embarrassed, without daring to admit your stupidity." Yet the purest possible position is the one that can never be seen and never be read.

In *Illusions perdues*, the novel that is perhaps Balzac's most cynical, for it is his first novel of disillusionment, his writing reaches new limits of zero-degree readability. At this point, one is inclined to agree with Georg Lukács's assessment: "This new type of novel was the novel of disillusionment, which shows how the conception of life of those living in a *bourgeois* society—a conception which, although false, is yet necessarily what it is—is shattered by the brute forces of capitalism" (47). Having attained the zero degree of readability, where what he himself is writing is also subsumable under the contract of exchangeable commodities, Balzac has reached the limits of his representation of reading as engagement. It is thus a short step for Flaubert to remove the pinions that uphold even this last illusion and to turn the dyslexic exchange system of *Illusions perdues* into the functional illiteracy that informs not only Charles Bovary but also the whole of the novel into which he fits.[15]

Elsewhere Balzac has proposed other forms of dyslexia for the novel. Between the two extremes—zero degrees of reading and cautionary tales—Balzac offers various hybrids of dyslexia. These hybrids are the misappropriation of writing rather than the full exclusion of a proper act of reading. In such cases there is a proper act of reading when and where the writing has reached its appropriate receiver, but this proper act is seconded by an improper one. One version, though a rare one, maintains the integrity of the communicational system on the surface, but changes the message in a fictitious manner. There is no better example of this anatomy of misreading than in *Le Cousin Pons*:

At the very moment that Pons was looking for one of those flattering answers that always came too late when he was visiting one of the Amphitryons he feared, Madeleine entered, gave a small note to the *présidente*, and waited for an answer.

This is what the note said:

If we were to suppose, dear Mother, that this brief message has been sent from the Palace by my father who was telling you to dine with me at his friend's house to re-engage the question of my marriage, the cousin would leave. (7:517)

This hybrid form of misreading blends proper and improper; it is tropic in its insistence on movement in two directions at once, and it can thus be used to further the plot of the novel. A kind of misreading thus is a tool for the author to place conveniently in the hands of his characters, who manipulate writing for him.[16]

Indeed, a work like *Pierrette*, from 1840, shows us that misreading is the law of the land, to the extent that a refusal of misreading brings about a return of violence that had been safely kept at bay. In that work, Sylvie, one of Balzac's most embittered *vieilles filles*, has her cousin Pierrette living with her. Sylvie is so suspicious and jealous of the naive, innocent Pierrette that she spies on her. At one point, which becomes the turning point for the plot, Sylvie decides that Pierrette has unfittingly received a letter (4:140). Sylvie actually tries to wrest the letter from Pierrette's hand, drawing blood in the process, ensuring Pierrette's eventual martyrdom and death. By insisting on her own right to read her own letter, Pierrette remains the naive prisoner of a system of reading in which there are appropriate and inappropriate readers; she thus ensures her own death. At the same time, the impossibility of a dyslexic reading brings out the physical violence that had elsewhere been turned into a war of words of Sylvie (and her brother) against the guileless Pierrette.

This hybrid version of dyslexia is most important in *La Cousine Bette*, which incorporates it into the exchange system and in which key points in the plot depend on misappropriation of writing. At least ten examples of this improper version of misreading can be found in this novel. Together they are the nodal points or the plot twists that bring the novel to its conclusion; they could be considered to be the very skeleton of the plot. The examples are as follows: Bette reads a letter of the supposedly moribund Wenceslas (7:110) that he leaves as an apology for his earthly existence; she is an improper reader in that the original destinataire is no one in particular and therefore not her. Second, Bette reads a letter that Hulot has dropped, an action that quickens her resolve to act (204). After that, Crevel shows Hulot a letter from Valérie that gives evidence of the Baron Valérie's duplicitous nature (232). The next instance is triple: Hortense reads a letter meant for her husband, which causes her to leave him (277); the author of the letter, Valérie, has already shown it to Bette before sending it (275); Wenceslas then shows Valérie the letter Hortense wrote him as a result of her own misreading (280). Valérie even suggests that Hulot ask Wenceslas for the same letter (284). The sixth instance occurs when Marneffe shows Hulot letters that prove that the latter is the father of the baby that Madame Marneffe is carrying (305). It would seem that everyone, including the police, is involved in the misappropriation of writing: the police inspector shows Hulot a letter—actually addressed to him, so that the proper reader improperly reads his own mail—that Madame Marneffe conveniently left for her husband to read (308). For the eighth occurrence, the baroness tiptoes into her husband's room and reads a letter that he has received from her uncle that details his monetary problems (315). In the ninth version of the same trick, Hulot reads a confidential letter that the prince gives him in order that the former be enlightened about his brother (343). One misreading deserves another: Hulot shows his brother a farewell letter he has received from Johann Fischer (344). And finally, Montès reads the facsimile of a letter sent by Valérie to Steinbock (413). In each case, the improper reading of writing, specifically a letter, produces an important plot change.

In general, *La Cousine Bette* is a novel about the misappropriation of writings and voices, starting with the fact that "the cousin even nicknamed herself the family confessional" (84). Wenceslas calls himself an author (129) of a sculpture; Hortense steals him from Bette and says that "I promised nothing for the author" (132). Later, "Hortense naively told the novel of her love to her cousin" (170). Balzac also notes that Bette, who is like a spider, reads the souls of Hortense and Victorin (207). Disruptions of the communicational model abound in the novel, starting with the fact that Madame Hulot says that she got an anonymous letter that she then burnt (95). In one case, for example, there is a disruption in the production of writing: "Josépha the maid contributed, through a letter whose spelling betrayed the collaboration of the Duke of Hérouville, to Adeline's complete recovery" (425). In another case, it is a question of pen names. At the beginning of the dénouement of the book, Hulot has disguised himself as a public scribe: "Where you see the two words '*Public Scribe*' written, in large script on white paper hung in the window of some mezzanine or muddy ground floor, you may well think that the neighborhood has lots of ignorant people" (437). After she discovers her husband hiding under a *nom de plume*, Adeline finds a letter, which is thus belated, giving her this very same and thus superfluous information (447).

There are even cases of a correct reading, but even that detours the information away from an appropriate, moral, or correct action. Madame Saint-Estève, who happens to be Vautrin's aunt and who is thus related to the best reader in the entire *Comédie humaine*, is hired to break up the proposed marriage between Crevel and Madame Marneffe after the publication of the banns (386). Madame Saint-Estève is supposed to misuse the language of the banns, which are the prelude to the performative action of the marriage ceremony, by preventing the marriage from occurring. Even the absence of misreading is remarked by Balzac: "In a conversation at loose ends in which Valérie and Steinbock had thrown themselves since Crevel's departure, it is like those long literary works in our time, on whose frontispiece [*fronton*] one reads: *Reproduction prohibited*" (396–97). And finally, Michel Foucault would undoubtedly add yet another example of misreading that concerns doctors as readers of symptoms. When Crevel and Valérie are dying, there is a difference of opinion on how to interpret the etiology of the disease. Balzac notes that the doctors were divided into two camps and then proceeds to list three different medical opinions (431).

Thus the act of misreading turns an undecidable point, a *Leerstelle* in the story, into a strategic moment; the narrative possibilities are condensed into one as the novel takes off in a new and unforeseen direction. At the same time, at least potentially, the misappropriation of writing by an internal narratee or destinataire helps produce a proper reading by the external narratee, the implied reader, and/or the ideal reader. The act of improper reading maintains its impropriety within the story, but determines propriety at the level of discourse. Yet the impropriety of the action is part of the exchange system and thus, for the story, there is a distinction between proper and improper readings. At the level of discourse, the improper and the proper are included within the same realm. It is not that the production of writing for Balzac has become an amoral action; it is rather that the necessary difference at the heart of the production of writing and its reception in an act of reading founds both discursive possibilities. In that this is the case, one would be tempted yet again to redefine terms in order to include the improper within the realm of the proper, for some distinction must be made between the improper readings that are plausible or includable and those that are not. One can imagine all sorts of improper readings that are not allowed, such as, for example, the reading by Bette of a letter by Pons or a short-circuited reading in which Valérie reads a letter by Bette, but to no end. There are undoubtedly possible cases that are not included, or cases that test the logic of proper versus improper: has Pons, like Julien Sorel, read Las Cases? And if so, or if not, what are the consequences? More intriguingly, have the later characters in *La Comédie humaine* read the works about earlier ones?

To preserve the integrity of the writing, the improper is scapegoated by the textual system. As I have already suggested in the discussion of Iser, the development of the benevolent system of communication and knowledge necessary to the eighteenth-century English novel may relate to the active exclusion of all that is perceived to disrupt the system. Whatever is perceived to be illegitimate is excluded from the outset, both from the system within the novel (any novel) and from the initial development of the novel as genre. Thus the repression of the dialogical elements in the novel and the reduction of aberrancy relate both to the novel's mimetic function of representing a system and to its social function of reproducing the stable values of the system. It is thus not at all irregular to see the development of this scapegoating mechanism at a profound textual level, found both in the work of the innovators of the novel in the eighteenth century and the conservative yet ironic Balzac in the nineteenth. Ultimately the impropriety in the story redefines the possibilities of exchange within the work and the limitations of discourse for the work.

The final version of dyslexia that has an important role in the development of the Balzacian system of writing is found in *Modeste*

Mignon. Remarkable here is the fact that the whole novel is built on a comedy of dyslexia inspired by a strategy of miswriting. Modeste is writing letters to the poet Canalis and he is answering her correspondence. But Modeste signs her letters "O d'Este-M.," thereby implying that she is a rich noble of Italian descent. In turn, Canalis is not answering this fan mail that rapidly turns into love letters; in his stead, the mail is answered by his secretary, Ernest de la Brière, who begins to fall in love with the correspondent himself. The secretary is feminized by the real (though silent) authority, Canalis, who calls him Mademoiselle de la Brière (1:575). Thus instead of the singular twist of the plot in *Le Cousin Pons* or the multiple twists used by the author to turn *Leerstellen* into strategic points in *La Cousine Bette*, in *Modeste Mignon* we have an entire novel whose plot is based on the figure of misreading.

The act of misreading has taken over the system of exchange of narratives for this work that has been economically streamlined into the improper exchange of letters built on a double substitution. In the one case the language of the letters substitutes for the inexpressible desire of Mignon for her poet. In the other case, the language is substituted for money: the poet who is improperly/properly reading the letters sent and received by his secretary believes that the correspondent is a rich heiress. Whereas it is not uncommon for Balzac's plots to relate to the acquisition of money, this work intimately relates money and narrative power. Both at the point of emission and at the point of reception, the use and misuse of language develop coterminously as an economy in which language is substituted for, and associated with, both desire and money. If the laws of desire and success are the laws of the Balzacian universe, the algorithm of those laws, themselves inexpressible, must be the use of language. And specifically, this is "written language," in that its very being (*sous rature*) implies an absence that can be filled after the fact with the desire or will to success of which it purports to be the vehicle.

Although Balzac bases the plot on a series of misreadings, he wants to ensure that the real (ideal, implied) reader will understand and read "properly":

Here, as you will see, nature, social nature, which is a nature in nature, gave itself the pleasure of making a story more interesting than the novel, just as torrents draw fantasies forbidden to painters, and accomplish feats of strength in arranging or polishing stones to surprise sculptors and architects. (1:480)

Balzac substitutes the possibility of contradiction for the act of benevolence with which the novel had theretofore burdened itself. Whereas the act of representation had to be univocal in its attempts at allegiance, Balzac sees fit to reinclude the improper within the act of representation.[17] Similar to the painter whose action separates from direct representation just at the moment that representation itself is put into question, Balzac proposes a difference from the novel as received genre and praxis in which the improper and proper are simultaneously inscribed at the same point. In so doing, Balzac is not completely dissociating himself from previous novelistic praxis; in fact, he uses old-fashioned techniques of the epistolary novel to further his writing, such as developing an overt system of misdirection of writing that is straight from the works of the eighteenth century: "Modeste wrote a short, polite letter to Dauriat, the editor of Canalis's poems, in which she asked him, in the poet's interest, if Canalis was married. She then asked that the answer be sent to Mlle Françoise, *poste restante*, in Le Havre" (1:511). This is further enforced by a "directed" misdirection within the correspondence. As if the discourse of misdirection were not enough, the charge is included within the story, as Modeste writes Canalis (1:514).

Nor is Balzac immune to pandering to some of the other conventions of the novel. For example, he appeals to the theater as a direct form of representation of which the novel is merely a variant. But it is not at all coincidental that the play to which he appeals, Beaumarchais's *Le Barbier de Séville* (1:500–501), depends so much on the misdirection and misappropriation of writing. In *Le Barbier de Séville* and in *Le Mariage de Figaro*, the letters help overturn the system: Rosine's letters to the count disguised as Lindoro; the letter in Suzanne's hand dictated by the countess to undo the count with a secret tryst in the park; love notes sent between Rosine and Lindoro; and especially, the various letters that Figaro has on his person: a four-page letter from Marceline, a letter from an imprisoned poacher, as well as Chérubin's commission.

Perhaps even more central to Balzac's continuity with generic praxis is the fact that Balzac provides his readers with a detailed version of Modeste's reading list (1:505) in a strange foretelling of Emma Bovary's reading habits. Most significantly, Balzac tells the readers that Modeste undergoes a process of identification with the heroines of the romantic novel she is reading: "Having become the heroine of a dark novel, she loved either the hangman or some scoundrel who wound up on the scaffold" (1:506). At the same time that he is allowing for this process of identification at the level of the story, Balzac is disallowing its possibility at the level of discourse: for Balzac's reader, there is a torrent in place of the benevolence of older prose and there is always a degree of impropriety in the act of identification and the act of consuming the writing.

Balzac underlines the dissociation of story and writing by introducing an intradiegetic level of metatextuality: the characters comment on the act of letter writing. This metatextuality is neither pure nor abstractable to our level of reading. The possibility of such pure abstraction is excluded by the author. For him there will always be a confusion of levels with a mixture of proper and improper: even Canalis exclaims to La Brière, his "lieu-tenant" and scribe, that "every anonymous letter is a beggar!" (1:521). The communicational schema is as bankrupt as the letter that goes begging because the failure of idealistic communication underlines the lies of the system. Certainly the receiver of the letter is being lied to, but also the signer, absent though he is, is lying in not signing his correct name. The system, as well as each individual letter, is also a lie in its totality: it is an impure object for the extradiegetic reader to consider as a mark of the textual ambiguity that it signifies. And thus, in its improper, lying state, the communicational schema is telling the truth about the production of novelistic prose once the state of benevolent purity has been eschewed by the author.

Numerous examples of this internal metanarrative are self-explanatory. One should think, for example, of the comment of Modeste to the false Canalis:

Would you have written the letter that I have as an answer to mine? Would your ideas and your language have been the same if someone had whispered in your ear something that might be true: Mademoiselle O. d'Este-M. has six million and does not want a fool as a master? (1:526)

Again, there is the letter from La Brière that serves as an answer: "You are not a d'Este. Does one owe the revelations you ask for to someone who lies about herself?" (1:527). Certainly, in that this is a comedy of manners, we have every right to expect an observation of conventions that at one level seems merely a commentary on epistolarity. But on another level, Balzac is using convention to talk about the very nature of novelistic writing. As Louis Marin comments in his study of Poussin's *The Arcadian Shepherds*, "The fact that in Poussin's painting nobody is looking at us allows us to state, according to our hypothesis, that the represented scene operates in its propositional content the 'negation' of all marks of emission and reception of the narrative message" (Suleiman and Crosman 306). Indeed, the disposition and uses of convention and the flouting of those uses may tell the reader or observer more about the writing than any content-oriented proposition.

A consideration of Balzac's rhetoric of dyslexia in the novels shows how this calculated strategy brings with it the very possibility of an identification that will provide a misreading. The dangers of reading correctly will cause the reader to misread the novel in a way, perhaps, that the author would not wish. In *Modeste Mignon*, Balzac puts the matter emblematically in a letter written to Modeste, with whom we must and must not identify ourselves:

Do you thus believe, Mademoiselle, that letters, more or less true relative to life as it is, more or less hypocritical, for the letters we would write one another would be the expression of the moment they left us, and not the general meaning of our personalities; do you believe, I say, that, however beautiful they be, they would ever replace the experience of self-discovery we would have in witnessing everyday life?

Man is double. There is the invisible life of the heart for which letters may suffice, and the mechanical life to which, alas, more importance is attached than one believes at your age. (1:540–41)

In referring to the double, Balzac recuperates a figure he uses effectively in many of the early *Etudes philosophiques*. In this case, he introduces the reversal of the figure as part of the realist rhetoric. It is a means of separating what he had amalgamated in the figure of the improper in *Modeste Mignon*, and of putting everything, so to speak, in its place. Yet a revisionist return to a dualism where he could prop his writing on a benevolent universe is not an acceptable solution; there is no return after the improper. One could perhaps explain this return by the fact that none of the other choices seem to have worked in the development of the various strategies of *La Comédie humaine*. That is to say, the strategies that Balzac uses throughout his production have never guaranteed the absolute result that he wanted. In the narrative world of *La Comédie humaine*, even if Balzac moves benevolence from the realm of the universe in general to the realm of the reader in particular, the author is still incapable of assuring himself that dyslexia will not surface at the wrong moment. And as I have indicated in a discussion of this presumed benevolence in the reader in an article called "The Unknown Subject," there is a necessary rhetoric of capturing this benevolence, the *captatio benevolentiae*, a rhetoric whose very nature forces a misreading of the work because it depends almost entirely on the collusion of narrator and reader.

HOW TO AVOID MISREADING

One other strategy that Balzac consistently uses throughout much of *La Comédie humaine* likens the novel to the theater: the novel is made to resemble the act of making present that is the performance of a play. Misreading could therefore be avoided. But that too is now seen as not sure-fire. In fact, in the play *Vautrin*, where Balzac tries to solve his narrative dilemmas directly by theatrical means, the work is by all measures a fiasco. What does remain from that theatricality, most evident in a work like *Le Père Goriot*, is a turn to the sublime, which for Balzac is a product of theatricality. So the return of the sublime in *Modeste Mignon* is an uncomfortable or improper one, which develops within the novel out of misreading, but which has as its antecedents Balzac's own reference to the sublime as an offshoot of the theatricality he invests in some of his fictions.[18] We cannot therefore understand Balzac's turn to the sublime as part of the comic solution in *Modeste Mignon* without first seeing where it comes from in Balzac's inscription of the sublime in a tragic mode.

To associate the Balzacian narrative with the forms and languages of the theater is to propose an entirely different frame of reference for the writing than that of the novel. It also posits different modes of representation. By using a rhetoric of the theater, Balzac negates the diegesis of the work and thereby denies its fictional nature. He asserts the truth in representation of a world that is no longer a narrative construct but rather a theatrical presentation. Balzac's casting of his writing as drama yields a theory of direct historical representation: the writing is posited as the image of society, the mimetic representation of the events of the nineteenth century. Society and its history are considered to occur in the form of drama with an exposition, a conflictual event, and its resolution. Instead of multiple causalities and the varied paths of narrative, events are reduced to a few select, salient features. Finally, the rhetoric of the theater circumvents both the accusation of careless writing and the secondary value placed on the novel as a genre: narration is seen as a series of didaskalia and the novel is elevated to being a variant of theater. In short, Balzac's theatricality excludes dyslexia.

It would seem, then, that the primary function of theatrical rhetoric is as a means of avoiding a framework of narrative by which the signs of narrative imply fictionality. Despite the dramatic excesses of the melodramatic imagination and despite the eventual foundation of a semiotics of fiction through the intermediate rhetoric of the theater, the theater is the locus of a simulacrum of the truth that neutralizes the falsity of fiction: "Ah! Know ye well: this drama is neither a fiction nor a novel. *All is true* [in English in original], it is so true that everyone can recognize elements of it in himself, even perhaps in his heart" (3:50). Whereas fiction leads the reader astray through guile and exaggeration, drama leads back to the truth in one's heart. But also, the rhetoric by which fiction is presented as drama—as that in which all is true—is self-erasing. Communication with the heart and recognition of truth are nonlinguistic and immediate. So the function of the rhetoric of theatricality is to erase all rhetoric and all difference in the acts of presentation.

The appeal to the theater means an appeal to a truth beyond the artifice or machines of fiction. Within the novel, theater represents a movement by which language dissolves into life; through rhetoric language disappears, to telescope fullness and completion into an immediacy of emotion. Emotion replaces language as the vehicle for communication; emotion communicates without the clinamen between presentation and representation associated with fiction. Because it is impossible to distinguish among plenitudes, and because there is no linguistic frame to limit emotion, the emotional field can overflow permanently. Yet the introduction of a rhetoric of the theater into the novel allows Balzac to exceed the limits imposed by fiction whose analogue is the bourgeois drama, and to change this drama into tragedy. He begins with the exposition where "all is true," and there posits a drama, and ends the first part with the transformation of the drama into tragedy: "Here ends the exposition of this obscure, but frightening Parisian tragedy" (3:126).

To transform the banality, clarity, and embourgeoisement of drama into the transfiguration of tragedy, Balzac introduces the sublime. The sublime resists inscription in a textual semiotics since it does not participate in a textual economy. Tragedy occurs apophatically: it occurs without language and without rhetoric. Within the novel, the tragic moment is a defining limit and an unattainable ideal for Balzac. If this ideal remains unreachable or only inscribable as a silent negativity, this very silent gape opens up a hypothetical trajectory for language along a curve that approaches but never reaches the asymptotes. If through its rhetoric drama defines a possible field for language and its attendant analytics, semiotics, social structures, and value systems, the tragic sublime defines the endpoint of the game. The rhetoric of the theater allows Balzac to express what he does not allow himself to express in a rhetoric of fiction. But at the moment of sublime tragedy, there is no more room for this rhetoric.

Thus the sublime is the alternative to the dyslexia that Balzac builds into his system: Pierrette, who dies as a result of trying to prevent dyslexia, is in that camp: "The Rogrons [Sylvie and her brother] put themselves hideously next to the corpse of their victim in order to torture her more after her death. The poor child's body, sublime with beauty, lay on the bed" (4:158). The sublime is a mark of supreme silence, an absolute textual blank not marked by difference or impropriety. From this posited point Balzac can turn either to the pure tragic moment, as is the case in *Le Père Goriot*, or to the pure comic solution, which is, as in *Modeste Mignon*, the fulfillment of desire. There are as many instances of the sublime in *Modeste Mignon* as there are examples of misappropriated writing in *La Cousine Bette*. According to Modeste, the lithograph used for Canalis's publicity is sublime (1:510); for the narrator, Lamartine is the "leader with sublime cries" as well (1:512). Reciprocally, La Brière/Canalis is sublime for Modeste (1:523) just as Modeste is for Canalis/La Brière (1:526).

Modeste becomes "the beautiful, sublime image of Germany" (1:509). The Duchesse de Chaulieu inspires Canalis to write "sublime chants" (1:647). Even the tragic itself becomes part of the comic sublime: "the firm, soft physiognomy of this man reached the sublime of the tragic" (1:479). As there will be no tragic moment in this novel, the tragic is subsumed into the greater version, which is the happy ending. And in general, Modeste is "sublime with affection, at every moment" (1:494); moreover, the role she has assigned herself as the future wife of the poet is a sublime one as well. Referring to Eliza Draper, who sought to marry Crébillon fils in the same manner, Modeste becomes "the heroine of such a novel, more than once she studied the sublime role of Eliza" (1:508).

In *Modeste Mignon*, the sublime is everywhere. Whereas in other novels the sublime is introduced asymmetrically, here it applies, within the fiction, to all sides of the writing of dyslexia. Sometimes it is Canalis: "Having decided to find Canalis sublime, Modeste, dressed as she was the day this story started, remained astonished, and dropped her embroidery which was attached to her hand by a cotton thread" (1:626). Sometimes it is Modeste: "The aspect of Modeste's sublime beauty embellished by the trip, the sight of this young lady dressed as well as Diane de Maufrigneuse had lit the powders gathered by reflection in Eléonore's mind" (1:698). In this late novel, the sublime recuperates a totality that includes both personal history and History in the large sense. The sublime is introduced to determine, though apophatically, the ideal piece of writing: the writing is pure and the model is resolved as the ideal, yet this does not occur except at the point at which there is no language. This sublime solution is also an ironic one for Balzac, who is aware of the implications of completing a dyslexic model with a solution that comes from tragedy: the return to beginnings seen in the first quote, with Modeste dressed as she was at the start, and the empty reflection seen in the second, both underline the hollowness (or at least the irony) of introducing the sublime as a correction and a solution to problems. That the plot itself takes a comic turn that depends on the independent voices of the two characters of Modeste and La Brière also indicates that this resolution is not the solution to the problems of the characters but only a solution to the problems of the writing.

Thus if Balzac takes us, between *La Peau de chagrin* and *Illusions perdues*, from one version of zero-degree dyslexia to another, it is a mark of his genius to have inscribed various degrees of misreading in between the two. That he ultimately arrives at the reinscription of the point of noncommunication at which he started is no surprise; nor is it astonishing that the sequel to this final zero-degree work, *Splendeurs et misères des courtisanes*, is also, at least thematically, a sequel to the first novel. There is also a system of theatricality at work that seeks to compensate for the closure of understanding that occurs with the inscription of the zero-degree dyslexic reader at the heart of the Balzacian narrative. The natural or logical continuation of this rhetoric of theatricality is the inscription of the sublime: the point at which there is no rhetoric, the moment at which the specular disappears.

In *Modeste Mignon*, the sublime is directly related to the narrative of zero-degree dyslexia: the sublime is inscribed as a product of textual fiction, along with all the other results of textuality. From that point, it is but a short step to the *béance* of Charles Bovary. For if Flaubert removes all the ties to received ideas left by the remains of the Balzacian system, the sublime as a product of fiction becomes indistinguishable from the gap of nonunderstanding. The difference between *Modeste Mignon* and *Madame Bovary* is thus of degree and not of kind. Thematics aside, both works inscribe the truly denatured nature of fiction at their very hearts. And it is the sublime reader, turned hypocrite for a lack of recognition of his own fictionality, that is the same in the two cases. If Homais is awarded the *croix d'honneur*, it is perhaps only because Vautrin became head of the secret police.

CHAPTER 4

Romantic Interruptions

Nerval's Mad Intertextuality

> Today, a whole school, which truthfully has been
> useful, reacting to the reigning abstract logo-
> machy, has imposed a new game on art . . . in
> which one shall constantly be satisfied with sen-
> tences that already exist.
>
> (Proust, *Sainte-Beuve*)

The path traced through the mainline narrative writers from Stendhal through Balzac and on to Flaubert is neither exclusive nor complete. As much as one might see a development of a style, a set of
problematics, and a set of contents along that line, other praxes participate in similar and different narratives. Instead of seeing a developing textuality, an emerging monolith, as it were, it is more productive to see the practice of literature at that point as something in
which the various kinds of writing seek to close the gaps of writing.

One such interesting case is what could be called belated French
romanticism. A half century after the earliest French romantics, and
even a quarter century after the high romanticism of the twenties,
authors, including Gérard de Nerval and Alexandre Dumas Fils, are
still writing works that could be qualified, at least on the surface, as

romantic. Rather than accepting their work as some sort of nostalgic and belated production honoring a dead system, these two revive their late romanticism with the same writing techniques, processes, practices, and schemes that develop in realism. Indeed, for all his nostalgic, Rousseauistic longing, Nerval shows almost a maniacal need to be Julien Sorel, free of the father's language. As I have demonstrated in an article on his translation of Goethe's *Faust*, Nerval's self-definition comes through in two different lights in the translations of *Faust I*, written when Goethe was still alive, and the idiosyncratic translation of *Faust II*, written after Goethe's death. Caught in the traps of his own writing, Nerval will become the negative image of that realist writing that has been the subject all along: he will insist obsessively on textuality, on its foundation, and will find, much to his chagrin, that the gaps and threads of textuality are one and the same thing.

So too will Dumas Fils attempt to limn a realist picture in a now-forgotten work called *Diane de Lys*. In this case, the author takes the standard romantic narrative built on longing for a woman and translates it into an allegory of the writing process. But this is not the writing process of romantic inspiration. It is rather—and quite astonishingly several years before *Madame Bovary*—a sketching out of realist writing's space of production. The subject may be romantic; the production is unabashedly and consciously realist, even materialist in its disposition.

WHO IS SYLVIA?

Often studied in the work and life of Nerval is the question of sanity and madness. Can sanity, critics have asked, include madness? Does madness find its definition in the primacy of sanity, or is it something unto itself? Moreover, can there be an act of recuperation in Nerval's writing? Can the author or narrator, through his writing, make the journey from sanity to madness and back again? Can he, in fact, recover through writing? These questions lead us onto the various common grounds of Nervalian criticism, in which rational prose and sanity, combined with narrative control, are on one side, and a grab bag of madness, myth, hallucination, dream texts, and fantasms is on the other. These questions of madness are often taken into the realm of the literary, as if literature, even in its "mad" guise, could directly represent all these rather heterogeneous categories, suggest their irrational and amorphous qualities, yet still maintain the "literarity" of the writing. Without being forced into all-or-nothing versions of the rational and the irrational, the literary process of intertextuality explains problems in Nerval's prose, often described in terms of myth, dream, and madness.

As Kevin Newmark notes, one can classify the strong readings of Nerval into two categories. Writers like Michel Jeanneret and Ross Chambers see the possibility of recuperation through narrative; Rodolphe Gasché and Christopher Prendergast, on the other hand, "call such a resolution into question" (39). For his part, Chambers (*Story* 110) warns the reader that he is not going to show "the ways in which the text of 'Sylvie' lends itself to a reading that focuses on its repetitive structures, its thematics of similarity, its temporal minglings and confusions of period with period." As soon as one has entered the world of Nervalian criticism, one is caught up in a series of references. If this is the task of the critic, who must show that he or she has read what has gone before, it is also, strangely enough, the figure of Nerval's writing, whose literary mechanism depends on a figure of intertextuality that runs throughout his work, from the translation of *Faust* through the *Filles du feu* and ending with *Aurélia*. I say "throughout his work," but the exception would be "Sylvie," where it is usually kept under control.

"Sylvie" seems to make sense because the figures of intertextuality are kept in check. Somewhere between the same and the other, Nerval's intertextuality collapses oppositions and requestions categories. Intertextuality in Nerval is the point at which the writing is endlessly ruptured and at which those ruptures are remarked as milestones in the writing. Following the generic patterns of the work, Gasché puts its representativeness into question. He notes (103) that Nerval had written to George Sand that "Sylvie" "is a short novel which is not quite a tale." Thus, says Gasché, this work "can be seen simultaneously as a part of the ensemble of *Les Filles du feu* and as a representative part of this ensemble." But this does not sit well with Gasché, who finds it "difficult to consider 'Sylvie' as an organic

whole." Reflecting on mimesis and representation in "Sylvie," Prendergast shows the problem at the heart of representation in the story:

> The "mimesis" produced by *Sylvie* is an internalised one; it is internal to the
> text, to the mind of its narrator, and takes the form of a series of "chains" in
> which part is constantly likened to part within a textual whole, which itself,
> however, *as* whole, suspends all possibility of a direct "referential" passage to
> a world beyond the text. (150)

Following Kristeva in *Le Texte du roman*, Prendergast (176) sees the
narrative as being nondisjunctive; it does not decide, adjudicate, or
define; it is dialogical at its very heart. Still, in "Sylvie" there is a possibility of framing the questions. As the same critic notes: "All the
major themes of ['Sylvie'] are 'framed' by the logic of the question
without closure. The questions it implicitly poses include the following: what is madness, what is the dividing line between madness
and sanity" (175).

Both the recuperative and nonrecuperative critics wind up at the
same point, understanding the play between reason and its other as
relating to the writing project. Gasché puts the opposition in question when he says that "the play between the same and the other, its
almost abyssal specularity, is *already* madness" (121). On the other
hand, Chambers sees "residues" (*Story* 116); bricolage (97); and an
intertext, the episode of Paolo and Francesca from *The Inferno*, announced and simultaneously denied (118). "Sylvie" does not get
caught up in the Babel of works like *Aurélia* or "Angélique." As
Chambers points out, the latter is a story in which "the book disappears in the labyrinth of libraries, bookstores and archives"; out of
that comes a "sort of Babel of quoted voices" (*Mélancolie* 105).

Though neither necessary nor emblematic, since the tale could
have survived very nicely without it, the parrot that appears toward
the end of "Sylvie" may be seen as an incarnation of the limitations
of language. Newmark has recently pointed out the importance of
the parrot to the story:

> What is still alive in the parrot is precisely that aspect of *Sylvie*, or any other
> text for that matter, that *cannot* die without entailing its utter dissolution as
> text. Like any author, the speaking parrot can live on forever because he lives
> off language as the written traces of memorized signs that can always be pro-
> jected onto a future act of recognition and understanding. (59)

The parrot is also an excellent figure for the actresses, speaking the words of another, and for the theater as a whole, which figures so prominently in the tale. This is not the only bird in Nerval. There are at least three other allusions in his prose to talking birds. In *Les Nuits d'octobre*, it is a question of the language of birds (401).[1] In "La Pandora" Nerval notes "a parrot passing by as swiftly as possible . . . had swallowed several [pomegranate] seeds I had rejected" (744). And in *Aurélia* (781), right after Aurélia's death and a series of references to Dante and Virgil, a talking bird appears: "Passing by a house, I heard a bird speaking several words it had been taught."

Now as Newmark remarks, "the narrator is forced to note, to mark, to write, a potentially disruptive *resemblance* between the parrot and the man of experience, which in this chapter also means the entire tradition connecting Montaigne, Descartes, Rousseau, the uncle, and of course the narrator himself" (60). But the critic has not gone far enough when he sees the parrot as a sign of the "man of experience." Indeed, I would see the parrot as the sign of the vortex of intertextuality in which Nerval constantly finds himself. For in each case, the reference to the parrot is accompanied by a reference to some previous literary endeavor. The passage from *Les Nuits d'octobre* swims in a sea of literary allusions that includes Homer, Dickens, and Diderot: the first of these will reappear endlessly in *Aurélia*; the last, at the end of "Angélique." In "La Pandora," the passing allusions are to Prometheus and to Jezebel. In *Aurélia*, the parrot comes fast on a complex of intertextual references that will be explored below. In "Sylvie" (613), both Rousseau and Virgil appear immediately after the parrot scene. Rousseau is caught in a chain of references to "those great names of thought that start with Montaigne and Descartes and end with Rousseau." Virgil is also caught in a chain that links him to Lucretius: "Fortunately, Virgil's privet still blooms, as if to stress the master's words written above the door: '*Rerum cognoscere causas!*'" (613).

Kept in check in "Sylvie," Nerval's intertextual vortex is also held back to some extent in "Angélique," with the *garde-fou* of a frame tale about a search for a book. The search for a lost book and for the persons that book is supposed to depict thematizes intertextuality, thereby making it safe. Except for a few spots in "Angélique" that I shall discuss below, Nerval does not get caught in a web of intertextual references. By *Aurélia*, there are no referents to seek, no books to close, and the disease of intertextual madness ravages the work. Almost boundless intertextuality destroys the opposition between self and other, refusing identity and clear doubling as well, and creating a fractal narrator who is more than one but not quite two. When he quotes, when he refers, when he falls into the abyss of intertexts, he is more than himself, but not quite in a dialogue: *nec tecum nec sine te.*

In order to understand the ramifications of the rupture and eruptions of intertextuality in Nerval's work, I am proposing three examinations of the manifestations of his intertextual disease. First, I shall look at the question of generic intertextuality and the references to a recent past in the form of Rousseau. Second, I shall examine the gyre of intertextuality in "Angélique." And finally I shall look at the mad cure for the disease proposed in *Aurélia*. The solution is a way of curing the problem of the search for the *Urtext* in a work like "Angélique," where, as Prendergast notes (163), it cannot be found. The solution is not the disappointment that there is no *Urtext* but that the *Urtext* is intertextuality "itself," literary *différance*.

A SIMPLE CASE: ROUSSEAU

The narrative of "Angélique" is doubly framed. The larger and more important frame is a long exegesis on the search for a unique book, a discussion of the denizens of the library, and the final hallucinatory comments on Virgil. The immediate frame for telling the tale is Rousseau's writing; a chance encounter with a Rousseau work entitled *Anciennes Chansons sur de nouveaux airs* sets into motion an intertextual system that functions as a thread of continuity: "precious autographs like those of *unpublished* letters of Voltaire and a collection of songs set to music by Rousseau and written in his hand" (525). This random event authorizes Nerval to write, not because Rousseau has already written, but because Rousseau had himself taken preexisting writing as a pretext. Rousseau's voice is given as one of absolute presence: Rousseau re-voices and re-presents the older writing in a present mode; his writing is related to music and not to the act of literary representation. The writing of music does not mark an absence made present or a past reborn; rather, it is the potential of bringing the human voice to full presence (Gordon 53–58).

By setting himself up under the sign of Rousseau, Nerval hopes to accomplish several things in telling the truth. He can bring the writing of times past to full presence, especially that of Angélique herself. He can also repeat the act invoking inchoateness of Rousseau's own *Confessions*, at the beginning of which (5) Rousseau makes a claim for uniqueness in that no one has preceded him in this endeavor and that no one will follow. The re-inscription of the writing of "Angélique" is analogous with Rousseau's own coming to presence: "this yellowed notebook, entirely written in her hand; since she was the daughter of a great house, this is perhaps more daring than the very *Confessions* of Rousseau" (526). Doubly inscribed under the work of Rousseau, the hybrid work of Nerval rewriting "Angélique" *with new airs* is posited as a potential fulfillment. Nerval sees his own work as the voice and writing that are even more true than Rousseau's confessional mode and even more present than Rousseau's act of presence of the *Confessions*.

Even as he formulates the paradigm for this project, Nerval undercuts the efficacy of the exemplary, framing narrative. No sooner posited as the author of a repeatable *Urtext*, repeatable despite Rousseau's own indication to the contrary, Rousseau is buried; the reference to Rousseau gives the narrator the idea to go to Ermenonville. Just as Nerval honors the memory of the dead Goethe with the thanatopical translation of *Faust II*, he buries Rousseau, even if he is to be honored in this rewriting. Rousseau is introduced to provide the lead in writing, but also to be buried, so that the writing of the would-be son can in fact exist. But burial is not so simple, for, as is well known, Rousseau's tomb is empty; Rousseau persists as a disembodied ghost that haunts the living would-be author.[2] Rousseau will continue to haunt him even as Nerval tries in vain to reduce his predecessor to the role of the dead textual father. The absence itself must be inscribed; along with the desire to revive Rousseau for his own purposes is the desire to bury him; there is no better example of what Kristeva called nondisjunction: *nec tecum nec sine te*. Both Rousseau's body and its absence haunt the work. In fact, the old bones rattle, making new music for old heirs; Nerval notes the little bells called *ossements* that are both a death knell and Rousseau's own music, "a sweet melancholy in Rousseau's soul" (566). The name of death associated with these bells is a catachretic sign for a truly ab-

sent skeleton in the tomb; the writing on the tombstone is a synecdoche for the dead writing of Angélique's manuscript and Rousseau's
Confessions.

The tombstone is the locus of the signifier that refers to no signified. On the thematic level, Nerval has not revived Angélique in his
new airs; he has reinscribed her death in writing, just as he has reinscribed Rousseau's. On the theoretical level, things are even more
troubling, because the dead textual father, not content to be dead,
stalks the writing and in this fractal haunting, underscores not only
the nondisjunction but, more important, the "neither one nor two"
figure that we have already indicated as the hallmark of intertextual
madness.

THE ELUSIONS OF GENRE

Between the death knell of Angélique's signature and the hollow
ringing of the bells at the blank of Rousseau's tomb, Nerval gives the
formula for the proposed transformation into writing, from *fille du
feu* into *feuilles du feu*, which translates the women into sheets of paper: "The bibliophile . . . was worried about a four-volume folio edition entitled *Perceforest.* . . . 'My friends,' he said, 'has *Perceforest* been
burned?'" (564). Since this is "one of the novels of the Arthurian cy-
cle," the Grail legend is now potentially a *f(eu)ille du feu.* Nerval's
writing insists on condensing the *fille du feu* and the sought-for object of redemption (the Grail) into the writing of the tale.

If the ultimate redemption through transformation does not occur, this failure is prefigured at the site of the previously existing
writing. Just as Nerval has reworked *Faust I* implicitly and *Faust II*
explicitly, and just as he has transformed Rousseau's supplementarity
posing as presence into the inscription on a tomb, he insists on the
transformation of the quest narrative itself: "I demand that the four-
volume edition of *Perceforest* be respected . . . a singular edition, with
two transposed pages and an enormous ink spot in the third volume"
(564). Just as the pilgrimage was to be accomplished respectfully, respect is demanded for the *Urtext,* the writing of the father. But the
original writing is no longer that, having been marked, sullied, and
transformed; the generic *Urtext* is what we might call an "elusion":
an illusion, an elision, and an allusion. If these be the comforts pro-

vided by intertextuality, Nerval certainly does not gain measurably from them. For if one understands intertextuality as the transformation occurring in the chronological, spatial, economic, textual, and ideological difference between the original writing and the rewritten one, here the intertextual transformation has already taken place.

The beginning is already transformed in the work and there is a black spot somewhere toward the middle that covers up what is behind, beyond, and before it. The Eucharist, of which the Grail legend is a metonymy, stands as the original emblem of transformation: from the real to the symbolic, from the linguistic to the objective (or to the subjective), and from the worldly to the redemptive. As Marin points out on the question of origins:

It was necessary for the Eucharist to show, in the *Logique de Port-Royal*, that language was a particular version of a more general problem; but at the same time, it was also necessary to cut off this positing of the problem from its origin, or, more precisely, to include the origin as a simple illustrative element of the problem whose positing it permitted. (55)

Here the transubstantiation is reduced to a shell game of inexplicable transformations. The angelic messenger that is the vehicle for transformation and transfiguration is spilt ink, not the wine, not the blood of the chalice, and certainly not the chalice itself. It is rather the very definite mark of the human, the act of inscription that is difference from divine writing. And, as for the one in search of the book that is the very key to generic transformations, "he was taken for a madman" (564).

Thus the realization of transformation or its ambiguous origin is inscribed within the madness of the bibliophile. Little matters beyond Nerval's bibliomania; whether there are three volumes, three out of four, or all four (565), everything sounds banal after the reinscription of the act of transformation of the original. No redemption will occur and every move in the work toward clarity and closure will instead endlessly repeat the shell game. This multiple closure that is not closure to the story of Angélique herself endlessly refers us back to the frame tale. Inscribed as an intertext, the Grail legend becomes the emblem for the whole story. But it is still not the necessary writing that grounds and authorizes; it is not "a singular book" (*un livre unique*) (504) sought from the very first.

The search for origins is transformed into a search for textual origins, a quest for the grounding writing that can justify the present act of writing. Yet the position of the preexisting writing is always ambiguous, for if it justifies the current act of writing, it also necessarily precedes this action. Thus this act of writing assumes a position subservient to the original. But if the act of writing does occur, and if in its unfurling it gives an account of the search for the original work, this original work of the full and present word assumes a position secondary to the current act. By positing the original work as something potential, an a posteriori construct that can only validate recursively, Nerval can escape from the vicious circularity of attempting to write when writing has always gone before. The risk involved is great, for Nerval then posits his writing as being unanchored and unfettered. Separate and apart from the recursive effect of the authoritative writings that are eventually incorporated into the Nervalian system, Nerval's work risks a total unbound madness or *folie*.

The only solution is to seek the necessary work, but in seeking it, not find it. Finding the *Urtext* will produce an act of closure and reinforce the situation of the writer subservient to past works. Despite all the peripeteia, it would seem that *the* book is finally found:

The book I have just bought at the Motteley sale would be worth much more than sixty-nine francs twenty centimes if it weren't so cruelly trimmed [*rogné*]. The new binding has this title in golden letters: *Histoire du Sieur Abbé comte de Bucquoy*, etc. The value of the duodecimo comes perhaps from three thin brochures in verse and prose, composed by the author, and which, in a larger format, had their margins cut to the text, which still remains readable.

The book has all the titles already mentioned, listed in Brunet, Quérard, and Michaud's biography. Facing the title is an engraving representing the Bastille, with this title above it: The Hell of the Living, and this quotation: Facilis descensus Averni [*sic*]. (587–88)

The goal has been reached: the writing is there and the story is thereby recursively grounded. Or is it? The writing found is reduced to a physical book; it is not the transcendental logos that had been sought but an object with a market value. Moreover, as a physical presence, it is misleading, since it has been rebound, and it is incomplete, as the pages have been cruelly cut. And its value, reminder of the book's status as a commodity, is other, for it comes from three fragmentary supplements of mixed generic heritage. All of this is as motley an array as the name of the sale itself. And finally, as if all that were not enough, Nerval's work ends with the misquoted writing of another, the "sweetest father," Dante's guide, Virgil himself, who writes that "the descent to Hell is easy [*facilis descensus Averno*]." Nerval skips the conclusion, which his readers could undoubtedly have recited by heart: the return is what is difficult, for there is the work and the labor: *hoc opus, hic labor est.* (*Aen.* 6:124–29).[3]

A recuperative reading would take this intertext as a metaphoric description of the trip from sanity to madness and back again. It could be a trip from ideal writing to the world of appearances and simulacra, the wasteland of false bits of writing. This voyage is followed by the quest that is difficult to accomplish, the return to the perfection of the logos. And the return would be borne as an angelic message, the production of the poetic work, which would then be the logos itself. But the recuperation occurs at a loss, for the book found is not the book that has been sought. Adding to the nonideality of this copy of the book are the distressed state of the book and the misquotation from Virgil. And so generic intertextuality is a failure because it needs a complete recuperation that does not and cannot occur.[4]

THE ABUSES OF THE LIBRARY

The problem of textual nonidentity is fully set out in the very first chapter. In this textual world, the ego is never fully identical to itself and language and textuality shatter; the world is "abyssally" situated in the library of Babel or babble (Destruel). The multiple and fragmentary nature of this world is institutionalized as the collection of writings. The abuses of the library are not only the perfunctory attitudes of the personnel consumed by the textual machine, but also the abuses perpetrated by an institution that appropriates writing for itself. The library sets itself up as institutional master of the word and thereby asserts its primacy as a simulacrum of a totality, the logos itself. The fragmentary nature of the library is underlined by the anaphoric use of the word *partie*, repeated three times in a short descriptive passage (510). The library is composed of fragmentary works that, even taken together, are an insufficient origin for Nerval's own. In contrast to the "singular book," the single author, and the single reader that form the ideal communicational system of the complete message, sender, and receiver, there is a multiplication into a congeries of hundreds of readers, multiple authors and editors.

If Bucquoy's book were the unique piece of writing, then Bucquoy would be the unique author, the one who does not need to rely on an intertext. His writing would be grounded in, of, and for itself. But if this is so, what can be adduced about Nerval's own writing: do we thereby assume that it is proffered as the unique ideal work that has supplanted that of Bucquoy, whose work would be reduced to being a simulacrum of Nerval's? If Nerval's is the ideal work, it is hermetically closed; his is the ideal message of which he is the ideal sender and receiver, the ideal writer and reader. And then Bucquoy's, still a foundational work despite its displacement, could not be recursively validated as a ground. The asylumlike closure of the library is supported by reason itself: "It has been said and rightly so [*avec raison*] that a singular establishment like that one should not be a place for the public to warm itself, an asylum room, most of whose guests are dangerous for the existence and conservation of the books" (510). For the communicational unit of ideal sender, message, and receiver to exist, it must be isolated in an asylum. Reason confines the madness and streamlines the system. But just because the madness is confined, it is not necessarily restrained. It multiplies and explodes:

This quantity of vulgar idlers, retired bourgeois, widowers, solicitors without jobs, schoolboys who come in to copy their translations [*version*], maniacal old men, like that poor Carnaval who came every day in a red, light blue, or apple-green suit, and a hat decorated with flowers, undoubtedly merits consideration, but aren't there other libraries and even special libraries to open for them? . . .

There were nineteen editions of *Don Quixote* among the printed volumes. None has stayed complete. (510)

Nerval unfolds everything in this extraordinary passage. Destructive and dangerous forces that constantly threaten to take over from within are multiplied within the institutional confines. The library is home to all those who do not fit into the ideal communicational system: the "retired bourgeois," nonproductive members of a productive society; the "widowers," bereft of a proper receptacle for their messages; the "solicitors without jobs," mechanical producers of vulgar messages and bereft of receivers as well; the schoolboys who have no original messages; and the "maniacal old men," the multiple destroyers of a system. Madness is dangerous: even within the confines determined by reason, it threatens to disrupt explosively the ideal communicational model and to insert multiplicities of messages, senders, and receivers.

The "vulgar idlers" are ultimately less vulgar than they are common or popular. With its multiple points of view, its shadings, its explosion of difference, and its movement away from the law, the vulgar is dangerous and confusing. For the vulgarity is that of Vulgar Latin, the movement away from the ideal, univocal tongue of Classical Latin, which for Nerval remains the archetypal language of Virgilian communication. Elsewhere in the story, Nerval again metaphorically points out the danger of this vulgarity by referring to "la forêt de Villers-Cotterets" (584). Beyond any woodsy referentiality, the phrase refers to a sixteenth-century ordinance whereby all legal documents had to be written in the vulgar tongue in order to be clear and comprehensible.[5] The clarity turns into the darkness of the forest, the Dantean "dark forest" of confused, multiple intertextual references and allusions.

The writing may implode poetically: intertextual madness is a poetic device, threatening to disrupt from within by producing a maelstrom of references and beginnings. When Nerval writes of Carnaval, he sets in motion the destructive intertextual force within the work that is the first step of a literary descent *in Averno*. Carnaval is a character described by Jules Champfleury in a story of 1846 and included in his book *Les Excentriques*. Champfleury's character is also found in the library, where he is oddly dressed with "an unknown decoration around his neck and a steel chain and artificial flowers instead of a ribbon on his straw hat" (165). With his unknown decoration, the replaced ribbon, and the artificial flowers, Carnaval is the poetic figure of displacement, substitution, and interchanged signs. The action of displacement epitomized in the trope corresponds quite neatly to the insertion of the poetic at this strategic point in Nerval's own work.

Even more significant than the description of this eccentric character is Champfleury's intertextual pretext for *his* writing, given as the introductory paragraph to the description of Carnaval: "You all know Hoffmann's "Dog Berganza . . . [who barks], 'From a certain angle, every spirit, however unoriginal it is, is predisposed to madness'" (164–65). Champfleury's writing is not grounded as an absolute, but takes as its intertext a tale by E. T. A. Hoffmann entitled "Information on the Latest Fate of the Dog Berganza." Reason is called into question, for we have moved from the realm of human speech to the speech and writing of an animal. Even more upsetting to the grounding of Nerval's system is that we cannot get any further than Hoffmann's title without the introduction of another intertextual dimension, yet one further (un)ground. Appended to the very title of the tale is an author's note that refers us to one of Cervantes's exemplary novels: "See the tale of the two dogs 'Scipio and Berganza'" (51).

Through the process of intertextuality, the work now moves from questions of the rational, that is to say, the epistemological motivation of the writing, to questions of possibility, in other words, the very ontological grounding of a textual system. And before we get to ground Champfleury's and Nerval's works in Hoffmann, the latter author's note draws us irresistibly to Cervantes's first dialogue in "The Dogs' Colloquy" (241–42):

"Brother Cipión, I hear you speak and I know that I am speaking to you, and I cannot believe it, for it seems to me that our speech has gone beyond the limits of what is natural."

"That is the truth, Berganza, and this miracle has become even greater, since we are speaking with argued discourse [con discurso], as if we were capable of reason, being so much without it, that the difference between the dumb beast and man is that man is a rational animal, and the beast, an irrational one."

The introduction of the colloquy of the dogs shows the syntagmatic breakdown of monological discourse, prefigured in the ever-increasing introduction of intertextual referents. It is a process that amounts to the introduction of alterity within the realm of the same. Though discovered through the intertextual chain, Cervantes is already there to haunt us with his multiplicity and his fragmentation: "There were nineteen editions of *Don Quijote* among the printed volumes. None has stayed complete." Cervantes's writing appears as both multiple and fragmentary, buried and still around, in a whirlwind of mad textual production; we can go no further, for the path is no longer clear: *la diritta via era smarrita* (*Inf.* 1:3).

At this textual source, the monological finds its intertextual referent in the dialogical, in the realm of the doubled voice of the two dogs: it is the dialogical *différance*. Between Cervantes and Hoffmann there must be the suppression of one voice and the establishment of the other in a position of primacy. The resurgence of this redoubled voice is tantamount to the resurgence of the repressed voice, the other excluded by the monological discourse of power and reason. Yet even more important than the process of textual exclusion and the covering up of this exclusion within the work is the absolute fictional nature of the process of assuming a position from which to speak or write. The dog says that he cannot logically or rationally speak, yet in so saying, he speaks. Paradoxical founding of a system, the possibility of speech or writing depends on the exclusion, whether possible, symbolic, imaginary, real, or impossible, of nonspeech and nonwriting, of the only absolute ground, silence itself.

Even if Nerval pursues his "rigorous investigation" (511), there will be an eventual return of the suppressed intertextual multiplication that is also a reaffirmation of the arbitrary grounding of a textual and rational system. And finally then, after all the red herrings, multiplications, and peripetiae, there is another pretext. It is the pretext for the finding of the Book long sought but not identical to itself when found. As could well be expected, this pretext is another intertext. But in this case it is a meta-intertext, a means by which another dimension of eccentricity, of flight away from the center, and of intertextual folly, is proposed:

REFLECTIONS

"And then . . . " (That is how Diderot began a story, I will be told.)
—Go on.
—You imitated Diderot himself.
—Who imitated Sterne . . .
—Who had imitated Swift.
—Who had imitated Rabelais.
—Who had imitated Merlin Coccaïe . . .
—Who had imitated Lucian. And Lucian had imitated many others . . . Even
    if it was only the author of *The Odyssey* . . . (587)

As Bruno Tritsmans (432) comments, this list is both a deferral of the origin and a reference to the founder, Homer; with this gesture, Nerval remarks the absence of the origin. Raymond Jean remarks the "allusion to Penelope's canvas . . . a representation of the work its author is undoing as he weaves it" (96). This anaphora of imitation itself, the punctuation, as Chambers remarks, "'imitates' and repeats the staggered structure and episodic linking of the whole" (*Mélancolie* 109). Thus this meta-intertextuality reintroduces the dialogical within the monological, upping the stakes perhaps, getting the writer and reader into an ever-widening gyre of mad rushing around, increasing *ad infinitum* and *ad absurdum* the intertextual madness of the Nervalian production.

INTERTEXTUAL MURDER IN 'AURÉLIA'

Aurélia describes a labyrinthine purgatory in which the writer is lost. There are recuperative elements in *Aurélia*, not the least of which are the dreams and mystic images that might be considered to be escapes from the imprisonment of the kind of textuality discussed in this chapter. Ned Bastet, for example, relates the tale to a cure; Uri Eisenzweig, on the other hand, sees the return as being impossible, the indication of which, for him, is already visible in "Sylvie": "The failure that characterizes *Sylvie* is thus double: on one hand, the subject fails to preserve his non-identity and on the other, fails to find a world, a structure of the original space" (235). For me, the imprisonment never ends, but it is an imprisonment in the mazelike jail of letters, the Borgesian Library of Babel before the fact.

In the very first line of *Aurélia*, Nerval announces the father of Western literature; it is as if that intertextual beginning were inevitable. If in works by other authors we might have assumed that the reference to Homer was there to give credence and to allow the work to move on, we can be sure that here, given the history of intertextuality has already been unearthed, Homer is a warning of danger ahead. When Nerval sings of Homer, a shudder takes over: "Dreams are a second life. I could not, without shuddering, penetrate [*percer*] the gates of ivory or of horn that separate us from the invisible world" (752). Homer (*Ody.* 29:562–67) distinguishes between the two kinds of gates and their functions, but Nerval leaves us with an ambiguous "or."[6]

The path of choice will realize the dream and help the dreamer return from the dark night into the open light. Choosing this path means deciding, but Nerval cannot decide. Nerval's writing is inscribed in the undecidable; the writing occurs between life and death, as it falls fully into neither one category nor the other. What seems to be another Nervalian descent into hell is really a movement into the indifferent limbo of purgatory, not thematically or philosophically, but literarily:

It is a vague underground, lit up little by little; gravely immobile figures who live in this limbo stand out from the shadows and the night. Then a picture [*tableau*] forms, a new clarity illuminates these bizarre apparitions and lets them play: the Spirit world opens for us. (753)

This is the world of the Shades, the chiaroscuro world that is neither of darkness nor of light. Nerval has seen the father—Homer—at the beginning of the work, and nothing can be done about that; Homer's emblematic presence insures that Nerval cannot himself write originally and that a downward spiral will ensue. The only hope is that he can choose his guides through the downward spiral, after which he might return to the world of light and sanity.

In search of a guide, Nerval posits Swedenborg, Apuleius, and Dante as possible escorts through the labyrinth. Of the three, Dante insists the most: he reappears on the next two pages in mentions of the *Vita nuova* and of Nerval's habit of seeing a Laura or a Beatrice in the mundane world (754–55). There is an obvious affinity between Nerval's search for a goddess as guide and the *Vita nuova*, an observation made by several critics.[7] Dante insists textually not only because of the similarities between Nerval's quest and the *Vita nuova*, but also because of the insistence of the structures afforded by the male guide in the *Divine Comedy*. Dante himself has already been led through a labyrinth by Virgil; Dante's success implies Nerval's failure, since Nerval needs to find his own original writing. Being led by someone who has predicated his whole work on having been led implies a Pyrrhic victory or a double bind. If we had any doubt, we need look no further than the same first page, for Virgil too is there from the beginning, repeating the same lines, subject to the same laws of predecession as at the end of Book Six of *The Aeneid*.[8] Virgil rewrites Homer and turns Penelope's pronouncement preceding the eventual reunification of two lovers into the warning of a dead father (Anchises) to his son (Aeneas). Virgil will be Nerval's guide, or more precisely, Virgil with Dante will be Nerval's guides, but they will guide him only to the point at which Anchises' voice should be internalized as he predicts what Aeneas will do on his own (*Aen.* 6:888–89). For Nerval, though, there will be no independence, for the point at which the voice of the dead father is internalized is the point at which Nerval cannot be an original author.

Having entered the Library of Babel where all his references are always compellingly, obsessively, and insistently present, Nerval perceives this world as the glorification of the memory of past textuality. This textuality becomes an all-consuming whir that allows no signals to appear other than those caught within the buzz of its remembered pieces of writing: "The lessons continued on Greek and Latin authors, with a monotonous buzz that seemed to be a prayer to the goddess Mnemosyne" (757). The prayer to memory reawakens the past and brings it all abuzz into the present of the dream and into the presence of a voiced prayer. Like the previous invocation of the goddess (650), the appeal itself upsets the system, and not even the love of knowledge can resolve the situation. Nerval wanders along, like Dante's shades, with the others who are caught, meandering from one locus to another in this Piranesian prison of the mind in which the proper cell is never found.

In the dream world that has invaded the real one, and which has become conflated with the worlds of madness and literature, the nodal points are all indexed in the *Purgatorio*. This writing of origins is first of all the preexisting inscription of Nerval's figure of madness; it is also a means of figuring the often repressed and textually wrenching problem of the paternity of writing. The return to the writing of origins inscribes the family that Nerval somehow hopes to resalvage through his writing: "It was like a primitive and celestial family, whose smiling eyes looked for mine with sweet compassion" (770). The return of the family does not mean sympathy and solution, but rather the insistence of the paternal writing that is already there. The white-clad Edenic family is the repressed writing of otherness returning in full force. Significantly, in Dante, this is quite specifically described as a *sinister* image: "The water was taking in my

image on the left [*dal sinistro fianco*] and like a mirror reflected to me
my left side [*la mia sinistra costa*] if I looked in it" (*Purg.* 20:67–69).

Another dream that recalls the family is peopled with beings remembered from the narrator's past or from that of another: "Three
women were working in that room and represented, without absolutely resembling them, relatives and friends of my youth" (770).
But again the image is not clear; inevitably, when Nerval remembers
family, he is citing the *Purgatorio*. The past he remembers is the past
of literature; the family novel and the *Purgatorio* begin to resemble
one another: "Three ladies came dancing in a round at the right
wheel, one of them so ruddy that she would hardly have been noted
in the fire . . . " (*Purg.* 29:121–23). Dante's fire is translated into the
flames of a lamp, and the various exchanges in the position of the
lead dancer (*Purg.* 29:127–28) are fragmented into an exchange of
parts in Nerval's rewritten phraseology: "The contours of their faces
varied like the flame of a lamp and at every moment something of
one passed to the other" (772). Remembered bits and pieces of other
works, or even what will prove to be a closely followed version of
several key cantos in the *Purgatorio*, cannot be integrated into Nerval's writing. Nerval's work fragments what it receives by multiply-
ing the possibilities or by reinscribing every remembered whole as a
heterogeneous set of bits and pieces.

Nerval's writing seems to have the consistency of a dream, but the
conflation of the various worlds that could be represented prevents
the backward glance at representability from achieving what is desired.[9] In *Aurélia*, the material is not integrated as well as in a dream,
for it is the reeruption of what had been totally encrypted: the remembered authorial writing that splinters the representability of the
material. Rather than weaving his writing to separate it from the
dreamer or writer, by which a certain amount of neurotic elements
can be alienated from the dream, the narrator lets himself be imprisoned among the filaments, as he is caught in the gaps and ruptures of
the dizzying intertextual matrix.

So if it is not a dream, what exactly is done and undone, woven
and unwoven, written and unwritten? This nodal point of the reinscribed death and the refiguration of the writer as the iterative
weaver of dream is a chiasmus: the sought-for woman becomes the

unattainable transcendental Other; the quester becomes himself the sought-for woman of his own writing. At the node of the chiasmus, however, is not the solidity of meaning but an important gap. The writing refigures the point that has already been omitted in the system of reference, the space in Canto 29 of the *Purgatorio* between the woman in white and the three ladies dancing. Significantly, where Dante frankly *admits* intertextuality, Nerval *omits* a reference to Ezekiel. Dante tells us to go read Ezekiel if we want a good description: "To describe their forms, reader, I do not lay out more rhymes, for other spending constrains me so that I cannot be lavish in this; but read Ezekiel who depicts them as he saw them come from the cold parts, with wind and cloud and fire . . . " (*Purg.* 29:97–102). Nerval omits the reference as if he were hoping against hope that this act of omission would solve the problem of textual paternity.

Though seeking absolute authority in writing, Nerval functions as the impotent and often unwitting transcriber of writing that has gone before, the same writing that now serves as his prison. Nerval's path through literature now turns into a sterile iteration of previous writing. A descent into a limitless purgatory is not followed by the promise of paradise, with its light, fullness, and closure. Thus Nerval remembers patient Penelope, constantly unweaving what she has woven, getting nowhere, and finishing nothing. While Penelope has a goal and has certitude on her side, for she is sure that Odysseus will return, it is not the same assuredness that guides the narrator as he unweaves, for he does not believe that Aurélia will return: "I did more, I tried to figure, with earth, the body of the one I loved; every morning, my work was to be done anew, for the madmen, jealous of my happiness, enjoyed destroying the image" (775).

Nerval's version of the scene reverses the original at numerous levels. In the *Odyssey*, Penelope is as wily as her husband: she is able to weave and unweave her own work, while waiting for the absent subject once more to become present; in the process, she fends off the suitors. If Homer's work is taken as a metaphor for writing, the writer is seen to have complete control of the language and the power to control the desire of the other. The writer maintains sovereign right over the work while waiting for the imprimatur of the subject of authority. At that point, the writing itself will have become a useless supplement, for there will no longer be an absence to be marked. For Nerval there is always an absence; since Aurélia is dead, there will never be any coming to presence. She will not return like Odysseus nor will she be beatifically reborn like Dante's Beatrice.

Moreover, the very act of creating the writing is itself a violation of the absolute authority of the Other, who alone can determine what is figurable and what is not. And thus the passive suitors of the *Odyssey* turn into a distinctive collective Other that undoes what this new Penelope has done. Structurally too, the Nervalian writing is posited as a reversal of the original. Penelope's work figures a three-dimensional scene from the represented world on a two-dimensional canvas: Penelope weaves a scene from the world that, whether it is reality or myth, can be corroborated by common knowledge. But Aurélia has been only a textual figure, for which there is no external act of corroboration: no other writing, no tangible proof, and no received knowledge. And at the point of her death as a two-dimensional figure, she is transformed into a three-dimensional one whose very existence is inadmissible in this textual world of two-dimensional figurations. As a "writer," Nerval does not have the right to make graven images in his work.

A MAP OF PURGATORY

Nerval does not stray from the purgatory imposed by Dante's original except for the fact that for Nerval no Paradise will follow. *Aurélia* is not organized by a promised redemption but by a road map of references to the masterwork of the *Purgatorio*. At first glance, Nerval's allusions to Dante might pass unnoticed, seeming to be no more than the natural outgrowth of the late romantic and vaguely Rousseauistic setting he has created. As Nerval begins to set up this idyllic location, he quickly peoples the landscape with Dantean figures: "I peopled the hillsides and clouds with divine figures whose forms I thought I saw distinctly" (775). There is a sudden change from a first-person description where there is no subject of action to an active first person who, through his gesture, initiates the very act of creation. This quick change is symptomatically aberrant, a telltale clue for the reader.

In a corpus as large as the *Divine Comedy*, it is not difficult to find something that looks like Nerval's description. And so one finds such a passage of Dante echoed here: "When the flowers and the other fresh herbage opposite me on the other bank were left clear of those chosen people, even as star follows star in the heavens, four living creatures came after them, each crowned with green leaves" (*Purg.* 29:88–93). What might pass for overdetermination is anything but that; the intertextual reference is not serendipity, for the passage occurs in the same Canto 29 of the *Purgatorio* and indeed, in the same section of that canto that Nerval has already remarked: the point at which Dante remembers—and Nerval forgets—to tell us to read Ezekiel. Thus the reference underlines the exclusion that signals the most acute stage of the problems of intertextuality and the precedence of authority in *Aurélia*.

The obvious lapsus allows for the free flight of writing that now ensues. Since, for now, he is able to exclude authority (Ezekiel) at will, Nerval knows no limitations: for the first time, no preexisting authorial subject interferes with the act of creation. Writing is unfettered and unhampered; neither the weight of the past nor the constraints of form can interfere with the absolute act of writing. Nerval is so sure of this writing that he even allows himself the liberty of reinforcing his reassurance with the definitive declaration of metanarrative judgment: "I was given paper, and for a long time, I busily represented, through a thousand figures accompanied by stories, verse, and inscriptions in all the known languages, a sort of history of the world, mixed with memories of studies and fragments of dreams" (775–76). In control, Nerval claims to produce the total infinite work, written in every language and every genre, and combining written and pictorial images. This work announces itself as a self-identical act of representation that makes present what is absent and for which the act of making present is the act of representation itself. The scriptorial "I" has finally been rewritten into the authorial "I," as the work is reoriented toward a new mode of representation that is also an act of totalization under which all is subsumed.

Can it be so easy? Assuredly not, for to forget Ezekiel, he must remember Dante, who includes Ezekiel as a predecessor in writing. The "elusion" of Ezekiel haunts the writing; it allows Nerval to write and have his miracle, but this comes at a price. Nerval can posit a new kind of textuality, his original work, only if there are other encrypted remains. Needless to say, these hidden writings are by Dante and Virgil. Nerval introduces his Orientalism and the rebirth of his work between parts of his writing that intertextually refer to two points of light in Dante: the light at the beginning of Canto 29 of the *Purgatorio* and that of the reappearance of Beatrice at 30:73. Between these two points of light is the most famous section of the *Purgatorio*, the disappearance of Virgil:

> I turned to the left . . . to say to Virgil, "Not a drop of blood is left in me that does not tremble: I know the tokens of the ancient flame." But Virgil had left us bereft of himself, Virgil sweetest father, Virgil to whom I gave myself for my salvation; nor did all that our ancient mother lost keep my dew-washed cheeks from turning dark again with tears. "Dante, because Virgil leaves you, do not weep yet, do not weep yet, for you must weep for another sword!" (*Purg.* 30:43; 46–57)[10]

Virgil appears twice more in Dante's work at points to which Nerval himself makes direct or indirect reference. At the beginning of the disappearance of Virgil, Dante himself quotes the master by recalling the Aeneid: "Agnosco veteris vestiae flammae." And just prior to Virgil's disappearance in Dante, it has been a question of a reference to the *Aeneid* (6:884): "All who cried, 'Benedictus qui venis' and, scattering flowers up and around, 'Manibus, oh, date lilia plenis'" (*Purg.* 30; 19–21). The phrase "you shall be Marcellus [*tu Marcellus eris*]" that is the missing intertext for Dante's quote is found only nine lines before Virgil's version of the gates of ivory and the gates of horn (*Aen.* 6:893). Even in this act of closure on Virgil, Nerval returns to the inescapable loops sets up from the beginning.

For Nerval, it is now impossible for Virgil or Virgil's work to appear, for that would be a reminder that the strategies of writing have failed to reach a desired goal; yet they cannot wholly disappear. When "Virgil," the character in the *Divine Comedy*, disappears, Virgil-as-writing must disappear as well. Yet through the omission of Dante's story of the disappearance of Virgil, Nerval has been aided by Dante himself in suppressing the "sweetest father." And at least for several pages, Nerval will allow Dante to take the blame or credit for the exclusion of the Virgilian writings. It is only when Nerval realizes that he too has participated in this act of suppression and patricide that the repressed Virgil reappears.

Just as he has excluded reference to Ezekiel as the textual father, Nerval also excludes a direct reference to Dante's telling of the disappearance of the master, the "sweetest father [*dolcissimo patre*]" who is the voice of authority. By omitting all direct allusions to the strategic intertext about the disappearance of the father, Nerval repeats the act of exclusion of his textual father: he excludes the position of a previously existing textual authority. As in the ironic double bind of "be independent," he uses what he excludes to perform that exclusion. Nerval excludes Dante, though not entirely; there will be echoes of Dante in Nerval, just as there continue to be echoes of Virgil in the *Paradiso*, long after Virgil's disappearance as guide. Nerval excludes the insistence and control of Dante; he refuses the authority of the already established author. It is precisely this act of exclusion that can never be announced as such. It must be marked over and encrypted by another discourse, one of the reoriented cosmology that comes to stand in the spot where the disappearance of Virgil should have been. At most, the turnabout can be alluded to metaphorically or sylleptically: "It was the signal of a complete revolution among the spirits who were not willing to recognize the new possessors of the world" (777).

Thus the discourse of tradition, the Occidental forms and logic by which Nerval would ordinarily be bound, is the discourse against which the silent textual revolution must take place. In that patricentric discourse, power eventually passes, by devolving and not through revolt, to the son who is redeemed by love, about which he too can write. Yet Nerval cannot overtly state the act of defying textual authority. It is not simply that the position of the object of desire for whom Nerval writes is an ambiguous one: mother or beloved, mother and beloved; or absent or present, absent and present. An announced reversal would have to give clear definition to a figure and to an object of desire, which in all of Nerval's theorizations of textuality remain ambiguous. Moreover, a voicing of the revolt would endlessly reinscribe Nerval's fragilely reaffirmed ego in a double bind; the writer is caught by the trap of the instructions given by authority to "be independent." Affirming his own position is a denial of the position of the other, and the creation of an impossible solitude in which his writing has no function. Allowing the position of the other necessarily recalls the other impossible situation: the priority of the authoritative subject who has already desired and already written. In such a situation—the subject coming after—the rebellious filial subject bound by *Nachträglichkeit* is totally impotent and his writing is totally useless. With Homer, Virgil, Goethe, or Dante, Nerval may approach impotence; without them, the speechlessness of infancy befalls him; once again, *nec tecum nec sine te*.

The signal that appears is telling and epitomizes the problem for Nerval of the nonidentity of the subject to itself, taken as a subject of enunciation, and the nonidentity of the writing to itself. This latter is taken as a production, but also partly as a reproduction, of writing that has gone before. Signaling an infinite textual regression, the open-ended quote points to the problem of nonidentity. In asking if he is good or bad, he recalls rhetorical questions from "El Desdichado" as well as those from "Artemis": "For are you queen, you! the first of the last? / Are you king, the only or the last lover?" (702). Nerval opens the act of textual recycling, but in so doing he recalls his own serious literary ventures, and especially the act of self-liberation that is the translation or adaptation of *Faust*. Here then the insistent poem returns to point to the continuing anxiety in the fallen one (*desdichado*) who cannot accomplish what he wants through writing. Nerval had a measure of control of himself and his work while translating *Faust II*. But here it is his own earlier works, now alienated from him, that have joined the Legion (Matthew 5:9) of alterity. There is no escape from the writing of the past, for it now includes the writing that was his, effectively the writing of what is now perceived as an alter ego. Alterity is now all else but the present moment, which of course is one of total absence.

REPETITION AS DESTRUCTION

Signaled emblematically by the return of "El Desdichado" and "Artemis," the theory of writing here begins with the act of repetition that is the second part of the story. What is told consistently becomes a retelling. The iterated vocative of "Eurydice! Eurydice!" used as the epigraph to this part of the story exactly repeats the plaintive cry of Glück's *Orfeo*; yet in repeating Glück, Nerval is unluckily remembering the obsessively returning father or grandfather, Virgil, in the *Georgics* (4:525–27), which I am quoting in the Latin to show the word order that will be repeated by Dante:

> . . . Eurydicen vox ipsa et frigida lingua
> a miseram Eurydicen! anima fugiente vocabat,
> Eurydicen toto referebant flumine ripae.[11]

There is a grammatical or syntactic imperative in the intertext that corresponds to the textual problems in Nerval's work. Glück is *an* intertext; Virgil/Dante are *the* intertexts. For in the story of Virgil's disappearance as told by Dante, there is a triple "Virgilio" that itself echoes the triple nature and the form of the quote from the *Georgics*:

> Ma Virgilio n'avea lasciati scemi
> di sé, Virgilio dolcissimo patre,
> Virgilio a cui per mia salute die'mi
> (*Purg.* 30:49–51)

Dante consciously adopts the form of alternation found in the Latin original by placing his vocative in the same relative positions that Virgil used.[12] Nerval cannot think of one without recalling the other. Linguistic evidence is there as well: Nerval's "on her lips. It flowed [*sur ses lèvres. Il en coulait*]" (788) recalls the *vox ipsa* and *flumine* in the passage from the *Georgics*. The now inevitable insistence that is the rememoration of the encrypting of the subject of authority appears here at its clearest:

If it were nothing . . . God willing! But God himself cannot make death be nothing.

Why then is this the first time in a long time that I have thought of *him*? The fatal system that had been created in my mind did not allow for this solitary royalty. (788)

Nerval recalls the act of rebellion, but can do nothing about the return of the repressed. Remembering the exclusion of the subject and the making of his own world in the "fatal system that had been created," Nerval annuls for himself any positive writing, however ephemeral, that he had theretofore produced.

The library of burnt books now reappears in force. The *filles du feu* have been consumed, never to be reconstituted, and the successful writing of the *filles du feu* is impossible since there can be no valid theorization of the project itself. The books of the past, thought to have been consumed—internalized and destroyed—and overcome, now come back to show themselves to have been impervious to flames. First is the *Urtext* of Goethe: "What have I written there? Blasphemies . . . A pact with God himself? . . . Oh science! Oh van-ity!" (789). The books of witchcraft and Kaballah that now appear, digests of the knowledge of the esoteric, are mute testimony to the predating (to Nerval) of the "fatal system" that he himself created. The system of alterity is codified, and even in alterity, he cannot escape previous writing: "My conviction about the existence of the outside world coincided too well with my readings for me to doubt the revelations of the past any more" (790). Yet the act of certitude is an act of submission to previously existing writing, equivalent to weakening the strength and value of his own writing. Using the logic of the Occident to overturn the pressure of this too codified alterity will perhaps provide a solution:

Still, I told myself, it is certain that these sciences are mixed with human error. The magical alphabet, the mysterious hieroglyphics come to us incomplete and falsified either by time or by those who want our ignorance; let us rediscover the lost letter or the erased sign, let us recompose the dissonant scale, and we will gain strength in the spirit world. (790)

Another angelic quest is needed, a search for the unique writing that is *fons et origo*—foundation and origin—writing that is and is not writing, the lost letter that is presentation and representation, the signs born of fire. As far back as *Angélique*, it was obvious that the sublime book could not be found. The very act of inscription, the representation of the original and not yet oppressive writing in a falsified alphabet, will never allow the rediscovery of the absolute *Urtext*. Though repressing the consequence of the fact, Nerval is in the process of realizing that every writing, even that of the immortals, here called the Eloim, who are part men and part gods (791), pretends to a position of absolute authority. This pretense is a theatricalization of the real authority that is absent: "the theater in which physical actions were accomplished" (790). Nerval's writing could be like that of the Eloim, but he is blinded by the fire, the *feuilles du feu*, that the Eloim have produced: the *Aeneid*, the *Commedia*, *Faust*, all masterpieces of success that (double) b(l)ind Nerval, making the realization of his own theories of textuality and the accomplishment of his goals an impossible task, doomed to fail: "—God is with him! I cried . . . but he is no longer with me!" (790).

Thereafter, the writing of the other and the collective authority of the Other takes on a phantasmagoric aspect. At times it is invisible, as even the necrography returns only to disappear. Nerval's ancestors can no more be adored than can Jean-Jacques Rousseau in *Angélique*; the tombs that are the inscription of the dead body have been moved "far from their origin" (793); even Aurélia's tomb cannot be refound. There are no bodies, no crypts, no tombs, and no hope. Everything is always elsewhere. Even if at times the writing becomes sacred, it is still useless: "In a little box that had belonged to *her*, I kept her last letter" (793). He cannot reconstitute a body from the characters she wrote. Writing is endlessly repeated, but since there is no power attached to it and since no power can come from it, it is disseminated into nothingness: "I immediately resolved to destroy the two papers I had taken from the box the day before" (795). The *feuilles* disappear into the fire (796) to be followed, not by the Other who creates, but by the writing of the Other that commands and condemns to an eternal hell: he destroys the letter and then the official paper about the location of Aurélia's tomb. We have moved from the relative comedy of Glück's *Orfeo* to the nihilism and condemnation of Mozart's *Don Giovanni*: "After the visit of the *stone guest*, I filled myself at the feast!" (797). As we know, after the Stone Guest arrives, there is no more feast, just the flames of hell. Now, eternally in a whirlwind of purgatorial condemnation edging ever closer to the fires of hell that burn but that do not consume, Nerval can do no more.

Nerval remembers Dante anew: "I want to explain how, distant for a long time from the true path, I felt myself drawn back by the dear memory of a dead person" (799). But this is the Dante of error: "Midway in the journey of our life" (*Inf.* 1:1); this is the Dante of loss: "There is no greater sorrow than to recall, in wretchedness, the happy time" (*Inf.* 5:121–23). Whatever Nerval does now to try to overcome loss, we are sure that it will be the loss itself that is endlessly reinscribed. There will be no Beatrice. The paternal figure will always be there and the seeming ray of hope that recalls Paolo and Francesca is really now no more than momentary hallucination. Nerval cannot write; in fact, he can barely talk or read. The narrator becomes dyslexic and aphasic, completely dysfunctional in his relation to language and his alienation from it. The world itself and all its signs start to become incomprehensible. His distance from understanding and normality rapidly increases; he can hardly talk; he can-

not read and understand ten lines in a row; he answers with non se-
quiturs (*quelques phrases décousues*) (799). And finally, absolute and
pure redemption through language is denied: wishing to confess to a
priest to gain absolution through an exchange of language, he is told
that the priest is from a different parish (802). The world has the
truth of language now; everyone but Nerval has this truth, which is
the truth of innocence, of salvation, of unity, and of pure and complete presence: "Children's voices repeated in chorus: Christe!
Christe! Christe!" (803). Kristeva comments: "Like Christ, the narrator goes down to hell and the text stops with this image, as if he
were not sure of gaining pardon and resurrection" (*Soleil* 179). But
for Nerval no salvation through Christ or through language exists.
There is nothing for him now except hollow words and a final textual abyss from which he will never escape.

Art Lovers

> J'ai un amant.
>> (Diane de Lys, 1855)

> J'ai un amant! un amant!
>> (Emma Bovary, 1857)

In 1855, Alexandre Dumas Fils published in book form a now-forgotten short novel entitled *Diane de Lys*. Literary history has been
less than kind to this author of popular literature. Often, we remember nothing more than his first spectacular success, *La Dame aux
camélias* (1852), but even that novel escapes its author, for it is better
known in later avatars: Verdi's opera *La Traviata* and *Camille*, the
1936 film starring Greta Garbo. *Diane de Lys* has met a different fate:
with neither Verdi nor Garbo to give it life or to resurrect it, this novella has been completely forgotten, even more than Dumas's plays,
for which he has always kept a minor, though marginal, literary rep-
utation. A classic literary historian such as Gustave Lanson, known
for his encyclopedic approach, is typical in his assessment of the author. Lanson, who curiously classifies Dumas among the naturalists,
devotes several pages to the plays, but merely says in a footnote that
Dumas started his career with novels; no mention at all is made of
Diane de Lys (1052–54).

Why revive a forgotten work? Among the many possible reasons are some obvious ones: the critic hopes to reformulate part of the canon, illustrate a thesis, or show the importance of what has been forgotten. In this case, the answer is that, though not an "important" work in its own right, this novella provides extraordinary insight into the gestation period of French literary modernism. As if it were the crossroads for various Foucauldian discourses, *Diane de Lys* is an illustration of the conflict between a retrospective romantic view of space as the locus of romantic effusion and a more modern view of space as the locus of objective, though recursive, production. It is the conflict of those two spaces, the rupture between kinds of representations of space, that I would like to discuss in this part of the book. *Diane de Lys* shows the transformation of the space of production by demonstrating how narrative organizes space in a midcentury work and how there is a conflict between various views of that space. Specifically, *Diane de Lys* deals with the eroticization of space and the development of the *lieu de rencontre*, a meeting or trysting spot, as a distention or interruption of discursive practices. Dumas shows how the space of production of the artist's studio is transformed from a space in which desire is the desire to represent to a space in which desire is the desire of the poetic—artistic and literary—subject. This desire is double, signaled in the oft-mentioned double genitive: there is a desire by the artist for the poetic object. And there is also a desiring of the artist *qua* artist by others, and specifically, by desire itself incarnate as a woman.

This novella is symptomatic of the changes occurring as a result of various forces at work in the disposition of public and private space: forces in the real world as well as forces that come out of art's codifications and its singular events. If Dumas's work does not remain with us today, it is perhaps because a work like *Madame Bovary*, coming just two years later, made us read in a whole new way. So perhaps we can read *Diane de Lys*, not as if *Madame Bovary* had not occurred, for that would be naive, but precisely because *Madame Bovary* did occur. *Diane de Lys*, a forgotten narrative, can be read somewhere between the pluperfect that makes it fade in the wake of Flaubert and the future anterior that allows it to shine again for us, as a work of art that illustrates the conflicts of representation of art, time, and space of which it is a prime example.

It would be too vast an undertaking in these few pages to try to define all the changes in the representation of space that occur through the nineteenth century and how, specifically, Dumas's piece is symptomatic of a sea change. We can, however, situate the question if we look at what might be the focus of the differentiation of space, not only between public and private endeavors, but also between various functions that might occur in segments of space. Therefore I shall focus on the elaboration of questions of space as they relate to the two themes of *Diane de Lys*. The first is the space of artistic inspiration and production: where does an artist work? what does he do when he is working? how does he produce art? Certainly, the clichés of romantic art are well known: the artist, inevitably alone, always male, and often in an isolation provided by nature as opposed to one built by man, produces art as an inspiration and/or a rememoration. Such are the received views about a poet like Lamartine. We read "Le Lac" and "L'Isolement" as if they were the result of inspiration by a muse, reinforced by the absence and solitude that surround the poet and that even force him to produce such poems as the testimony to that inspiration and rememoration. When the space is not the isolation provided by nature, it is figured as the lonely space within, a *sanctum sanctorum* in which some muse may come to visit as the poet burns the midnight oil: Musset's various "Nuits" and Poe's "The Raven" are spectacular examples of that variant of romantic production.

Romanticism views artistic production as a private affair: it is not visible except in its result, the poem; it is separated from all other activities. As the century goes on, and as, quite frankly, artistic endeavor becomes more and more openly associated with the functioning of modern bourgeois society, the sacred nature of artistic production begins to disappear. What an artist does, as Balzac points out, can be done at a newspaper. Or, as an illustration of the semi-public nature of an artist's work, there is Courbet's painting, *The Painter's Studio*, whose full title is *The Painter's Studio, a Real Allegory Determining a Phase of Seven Years of My Artistic Life* (*L'Atelier du peintre, allégorie réelle déterminant une phase de sept années de ma vie artistique*). This impressive canvas represents the roles of the observer and the artist-at-work, as Michael Fried has so elegantly pointed out (155–64). Though for many Courbet's painting signals the end of the artist's realist phase, it also suggests the possibility in another realm, that of literature, of the birth of realism and modernism: the recognition of the work as production, and not only as the teleological possibility of a more or less successful representation of the object.

The purported aesthetic of representation has begun to change. If previous aesthetics, including romanticism, see the work of art as a representation of something or some thing of the inner or outer world, object or emotion, Courbet's painting begins to illustrate the idea that art is, at least in part, going to be illustrating itself and not only something exterior to the sign: art begins to evince one of the hallmarks of realist production, modern self-consciousness in the work of art. Second, the creation of the work of art has in fact become a semipublic event, a performance not unlike Franz Liszt's invention, around 1840, of the solo piano recital, where he had the brazenness to play with no other artists and with the piano turned sideways, so people could see him produce the music. Third, and of great importance, is that there is a demystification of the work of art: if it can be seen in the process of being created, it is certainly less private, less sacred, more public, and more reproducible. So simultaneous with the making public of art is a resistance to that public face. As Baudelaire's elevation, Flaubert's self-erasure, and Courbet's "real allegory" all indicate, there is also a desire by the subject to produce something unique, something different, and something that does not depend on the preexistence of a real object "out there." This is the most profound rupture imaginable, for it involves a break with all other systems of integrating text and context. Thus, in the second half of the century, one finds an increased awareness of singularity and repetition as functions of a work of art. As the century frames art ever more publicly, there will be an ever greater temptation on the part of the artist to make each piece a singularity. In other words, the dynamics of the marketplace, or its metonymy in the bourgeois public, may make each event open, visible, and public, but the event is not repeatable.

Having said this, I would now like to proceed with a reading of *Diane de Lys*. Since it is a work that is unfamiliar to most readers, a synopsis is a necessary evil. The young Baron Maximilien, who is only twenty years old, is the suitor and eventual lover of the Marquise Diane de Lys, an older woman of twenty-eight, who is trapped in a loveless marriage with a man more than fifteen years her senior. Maximilien and Diane have no trysting spot; neither her boudoir nor his parents' house, where he is constantly watched, will do. Maximilien asks his friend Paul Aubry, who is an undiscovered painter, to lend his studio for the meetings between the lovers. The more Diane goes to the studio, the more she becomes enchanted with this painter whom she has never met. She arranges to buy a picture of his to help erase his indebtedness. On one occasion, she goes to the studio even though she has no meeting scheduled with Maximilien. At that time, she removes her ring to try on a pair of gloves she has found while snooping around; needless to say, she also reads his mail. Of course she forgets her ring and wears the "wrong" gloves home. As a result, thinking he is cheating on her, Aubry's mistress leaves him.

Diane also arranges for her friend, the happily married Marceline Delaunay, to have her portrait painted by Aubry, who proceeds to fall in love with his subject. Diane accompanies Marceline to the studio to see the final portrait, which Diane has paid for, and finally meets Paul. Diane lets slip that she already knows his work, though it has never been exhibited, as it was she who anonymously bought his painting. She then has Aubry come to her house to paint some panels for her dining room. When Aubry arrives, he sees Diane wearing the ring that had been abandoned and subsequently returned to Maximilien. He then concludes that Diane was Maximilien's mistress, an accusation she denies by saying that the ring is really Marceline's. Finally, Diane admits the truth and writes Aubry a letter in which she offers to be his mistress. At first taken with the idea, Aubry remembers that the spot in which he is standing, his own once inviolate studio, has been the profane *lieu de rencontre* of Maximilien and Diane. Aubry refuses her offer and the novella ends.

This overview of the plot shows that the focus of the novella's erotic mise-en-scène is Aubry's studio: it is where Maximilien and Diane meet for their trysts, where Aubry paints Marceline, where Diane leaves her ring and her gloves, where Diane purloins Aubry's letters, and where, reminded of all that has gone on in that very spot, Aubry finally decides not to continue the game. Everyone is familiar with Dumas's eroticization of space in *La Dame aux camélias*, magnificently evoked at the beginning of Franco Zeffirelli's film version of *La Traviata*. As the camera moves through the apartments of the deceased heroine, every object is a reminder of the love and lust that have taken place in that location. The film is suffused with an erototropic light: it is a pornotopia of luminous pleasure. In that, it is a faithful echo of the narrative version of that novel:

> The one in whose abode I found myself was dead: the most virtuous women could thus penetrate as far as her bedroom. Death had purified the air of this splendid cloaca, and besides, they had as an excuse, as if they needed one, that they were coming to a sale, though without knowing the person in whose abode the sale was occurring. . . .
> I wandered through the apartment and I followed the curious noblewomen who had preceded me. They entered a bedroom swathed in Persian fabric, and I was going to enter as well, when they came out almost as quickly. They were smiling as if they were ashamed of this new curiosity. That made me want to penetrate the bedroom all the more. It was the dressing room, which, with its most minute details, seemed to indicate to what extent the dead woman's prodigality had developed. (27)

The description is classic, even predictable: the narrator decides to "penetrate" into the deepest recesses of the woman's space: her boudoir. Like Courbet's lost-and-found painting of 1866, "The Origin of the World" (now in the Musée d'Orsay) the woman is seemingly placed in the space of representation for no other reason than to be penetrated by the male glance. Even when the ultimate secret is neither known nor knowable, the woman's space is the space of exchange, where the woman is made the subject by the male glance or gaze, without which "she" does not exist. He determines what her subject is and what space is hers.

This woman's space, the space of the stereotypical boudoir, is an all-too-frequent metonym for its resident; such is the case of the courtesan Marguerite Gautier in *La Dame aux camélias*. Even more clearly, her body is a metonym of the metonymy: no subject herself, she functions as the figure of the space that is the metonym of the nonexistent female subject. Marguerite's body is the locus in which "things go on"; she is penetrated by the man, her space is always violated by his probing. Though endlessly a mystery for the male, her innermost body always seems there to be discovered by the man's eye or by his other organs. The classic space of the woman, the boudoir or the *cabinet de toilette*, never is a solitary one equivalent to the male space that always maintains its impermeability and its inviolate nature. The woman is never wholly alone in her boudoir, for this archetypal locus of reverie is always penetrated by the watchful narrator who is, in essence, telling the male reader that a secret is about to be revealed and telling the female reader that she is never wholly alone, even in her most recessed spot. As Gilbert and Gubar sarcastically state, there is a "paradigmatically patriarchal library" that is "locked away from female contamination" (192). Yet a woman's space, as Dumas illustrates, is always subject to the patriarchal law. As Peggy Kamuf puts it, this space "is frequently broken in on" (163). The woman's space—her body, her room—is the space of interruption and intrusion.

Far from being a room of her own, the normalized locus of the woman's space is the spot in which Diane is first anatomized for the reader. That first encounter takes place in rather stereotypical circumstances:

The Marquise Diane de Lys, our heroine, was one of those women. At the moment we are making her acquaintance, she was seated by the window of a charming boudoir in the mansion she lived in on the Quai Voltaire. She had a book on her knees and was filing her pink nails. As to what she was thinking about, no one could have known, perhaps not even her. (2)

Now there is a bit of narratorial modesty, if not to say downright irony, here, as the narrator claims not to know what is going on in Diane's head. Not a logical Cartesian in her own right—that is, not a man—this stereotype could not know her own thoughts, for her identity and thus the univocity of her thought are always determined by another. But she has been or is reading, rather distractedly, I might add, and she is filing her nails. She is thus doing what women stereotypically do in novels, which is read other novels, abandon reality for fantasy, and generally fulfill the requirements for having a boudoir in any nineteenth-century novel worth its salt. Thus she ironically repeats, though in a sterile, hollow fashion, what romantic art tells us is the work of the artist: alone, dreaming of what is not there, *he* produces; alone, *she* just files her nails. Later, after her first tryst with Maximilien, she returns to the boudoir, and this time we are sure we know what she is thinking. For as she looks at herself in her mirror, several years before *Madame Bovary*, she says: "I have a lover [*j'ai un amant*]" (26).

There are no secrets here; the woman's space is that space of production in which production and reproduction coalesce, where even
as we repeat that there is a mystery about the place, we, the readers,
labeled as male penetrators, insist on knowing what is going on. In
contrast, for Emma Bovary, there are tantalizing mysteries that hover
between the known and the unknown, signs of a subject in the making who is tantalized by the very presence of that mystery: "She
would repeat to herself: 'I have a lover! A lover!' [*J'ai un amant! un
amant!*], delighting in this idea as if in another puberty that had come
to her" (Flaubert 439). Thanks to the renewed aesthetics into which
she is cast, Emma then will be capable of some production, whether
it be giving birth to her daughter Berthe or racking up debts that in
earlier narratives are generally associated with men. Emma succeeds,
so to speak, as a part of the new aesthetic, where Diane, certainly unaware of any artistic sea-change, can only appear to be the sterile
repetition of some older romanticism that is on the way out. When
Emma wants to keep a real secret far from the eyes of the doltish
Charles, she locks it away in a drawer in her secretary, one of the
models of secrecy, according to Gaston Bachelard (74–89). But there
are no secrets in Diane's archetypal boudoir.

Distinct in its hermeneutics from the boudoir, which readily gives
up its so-called secrets, is the artist's studio, which endlessly maintains its secrets, the most important of which is the secret of the production of art. As I have already indicated, the formula is already present in the gradual shift in this period between concepts of how an
artist produces. As the romantic formula of Lamartinean isolation
gives way to the making public of the artist, there is a simultaneous
secrecy: Flaubert allows Emma her locked secretary, Dumas shows
us everything in telling us nothing. We may penetrate the artist's studio with Diane, but without the crutch provided by vatic inspiration,
we have nothing to guide us. We have no better idea of how the artist
paints or writes than before we pried into his life. Does Courbet's
"real allegory" ever give a formula for how he paints?

The studio, however, is not wholly opposed to the boudoir, for if
one reveals and the other maintains its secrets, both engage desire as
a function of that space. Thus whereas the hermeneutic codes of the
two spaces are different (Barthes, *S/Z* 25–27), both are versions of
the space of desire. The artist's studio is hardly devoid of desire:

Balzac's "Le Chef-d'oeuvre inconnu," for example, and Courbet's nude models depicted in the "real allegory" of *The Painter's Studio* amply demonstrate this. In the studio, it is the artist, the master of the space, who is in control; it is the woman, always potentially nude and therefore always potentially vulnerable, who is imprisoned in a spot in which the artist's desire is possible but the artist's secret remains hidden. Again, "Le Chef-d'oeuvre inconnu" reveals the studio as the space of desire between Poussin and Catherine Lescaut, but refuses to yield the secret of the painting beyond the tantalizing foot that seems to have a life of its own (Didi-Huberman; Schehr, "Unknown Subject"; Serres).

In *Diane de Lys*, the artist's studio is the privileged space. It is always a space of encounter, even when it is habitually used by the painter alone as an artistic space. His studio is a "veritable street [*véritable rue*]" and, in fact, "a world [*un monde*]"; the possibility of representation implies the artist's power to turn his space into a microcosm. What encounters take place in this space? Certainly the artist meets his muse; his production depends on his inspiration. Moreover, it is a synaesthetic space that overflows with juxtapositions: "there was an open piano, covered with pencils, albums, and music" (14). The arts lie side by side, two corpuses—"*deux corps*"—in an aesthetic microcosm as variegated as a street that is an infinity of possible representations. Coterminous with "realistic" representation is its distortion, for this is a space of metonymies and fetishes. It holds parts that are seemingly endless in number: sketches, fabrics, and mannequins, material for artworks, indices of things to come and not wholly objects in their own right. Fragmented too is the language of the spot: both the language of art, its matter, and written language are spread out helter-skelter to fill the space: "Semicircular boards held statues, nudes, and anatomical drawings [*des statues, des académies et des écorchés*]. Names and addresses of models were written in chalk on the grayish wall and on the stove-pipe . . . " (14).

The studio is even defined as a theater, a space of representation intermediate between linguistic and visual representational systems. But nothing has happened yet; the play has not begun; the action is still backstage about to happen, as if actors were waiting in the wings to go on. In which space will this occur, according to what aesthetic, following the laws of which gender and what genre? Dumas allows the characters on stage, but no sooner is it described than the space instantly undergoes a transformation, as from six to midnight the artist's studio and rooms become a trysting spot for Maximilien and Diane. The spaces of work and desire, the spaces of production and meeting, are superimposed one upon the other. It is not the artist who seduces his model, but rather the nonmodel, the almost surreptitious visitor to a space never occupied by the artist when she arrives, who imagines being in love with the absent artist. Diane turns the studio into a boudoir, one into which she penetrates with no fear of being penetrated herself by the unknown. In having accepted the tryst with Maximilien, she has accepted the consequences, which could hardly be unknown to the reader of novels that she is.

The space of production and the space of meeting are linked as one signals the other, as one replaces the other, as one serves as a metaphor for the other. Both versions of the space—work and pleasure—are marked variants of some impossible neutral space that we never see. For Dumas, there is no possibility of neutral space: every locus is infused with discourses, art, power, relations, and love; every space is gender-marked as well. One of the most stunning examples of the impossibility of neutrality is the transformation of space and meaning that occurs when Madame de Lys invites her husband into her room: hers is an inhabitual invitation, a suggestion of fictionally illicit intimacy, the Marquis cuckolding himself. As an invited guest in this sanctum he becomes his own wife's lover, takes his wife as his mistress, and they have a date that lasts from midday on.

The singularity of the depicted space is defined precisely by what it is not: the space is not a woman's boudoir or *cabinet de toilette*. The space is not some neutral, innocuous, or public space, such as a hotel room that can be used by anyone for a price. In the strictest sense, the space is not a bachelor flat either, since this aspect of the studio is ancillary to its artistic functions. It is the studio, not the bedroom, that is the site of Diane's seduction by the absent artist. The artistic space maintains its privacy, even as a crossroads; it does not give its meaning freely. The eroticization of the artistic space has to compete with classical narrative images of the *locus voluptae*, as well as with the singular artistic space that produces according to other rules of the game: these rules are not known until a work is done, whereas the rules of erotic space are known before the action or production begins, even in the most extreme examples of classical, readable narrative, such as *Les 120 Journées* or *Histoire d'O*. Moreover, though it may be the most hidden, protected bedroom, the erotic space always has its privacy on parade. Diane's visit to this space is initially confusing, not because of the illicit sex, but because the space itself confuses. Even as the visit begins, the space and moment are suffused with anxiety and apprehension. An ignorance of the space certainly comes to the fore, but Dumas quickly and completely profanes the space as a space of the artistic production of singularities by positing repetition from the beginning:

> In a first visit like this, there is always a sort of material obstacle that usually disappears in the second. This obstacle exists far more for the man than for the woman, who does not have to concern herself with any of the preparatory details. Thus Maximilien, who was quite moved, dared say nothing. He silently opened his friend's door, let Diane enter, and followed her as he took care to remove the key and lock the door. (21)

The artist's studio is normally devoted to the mimetic and to the representations of a singularity, as a whole or as a collection of heterogeneous parts. But the event of that representation is itself singular, unique, and repeatable only through other means. At this point in the novella, the artistic space is replaced with a space of repetition that is the epitome of nonartistic space. Now, however, the space is desacralized and the artistic singularity gives way to a black box, silent, dark, and sealed, where repetition is the order of the day.

At least this first time, once the initial confusion has passed, during the hours from six to midnight—before the lovers arrive and presumably after they leave—this space temporarily takes on another identity. Nonetheless, the receding of the artistic nature of the space is only temporary. The space is confusing, the wealth of details of which we initially got merely a glimpse has become "a veritable maze [*un véritable dédale*]" (21) in which Diane is confused and uncertain. This is not her space, where things are known and ordered, but neither is it Maximilien's space, although he has taken it over for the nonce; it is a space whose rules they both ignore. But it is especially Maximilien, so blind to everything, who does not perceive that the space may be structured according to different rules.

The freedom denied to Diane in her boudoir is recovered in the studio. Since there is no lawgiver or no-sayer to structure the aesthetic space, Diane seizes the opportunity to begin to appropriate the space for herself. The space that she sees is some fantastic hybrid in which the erotic has been aestheticized and the aesthetic has been eroticized; and she cannot make the necessary distinctions between the two. Though there with her lover, she immediately becomes fascinated by the absent artist Paul Aubry and wants to know everything about him. Her fascination begun, there is no stopping her: "The marquise looked around with curiosity; from time to time her eyes focused on the young man who had fallen asleep at her feet" (22). The unknown is more fascinating than what she has before her: could it be that the situation of an illicit affair, which has no secrets to such a woman of the world, is far less enchanting than the mystic experience one normally, but wrongly, associates with the erotic? In the world of nineteenth-century narrative, there is a stereotypical opposition between the dreariness of marriage, with its basis in the world of feudal or capitalist economics, and the transcendental ecstasies, ineffability, and mysteries of passion (Rougemont).

Diane has begun to lose focus on Maximilien, her glance only landing on him as if by accident, in an ironic reversal of literary sex roles in which the woman-as-object, though marked as singular, is never a real subject for the gazing, contemplating, and penetrating male glance. So it is clear that there will be an end to repetition in that space; in the first meeting the last is posited: "She knew that sooner or later there would be a break [*une rupture*]" (23). Still, for now, the space is marked as the locus of encounter and romantic (or Romantic) love, completely distinct from everything around it: "The night was wonderful and full of the odors of springtime. That evening, like every other, many people passed in front of 67, rue des Martyrs, some going up, others down, some going to business, others to please, some happy, some sad" (23).

Despite the projected repetition and its discontinuation, Dumas posits a singularity as this tryst becomes an artistic subject; that singularity must be recorded, and, I would add, quite prosaically. Maximilien adds one more scrap of discourse to the heterogeneous collection of names Paul has written on the wall: "Today, 15 September 1845, at eleven P.M., two grateful happy people drank to the happiness of their host" (24). The initial tryst will be prosaically repeated;

the representation of the tryst will itself repeat as the imitation of a capharnaum of metonymies and improper names: the names of women-as-models, mere surfaces to be reproduced in art, subjects denied their own proper subjectivity as they become subjects of paintings. Artistic production in the studio becomes parodically re-doubled as Aubry's scraps, each of which is a sign of the singular and the modelable, are repeated as a notch on the bedpost, an index of the acts of repetition and the end of that repetition. Moreover, writing up the event makes it one that might serve the artist. By noting the event, Maximilien unwittingly makes Diane another one of Aubry's models, subject to his art. Diane thus occupies the space twice, once as an organizer and investigator in a world she does not know and again as a potential subject for art, thus possibly alienated from her own subjectivity. Later she will send her friend Marceline as a stand-in model: Diane has Marceline commission a portrait with Diane's money, for she cannot commission Aubry directly herself. Aubry's scribbles are openness insofar as production is concerned and closure insofar as repetition is concerned; Maximilien's note is the reverse. Yet confusion is possible, as the scribbles act as signs of the interchangeability of spaces, structures, and laws of production.

As the space of the first tryst with its *promise* of repetition becomes the *space* of repetition, it consumes an aspect of written language that has become a nuisance in its singularity: deixis has to disappear. For example, the idea of the two lovers is to be able to indicate to one another: "I will meet you there at nine P.M." Yet given the exigencies of safe, controlled communication, there are so many machinations to go through that deixis becomes almost an impossibility. There can be no signs of the subject, for the subject has been dissolved into the space of representation. In place of a discursive communicational system based on a model in which deixis is necessary but impossible because it takes much effort to have one sentence reach the receiver, the repetition of habit takes the place of the signs:

The visits thus continued to the house on the rue des Martyrs, on the order of once every three days. After five or six of these visits, the Marquise, in order to tell Maximilien that she would come to the meeting, forced to write to Marceline or to go out herself to post her letter, for she did not yet dare to write the baron, agreed with him that, in order to avoid all these difficulties, he would, quite simply, wait for her at his friend's place from eight to nine o'clock every evening. She would come if she could, and he would be even for having lost an hour if she could not leave her house. (35)

Signs have twice been banished from this new communicational model: the aesthetic signs of singularity that belong to Paul Aubry are hidden from understanding and the signs of the discursive structure that organizes the space for Maximilien and Diane have now also gone by the wayside. With no effort and no understanding of a foreign system, Diane becomes the possessor of the space, even as it continues silently and invisibly in its other guise, its original and originating role as the space of aesthetic production. This space of real production has become subject to temporality, as if the figure of time that now organizes the space by dividing it into "from six to midnight" and "the rest of the day" necessarily invades the other space. We witness Paul's artistic production as work over time: "Each day a new sketch appeared on Paul's easel" (35). By remarking the space, Diane has marketed it just as she markets Aubry's work. With a market, there is a real change over time, beyond the atemporal present of iterative romantic desire, where it is always nine o'clock. Time has begun to shape the various manifestations of the space. There can now be exchange over time; Diane even suggests that she be a self-serving Maecenas, in that the more money Paul has, the better she and Maximilien will be received (36).

Although she does not know him, Diane seems to be trying to include Aubry in this intimate lovemaking. The more he possesses, the more she has invaded his life, and thus, the more he becomes part of an imaginary *ménage à trois* of which both he and Maximilien remain unaware. As Diane becomes the "mistress of knowing everything in this young man's place" (40), she appropriates all that is his. So as she promises to free him from his debts and obligations with her commissions for artwork, she indebts him to her, so to speak, by occupying his spot. Not content with stealing a glance at his correspondence, she out and out steals a letter (41–42). As one character reads words destined for another and thereby occupies his or her space, the process of inappropriate reading turns into a power game.

Henceforth the space is hers. What had started out as Aubry's studio and become a *lieu de rencontre* now becomes a *lieu de jouissance* for her alone. Maximilien is put off, as Diane tells him to show up at nine o'clock (45) whereas she appears at 7:45 to be alone in her space of voluptuousness. Nothing escapes her glance, hands, or mind:

She went straight to the young man's dressing room and searched his pockets. She recognized the suit, for she found the clerk's letter in it, but the wallet had disappeared. Then the marquise was really embarrassed: she had not only wanted to read the end of the correspondence with Berthe but had also wanted to return to Paul the letter she had taken from him. For it seemed to her that he must care greatly about this collection and that, if she did not find the pack, she knew what to do for him not to realize anything. But Madame de Lys was not a women to lose courage so easily; she threw the drawers, boxes, and closets into such disarray that she finally found the wallet that Paul had carefully hidden in his dresser underneath his underwear. (46)

Sitting alone, reading a letter from Aubry's mistress, Berthe (which, coincidentally, will be the name given to Emma Bovary's daughter), Diane has temporarily transformed the studio into her own boudoir, as she falls into "an inhabitual reverie" (47). But the reverie is far from inhabitual, for our first meeting with Diane finds her rapt in the same sort of thought. The daring Diane has not shrunk from a thorough search of Paul's private apartments. The reader realizes, however, that the secret to the space is not there, but in the more publicly visible but less understandable space of the studio. Yet it is not enough to be an illicit reader. She wants to write *in loco Pauli*: "The marquise began to look for paper and pens" (48). The writing project is aborted; in fact, it is the first of two aborted writing projects, the second being Paul's interrupted writing act in the dénouement. Having started to write, she thinks better of it and stops, because it would be too daring (50). More relevantly, her writing would be impossible here, for she who does not know the secret of the space cannot write in it.

Thus by this point the space of production has been partially eroticized and the space of erotics has been partially aesthetisized. After all, the artistic production that is represented—that of a painter—is a mise-en-abîme of the space of writing. If the painter's art has often been chosen as the representative of aesthetic production—as in, for example, Balzac's earlier "Le Chef-d'oeuvre inconnu" and Zola's later *L'Oeuvre*—it is partly because it is describable without the threat of parasitism or incomprehension, risks often run when the artist represented is a writer or a composer. In works like Thomas Mann's *Doctor Faustus*, which deals with music, or in any one of a half-dozen stories by Henry James, which deal most often with the writer's craft, the problems relating to an artistic mise-en-abîme are far more imbricated and recursive in an immediate way than they are in a work dealing with painting.

Aubry's space, a vague intermingling of the erotic and the aesthetic, becomes almost a stereotypical space of escape and forgetting, as if the vague brushing of art against love necessarily produces a romantic locus par excellence. The more Diane romanticizes the space, the less she understands about its real nature as a locus of production. Her extended reveries that mark the space as some ideal version of what she reads in novels leave art in a chiaroscuro of incomprehension:

Yet at every moment, the door opened to the room in which Diane was found, to ask for her order, to bring her a letter, to announce someone. At Paul Aubry's place it was different. Once she had crossed the painter's threshold, nothing that surrounded her reminded her of her normal life. Not a servant, not a sound, of an intruder. Solitude, work, contemplation, a sort of melancholy life in that large room, in whose shadows were pictures and statues. There Diane's life had a new existence. (60)

Having taken over and having become at least at certain times the mistress of the territory, Diane inserts herself fantasmatically into the space as Aubry's mistress. Neither muse nor model, she must settle for being the reduction to her own lack of subjectivity and logical comprehension. She cannot inspire Paul, but only pay for him; she cannot be loved by him; she cannot understand him or his space. She can, however, fantasize that somehow, even piecemeal, all this is hers. Exchanging fetish for fetish, sign of one femininity for that of another, she tries on the gloves and slippers of Paul's mistress, Berthe, as if they belonged to her, as if *he* belonged to her; in fact, she keeps the gloves. At the same time, leaving her own gloves and her ring as if they belonged in that space, Diane re-marks the locus as hers. She, of course, has tried to possess the space as would a Maecenas, who is someone who can afford to abandon a ring "that she never took off [*qu'elle ne quittait jamais*]" (62). Through this exchange of gloves into which she comfortably fits, she also marks the space as if she were its mistress: her gloves, her cast-off clothing, now belong to this world as well as belonging to her. She has become territorial, even unto the most private—and thus most obviously public—locus, Paul's bed, the space of exchange: "And the marquise, keeping the gloves she had just donned, threw those she had taken off [*ceux qu'elle venait de quitter*] on the bed" (63).

Inasmuch as the space is becoming more and more the locus of mysterious exchange whereby Diane is the fantasmatic succubus for an artist unknown to her, and an unknown artist to boot, the aesthetic space itself, once sacred and inviolate, itself continues to become eroticized in, oddly enough, an act of repetition. Marceline comes to Paul's studio to be a model for a portrait, a situation arranged by Diane. The work space becomes a space of *coitus reservatus* with Marceline, the real woman and model, occupying the real place of the woman as object that Diane occupies for herself on an imaginary level. For herself, Diane becomes Paul's model, because it is she, through her money, who is controlling what he paints: she models his art for him. Ignorant of all that, Aubry develops an intermingled sexual and aesthetic desire as he becomes attracted to Marceline. Unaware of the new import of time to him, he nonetheless wants, like Marcel waiting for the maternal kiss in "Combray," to delay the final act as long as possible: "But as the portrait was being completed, Paul, who when he started was in such a hurry to finish it that he worked on it in Marceline's absence, Paul, as we were saying, worked on it as slowly as possible" (68). Complex locus of exchange where art and desire mix and where there are often a second receiver and emitter silently occupying the same locus as the first, the space has collapsed all its functions into a boiling mélange, still as closed off from the outside world as before, but now the two inner worlds have fully mingled. Time itself is out of joint in a Bergsonian compression of a period of hours into a duration of a minute, as Paul's work session "passed as if a minute" (72). Just as the artistic space finds its time collapsed by the very real presence of the object, the space of desire finds its time elongated by absence:

Diane had not, so to speak, registered the baron's absence. We told above of the conversion that had occurred in her, and the pleasure she felt in coming to dream for two hours in this studio, where no one, not even the person who lived in it, could suspect what she had come to do there. (72)

The meetings between the lovers that had been preceded by Diane's solitary visits that lasted one and one-quarter hours are now prefaced by two hours of voluptuous solitude. She is now closer than ever to Paul's time in the space as she follows him by an hour but precedes her lover by two. As there must be, there is an eventual meeting between Diane and Aubry, as the former joins Marceline to go to the artist's studio. After so many visits, Diane gets a case of the vapors as she thinks of entering the space when it is occupied by Aubry. At the same time, thinking he is meeting the woman he loves unrequitedly, whom he believes to be Marceline, Paul has changed from his artist's garb to something signifying he is an artist: "there was even something studied in his disarray [*il avait même une certaine recherche dans son négligé*]" (79). Thus in the intermingled space, along with the original artistic fetishes and the fetishes indicating desire, including the gloves, the slippers, and the stolen letters, there are signs attached to their referents. Diane wears a sign that, at least for the reader, indicates that she is aroused; Paul wears a sign that he is an artist. As at an MLA Convention, the space of meeting only fully becomes itself when the badges are out front, visible for all to read.

This is only the culmination of the apposition of the badge or sign and the object, for it has been a current through the story, throughout which the signs have served as metonyms of no real subjects that exist independent of signs others pin on them or as a set of signs they themselves emit. The most notable previous example consists of the scribbles of the names and addresses of Aubry's models on the wall of the studio. Along with Aubry's scribbles is Maximilien's self-commemorating testimonial. Aubry's scribbles mark the space with the indices of an artistic studio; Maximilien's testimonial says that it is another space, an erotic space whose conservation is that very act of writing. Along the same lines is the initial presentation of Diane, with her book open and unread, lying on her lap as the indiscriminate mixture of two signs: the sign of reverie and eroticism, the book juxtaposed with her most secret recesses and private parts, and the sign of aestheticism: the book as an artistic production.

This culmination of the investment of the meeting space shows it to be a locus where space and time are distended according to a semi-otics of desire. It is also a space of *corps mélangés*, mixtures of bodies and signs, confrontations of systems, and unbridlings of desire. Even in such a late-romantic novella, the space of *rencontre* has all the hall-marks of the distension given it in realism, the best examples of which will be found a few years later in *L'Education sentimentale*. The invaded space does not remain simply a space of *corps mélangés*. It is volatile as art and desire mingle all too unhappily. Still in the dark about whom he loves, Paul writes to Marceline, "I have left Paris, I fled my room where I constantly found the trace of your love for an-other" (105). He thinks that it is she who has visited so many times with Maximilien, she who has marked the space with her desire. But of course he is wrong: it is Diane who has visited, and it is not an-other that she loves but Aubry himself. Marceline has nothing to do with it. She is only Diane's lieu-tenant, the proxy of Diane, the stand-in for "she who cannot be painted."

Finally the space of *rencontre* does not itself emerge unchanged, for wherever there is a sign, there is a trace. If desire is fleeting, if it can mark a space, it is at most with a totally ephemeral *odor di fem-mina*. But a sign is forever. As Paul is finally about to allow desire to reenter, now that he has learned the truth, as he is about to seal his letter saying "oui" to Diane, he reads an indelible sign. The desire is gone, but the sign remains in the words that Maximilien had written on the wall: "Paul had only to seal the letter he had just written. He took a match on the table and approached the wall to strike it. Chance made it just at the spot where Maximilien had, a few months earlier, written the words that had never been erased" (122). The sign does disappear, finally erased by the helpful porter who cleans the apartment, but it is too late for desire to occur unchallenged by the forces at work, unrivaled by the laws of aesthetic production that need to maintain their secrecy (124). So the sign is indelible as long as there is a subject. But with the subject gone, the sign too is, like desires and mixtures, and like the space itself, gone with the wind.

What then can one say about a forgotten tale that has disappeared from even the tertiary literature? Perhaps like Courbet (who has not disappeared), Dumas discovered a truth in his 1855 work about the changing parameters of artistic production. Unlike Courbet, though,

Dumas could not engage the necessary aesthetic for his writing. He could not dissociate sign and body, nor could he bury the bodies in some unmarked grave to leave the signs to be read as the only marks of the writing. Thus despite a foreshadowing of certain aspects of the modernist aesthetic that is born in narrative with *Madame Bovary* (and despite the immense intertwining that links Flaubert inextricably to Stendhal and Balzac), Dumas does not fully engage the modern aesthetic. For him, the woman remains without a subject, the man remains the prey to desire, the sign must be an index, if not to say a full-blown romantic apostrophe. For Dumas, there cannot be a complete dissociation from a romantic praxis of representation that demands the act of making present as its *sine qua non*.

Literary history has consigned *Diane de Lys* to a shelf of forgotten works and was rather unfair to its author. Lautréamont, for example, wrote:

Alexandre Dumas Junior will never, absolutely never, give a high-school awards-day speech. He does not know what morality is. Morality does not compromise [*Elle ne transige pas*]. If he were to do that, he would have to cross out with a stroke of the pen everything he has written heretofore, starting with his absurd prefaces. (in Derrida, *Dissémination* 45)

We cannot, however, condemn the author for not being able to hand out prizes in the Third Republic, nor should we condemn him for not having been Balzac or Flaubert. We realize that Dumas fades (not fails) because he does not underline to what extent the contradictions embodied in either romantic or realist production, their aesthetics of representation, and their visions of the relations between art and the world around it might have been brought out. Diane de Lys is an old-fashioned romantic heroine disguised as a modern. The world in which the author places her cannot apologize for her contradictions, nor can she overcome the contradictions of that world. As a book, *Diane de Lys* has much the same fate: no longer the ironic contradictions of Balzac's novels that make the period of the Bourbon Restoration our first modernity, not yet the disillusions of Flaubert that invent a new modernity because the first had proven to be far too venal. If the artist becomes public property, so be it; Flaubert will respond in other ways. Caught between the desire to represent and the knowledge that self-conscious representation can occur if and only if the innermost secrets are *not* revealed, Dumas falls back on a mode of representation in which he has mastered the contradictions, for he cannot, *pace* Lautréamont, cross out everything he has written. Literary history will do that for him, but we can still read under that crossing out and rediscover a missing link of literary change.

CHAPTER 5

At Home with Flaubert

Flaubert's Disorder

In the years preceding his death in May 1880, Gustave Flaubert works assiduously on his last novel, *Bouvard et Pécuchet*, which ultimately remained unfinished. Along with being his final meditation on his own work, *Bouvard et Pécuchet* is an extended commentary on nineteenth-century narrative and the allegory of its strategies. Toward the end of the novel, having gorged themselves with stupidities about educating children, Bouvard and Pécuchet foresee "establishing an adult education course." To "expose their ideas," they intend to present a lecture at the Hotel of the Golden Cross (2:983). The conference never takes place, for Flaubert dies before being able to write it.

While the work-plan sketches out what is to follow, the novel stops brusquely in the middle of a sentence whose last words are "The Golden Cross" (La Croix d'or). A transcendental sign that would elsewhere have guaranteed the closure of meaning, a solid referent that in other times might have sustained the translation of the world into signs, an icon of the entire realist project, in another novel, this golden cross would have been the semiotic serving as a model and as an example of transparent readability. But in *Bouvard et*

Pécuchet, it is literally and figuratively another story. Suspended in everlasting incompletion, the work will remain forever open. The sign of the Golden Cross is a sign of an interruption, an incompletion, a rupture of the pact between author and reader, and in the last instance, between the writer and himself.

Flaubert's death at such a moment in his writing is certainly a chance event that in no way informs the contents and the structure of this novel, except in that it necessarily marks the work's incompleteness. Eerily, the gap created by this unexpected death repeats other gaps in Flaubert's writing. In other words, had he lived, Flaubert would have certainly produced a scene equivalent to the complete gap that is ironically and emblematically limned in the author's death. Written, imagined, or absent, the lecture that is a gap in writing reinscribes the author's own gesture at many previous moments in his work. Here the absence of writing is equivalent to the writing that could never reproduce a given reality nor successfully stand on its own. The golden cross means nothing more than the absence of both definitive denotation and transcendental value.

Throughout *Bouvard et Pécuchet*, the performative gesture of writing motions toward the gap of incompletion. It would be wrong to see the sign of some nihilistic absence in this gap of open uncertainty. It would be too easy to see Flaubert as the novelistic precursor of a Mallarmé, especially the Mallarmé drawn by contemporary criticism: the one who, in working on his poems, produces the nothingness of an "abolished object of sonorous inanity [*aboli bibelot d'inanité sonore*]." Far from it: the writing, the body, and the gesture of Flaubert remain *literally* in suspension. A mixture of solids and liquids, solid particles dispersed in liquid, a stretching yawn between closure and openness, this novel shows the total gap in being of a work that is always *in articulo mortis*, while the Flaubertian death has neither the solidity of gold nor the transcendental value of the cross.

With *Bouvard and Pécuchet*, writing shows the built-in suspension that comes with the Flaubertian gape: "Bouvard cleaned off the table, put paper in front of him, dipped his pen, stared at the ceiling" (2:836). Viscous ink stays suspended on the pen that has paused in midair; the ink does not dry on the page as it should have. Ready to write, Bouvard can only let textuality itself gape, as it repeats, not the losses of Frédéric in *L'Education sentimentale*, but the fact that Frédéric "permitted the idling [*désoeuvrement*] of his intelligence" (2:449). Suspension, gape, mixture, figures of the indefinite: these swirls in Flaubert's writing must be made as precise as possible. Thus we could conceive of a writing project in which it would be a question on one side of representing these *flous* somewhere between the presence unto itself of the object and the disappearance or the absence of the subject on the other. It would thus be a question of separating these *flous*, as a chemist might titrate them, allow them to precipitate the solid from the liquid, and determine the specific gravity of these mixtures.

This double figure of representation and solution becomes an impossible figure to trace. In other words, the figure of the *flou* in Flaubert's writing is nothing more nor less than the very impossibility of its own conception. The first figure of flow in Flaubert is this stupid gap, the composite figure of the ink drying on the tip of the quill and the whiteness of the page ever waiting. Yet this whiteness is not purity, but the author's anguish as he is faced with that whiteness, a white tornado, a cyclone that engulfs. Far from being some pure whiteness that recalls the white mythology of creation, it is the *flou* of the unfathomable and uncapturable gap of the world of representation, whose figure, in other writers, might be the whiteness of Melville's whale, the white tornado in Zola's *Au bonheur des dames*, the snow in Mann's *The Magic Mountain*.

Thus it is a question of sketching out the figure of the *flou* in Flaubert's last writing. More precisely, it is a question of showing what is involved in representing this *flou* and in showing how what is at stake in Flaubert's work can be seen in this last challenge to and of representation. Representing the *flou* will be finally the work of articulating the gap, as it is as much the sign of the system of representation, indeed of "realist narrative," as it is the demonstration of its failure.

First of all, a preliminary historical question: what does the *flou* represent for the nineteenth-century novelist and how can he represent it? We have seen what Stendhal and Balzac do with the mud that spatters their novels. So for the moment, we shall remain at the level of the project of any male novelist, to protect his typicality. From all accounts, the typical nineteenth-century novelist is the sworn enemy of the *flou*. To tell a story means trimming it, printing it, or making a coping stone or a jewel of it. Perhaps a too easily found phallic symbol shows up, but the word "recount" (*raconter*) and the word "castrate" both come from Indo-European words that mean "to cut." The nineteenth-century novelist castrates himself, as did Origen, to eliminate the flows. Castrating oneself or castrating his writing: to lead out, to eliminate the liquid to make the solid. Eliminate dissemination, the testicular flow, to produce solid testimony, to produce some thing, to force into a frame a flow that will solidify. The ink flows to represent the so-called real world, that of objects, codified emotions, concrete psychologies. The author's project consists of pinning down these objects, to "say" them correctly, or to crystallize an emotion (Stendhal), to write the zoography of the human species (Balzac), to give the social history of a family under the Second Empire (Zola). The novelist tries to contain what flows, attempts to stop it for a moment to produce what Proust will call "a conic section taken out of a rainbow-hued spray of water" (1:86). The goal of the writing will be to capture a moment, to fix it, frame it, and insert it in a paradigm.

In Flaubert's writing the referent is always already impure, for it is always parasited by signs: the object is polluted by discourse, threatened by language, and crisscrossed with images of a production that exceeds materialistic and positivistic models. If the object is always marked by language, language too is simultaneously treated as another object, fleeing, never wholly capturable. Though they may abound, the free-flowing signs, ready to serve to pin down or label an object, cannot be so easily grasped. Signs depend on a law of the signifier that calls an elsewhere, that invokes and convokes other signifiers, and that, in the end, cannot be recounted. The signifier always is dis-counted. It slips and slides all over the referent; it refuses to be pinned down; it participates in a sliding that doubles, in the paradoxical irony of realism, the sliding of the referential world.

Refused as such because it cannot be mastered at the level of the represented, the *flou* is the metatextual sign of narration. This is a conclusion that is both logical and impossible, and one that every nineteenth-century novelist would have loudly opposed. Each would have opposed the *flou* on several levels: on the level of the referential object, the represented, or the narrated, the novelist would have sought means and figures to channel. On the level of narration, the refusal would have taken the form of the law and the metatextual justification of the project. A third level is ideological, where it is a question of sweeping away the *flou*, of getting rid of it because it is that against which the modern state and its body of knowledgeable individuals fight.[1]

Motivated perhaps by a lack of faith in a *terminus ad quem* or a *terminus ab quo*, Flaubert cannot easily deal with the framing or channeling of the *flou*. He accepts as something to deal with once and for all the literally upsetting and disruptive nature of the *flou*. This is the project par excellence of the author: from *Madame Bovary* to *L'Education sentimentale*, including *La Tentation de Saint Antoine*, *Salammbô*, and the *Trois Contes*, it is always a question of the *flou* for Flaubert. But the question as such must be deferred until every other preliminary question has been resolved. One should not be astonished that Flaubert did not tackle this problem directly before *Bouvard et Pécuchet*, although it was often a question of mud, be it metonymy or synecdoche—but how can you speak of parts and wholes when it is a question of the *flou?*—of the unnarratable and its attendant problematics of representation, difference, and the discrete. Before trying to channel this mud, Flaubert takes it upon himself as an absolute prerequisite to dismantle ideologies, to undo the givens of the novelistic, and to sort out the laws and fictive parameters of realism. Having examined all the presuppositions of realism while simultaneously elaborating them through his own novelistic praxes, Flaubert is finally ready to discuss the possibility of narration itself. Even in *Salammbô*, where it is a question of narrating alterity, as I have discussed in an article on that novel, and even in *La Tentation*, where it is a question of narrating the fantasmatic, Flaubert never interrogates himself as deeply on narration *as* narration, on its possibilities and its limits.

For the first approximation of the *flou* in Flaubert's work, and thus as a first hypothesis, we can follow the critical observations of Jean-Pierre Richard. In his well-known study "La Création de la forme chez Flaubert," Richard deals with the images of creation both in the general and in the particular, that is to say, in the conjunction of creation with the creative processes used by Flaubert (117–219). Richard shows the coincidence between the presentation of creation and

the creation of representation. At first glance, one might be astonished that Richard focuses on the images of fluidity and solidity, but
the astuteness of the move is soon apparent. Richard justly establishes that Flaubert's work is not in general an art of the static, or a
"purely marmoreal art" (212), an oft-accepted purity that we must
eventually investigate. For Richard, Flaubert's art occurs in the creation of a narrative that conceives of life as a transition from metamorphosis to metamorphosis (153). Nothing is fixed; everything is
always in the process of changing and undergoing mutations at the
very heart of its being. Stability would only be a momentary effect of
the real getting stuck in the mud. In its comic version—*Bouvard et
Pécuchet*—the novel is a story of two characters moving from one
sticky situation to another.

This vision of Flaubertian creation is underpinned by an art that
must paint both the outside and inside of things, both what is visible
and what is hidden. Or at least that is the project announced by
Flaubert and subsequently asserted by Richard in his study. It is important to recognize this confirmation of the project by the critic; in
the metatextual framing that we mentioned above for other writers,
Richard's gesture would be the equivalent of accepting "as is" the refusal of the *flou* that Flaubert announces in his correspondence. Yet,
in Flaubert, this refusal is posited otherwise. The gesture underpin-
ning the project gives it the lie, at the same time as does the radical
proposal of Flaubertian metatextuality, which posits the gap between
fiction and referent a priori: every channel shows its own fictional
nature. To attain the inside in which the metamorphosis occurs, layer
after layer of descriptions must be crossed, each of which describes
more liquid than the preceding. According to Richard, this is how
the novelist shows the metamorphosis of things through description,
and how he always indicates the process of creation at work in the
novels. Fluidity would thus be hidden by the surface of things and revealed at the same time by the novelist's art, which allows the reader's
eyes to penetrate that surface in order to show the metamorphosis in
progress.

Richard repeats what Flaubert says of his project, and in so doing,
the critic seems to believe that this is what is actually occurring in the
narrative. The difference between the project of an author announced in his correspondence and the novel produced, however, is

so enormous that for us to say that the project is not accomplished says nothing. To the extent that Richard's critical gesture consists in repeating Flaubert's project, and thus in repeating the author's desire to create a totalizing epistemology, Richard is right. But it would be too easy to limit oneself to such a criticism of Richard's observations, as "solid" as they are. On the other hand, through such a thorough, subtle thematic reading, we can isolate the limits of such a method, the method of thematic closure, as well as the hidden contradictions in Flaubert's writing, both by the reading Richard gives and by the *hénaurme* specter of the project itself.

Richard's reading has three limitations that are reason enough for us to want to go beyond thematics. The model of Flaubertian description presented by Richard cannot account for the static side of those extraordinary Flaubertian objects, the list of his objects of interruption: Charles's cap, the first sentence of *Salammbô*, the stifling nature of the first sentence of *Bouvard et Pécuchet*, and the Renaissance cabinet of that novel as well as a grouping of static tableaux and petrified images. One might think that Richard seeks to establish a polemical point of view, set out against those who have seen Flaubert's art as being marmoreal. To make the object vibrate against the descriptions of traditional literary criticism would be essential to any renewal of thematics. Still, against Richard, one might posit that the art of Flaubert consists less in the revealing of the truth than in the multiplication of surfaces: after all, Salammbô's veil reveals nothing less, or nothing more, than absence. Flaubert's writing resembles, *avant la lettre*, the Cubist idea of juxtaposed surfaces; his work announces the fractal surface as Mandelbrot will describe it. In the end, to believe that the novelist's goal is to capture or to show a truth of the world is what we know from the beginning: the *flou* has no truth of its own and thus has no narrative truth. For the truth of the *flou* is always defined by starting from the truth of the solid, which, as we have already noted, can only describe the *flou* by inscribing it, by channeling it, and thus by removing the *flou*'s most significant feature.

A second objection is that the desire to represent this metamorphosis depends on the a priori existence of a transcendental signifier that guarantees the system: History, the subject of Absolute Knowledge, metaphysical plenitude, or even the Kantian sublime. Any one of these signifiers would guarantee the system of metamorphoses; but none of them is there. Flaubert systematically destroys all transcendental possibilities; from *Madame Bovary* on, all possible means for novelistic and philosophical transcendence are decrypted and removed. The third objection is that the world does not pass from solid to liquid by bifurcation. In Flaubert's work, solid and liquid are mutually distinguished, but only after the fact. Before being outside and inside, separated from one another, they are joined, outside-and-inside, undecidable situated between the solid and the liquid. Thus the Flaubertian object would be neither a composite object with surfaces and facts describable through marmoreal phrases, nor even the channeling object, one that englobes metamorphosis. The Flaubertian object would be the *flou* in its "own" realm, neither liquid nor solid, "purish" (*purâtre*) as Sartre (43) says in *La Nausée*, an always undecidable mixture far from thermodynamic possibility, far from the Northwest Passage.

In *Le Passage du Nord-Ouest*, Michel Serres writes with brio about the difficult navigation between two bodies of water or two bodies of knowledge. Yet for him, as difficult and disrupting as this navigation may be, it is always possible; it is never a question of splashing around in the mud. Flaubert is more pessimistic. He recognizes that navigation is not always possible, and that "the translation of muds" of which the entire century speaks (Corbin 135) will not occur. The Flaubertian object is the unnavigable *flou*, partly solid, partly liquid, but in which these parts are no longer decidable. It is a vast terrain, a wasteland, a marsh of muddy labyrinths without exits and without methods. It is the world of the viscous, as Sartre speaks of it, the *terra incognita* and *terra infirma* of magma and miasmas. Far from being the neutral term that guarantees the system, the *flou* is the third term that upsets the whole.

Instead of a totalizing epistemology repressing the contradictions of the *flou*, one can imagine an epistemology echoing the ontology of the *flou*. Far from being the thematic closure that is the textual guardrail, this new epistemology of the *flou* shows the epistemological failure of the system of description. In Flaubert's work, the *flou* is less the sign of creation than it is the mark of a paradox: for the *flou* to represent change, there must be a solid layer on which the *flou* is spread; yet, as Richard shows, this solid layer is rather liquid. In other words, this layer ostensibly established as a transcendental signifier is strictly nothing for Flaubert. It is not there and Flaubert's writing wavers.

From one moment to the next, everything will explode, be it a cadaver, a garden, or a scientific experiment. As Heraclitus says, everything flows; Flaubert's narratives would be an offering of some temporary plugs between two moments of disorder. For Flaubert, the torrents of nature are not at all sublimated. There is no admiration for the purification that comes with the *flou*, nor is there an attempt to categorize the *flou* once and for all. Flaubert's writing is always steps away from being engulfed.

In part it is a question of the subject: for Flaubert, stupidity flows endlessly in an unstoppable logorrhea, whereas the right words arrive painfully, one by one. This omnipresent stupidity is itself a metaphor for this *flou*, just as the *flou* serves as a metaphor for stupidity. All-engulfing, this logorrhea, this *flou*, this stupidity are *hénaurme*. Thus the *flou* and stupidity are inextricably mixed with one another, just as the so-called pure objects, constructions of a novelistic identity, are always infested, infected, at the very heart of their presumed purity, with language itself.

With *Bouvard et Pécuchet*, all pretense to this ideal of language disappears, due to the fact that this book is the veritable allegory of novelistic representation and of the narrative processes of realism. There is no book in Flaubert's corpus that is as muddy, as poisoned by miasmas, or as laden with magma as this last one. Trying with his well-honed stiletto or stylus to reinscribe the litany of man's stupidities, Flaubert tries at the same time to construct his novelistic edifice on a base that is as unstable as these quicksands of stupidity. His project of writing or constructing "the book on nothing" is only too familiar, but this nothing reappears over and over again, not to serve as a base, but to engulf the work and swallow up the project. Oddly enough, these blanks are inscribed in a precise, careful style, as if Flaubert, in his last stab, were making the textual illness even more acute. He seems to be marking the artifices of textuality, showing how constructions are based on and in this nothing and how they finally disappear into it. This nothing invades and engulfs the work, even if, from time to time, there are small victories. Pécuchet, for example, succeeds painfully in making his way through the mud:

"Pécuchet finally abandoned the cart, and, dog-paddling through the mud, forged ahead" (728). But the victory is shortlived; not long after, Flaubert's version of Venice, called Chavignolle, risks being totally engulfed in a deluge of slime: "Elsewhere in the garden, a sort of Rialto spanned a pond, offering, along its edges, incrusted mussel shells. So what if the earth drank the water! A layer of clay would form to hold it back" (750–51).

The novel is always about to succumb to the blanks, to the ephemeral, to the viscous; it is constantly running the risk of showing its true nature—or would be if there were a true rim, edge, or line that could be defined without deforming the writing. For Flaubert, every *flou* is upsetting and goes beyond the forced limits; the *flou* is expelled like the unstoppable language of logorrhea. Flaubert discovers an ironic truth: no matter how chiseled it may be, no written language can reproduce the *flou* as well as the infernal revving or buzzing of continuous stupidity that is the numbing *bourdonnement* that marks *Bouvard et Pécuchet*.[2] Liquid and solid mix when the work goes beyond the limits of categorization of the states of matter, goes beyond the margins and rims of representation. The *flou* and flows undo definitions, resist categories, push the narrative toward its own engulfing.

More simply, the problem comes from the fact that nature is always in a state of disorganization. Natural organization is merely a small anthropocentric illusion between two or several states of disorder. Even in one sentence, the author gives us clues when he proceeds from a primordial flow through a state of organization to end up, once again, at another state of flux: "How is it that the same sap produces bones, blood, lymph, and excrement?" (770). For there to be metamorphosis, there must be *morphe*; here the *flou* is called *flou*, becomes another *flou* with some solid bones amid a series of flows, all of which are destined to become yet another *flou*. Even on the surface, nature for Flaubert is much less a world of objects than it is a crucible of saps, flows, juices, and miscellaneous liquids.

After the disastrous studies of anatomy done by Bouvard and Pécuchet, one might have believed that it is man or, more precisely, his stupidity, that is at the origin of a second flow. In other words, the first flow, which could be defined as the productive magma to which one might associate the *od* of magnetism, would be the good creative flow, channeled by the universe into its interrelated vessels: things, nature, beings, Being itself. It would be only human stupidity that takes hold of this good flow fixed in an object; man destroys the worthy object with his stupidity as his unique tool.

Among these flowing liquids, we could insert the idea of a universe in the process of slow evolution, from the originary explosion of the Big Bang,which produces a flow that leads to order and creation itself: "Then volcanoes erupted, igneous rocks spurted out of mountains" (782). Magma produces the base of the earth, of everything that is solid; it emits its vapors and its gases to remain a pseudo-solid liquid whose dissolution will occur only at the end of the world: "Caves with stalactites will close, burning mountains will become extinguished, natural glaciers will warm" (780). The function of writing is to capture the world in its intermediary state between its two flows. In this world, to name is to pin nothing down; quite simply, naming indicates the absence of the acceleration toward entropy.

It would be too easy for Flaubert or his reader to accept this imperceptibly changing model of textuality. First of all, the named object, present like this liquid that flows ever so slowly, is also a sign, a mark of a flow more rapid than the preceding one, and of another to come: "All the hills were proof of the flood" (787). Thus the thing is both the thing as such and the sign of two disorders: the preceding one and the one to come. Flaubert cannot succeed with his project because the thing is of a hybrid nature, one part of which always refers to another, toward a past or future that are unnameable. The object always maintains a difference from itself, because it cannot be captured in an atemporal perspective. The novelist's burden is that time changes what he describes and that no signifiers set in concrete can make up for the two-way semiotic flow that every name or every noun has as a primary characteristic. The name of an object—a cap, for example—refers to other signs in the object, to the whole object, and to other signs. The process of Flaubertian semioticity is corrupted, made impure; this semioticity itself flows, for the act of naming implies slipping from one sign to another. The metatextuality of Flaubertian representation repeats his own act of representation and, in so doing, reveals the process.

The retrospective semioticity of the Flaubertian object puts into question the very possibility of it ever having been named. For the name signals the object in its static state, but if the static is only the supreme fiction, at no moment could the author name an object. Let us recall the dictionary definition of "magma": the solid object that remains once the gases have disappeared. But for Flaubert, one always refers to what has disappeared. That sign of alterity escapes nomination and corrupts the process of naming something: "The central fire had broken the earth's crust, raised terrains, made crevices. It is like a subterranean sea, with its flows and storms; a thin layer separates us from it" (788). Surface effects are nothing more than cheap fictions that are easy to undo. Everything else is *flou*. Every object is falsely named because it flows, and thus every object is itself suspect: "One supposes, in place of the sun, a great luminous hearth, now disappeared, and whose *aurora borealis* are perhaps only the vestiges" (794). White heliotropic mythology does not disappear once and for all; it would be impossible to find a beyond to the metaphysics of light (Derrida, *Marges* 247–324). But metaphysics is revealed through mythology, a fiction that, while incapable of reaching any external authenticity, now knows itself as fiction.

So the problem of nomination brings us once again to stupidity, despite the best efforts in the world. For if there is nothing that can be correctly named, every remark is as stupid as another. As every remark and every model of knowledge given in an "-ology" erect an object monumentally, they ignore the changes in the object, as is the case when haystacks undergo spontaneous combustion "like volcanoes" (743), when there is vomiting without reason (776), and when, despite the best philosophy in the world, there is slime, muck, mire, ooze everywhere: there is a layer of clay in the garden, oysters that taste of mud, and the very same mud or different mud is in the garden.

Thus the confusion doubles. It would seem that nature might bring us to a process of nomination, but this same process is false because it is heteroreferential and in that guise recalls signs of past flows and predicts those to come. This same process is stupid as well, because we stupidly believe that we can stop the movement of a flow and wipe up the liquid that drips from the object. We realize that naming is associated with flow itself, as if naming were itself an illness and a delirium that flow brought us: "the delirium of fertilizer,

Belgian liquor, Swiss leaching, detergent, sour herrings, kelp, rags, guano" (741).[3]

When all is said and done, the flow of a referential world between primordial chaos and final dissolution is for Flaubert repeated not as a part of the thing, but in its semiotic function, that is to say, what is figured in the sign. The referent that serves as a thing and as a sign of this flow recalls this absence and dissolution; in its semioticity it makes the referent necessarily impure. This impure referent is echoed in the flow and in the inadequacy of the signifier to its task. As there is no other means of proceeding, the author must always repeat the same gestures. In vain will the writing try to fix the signifiers in their places; each is a sign inscribed in the total system, and refers elsewhere, slipping from one signifier to another. Each signifier recalls for us the white page, and indicates before the fact the dissolution or the gape of meaning. Thus for Flaubert each signifier is found at an intersection of three flows, which we could represent as a three-dimensional geometric system, were there only some sort of stability, a zero point, a line separating positive from negative. The signifier refers to the referent caught in a process of flow between chaos and entropy. It belongs to a system of language that has been characterized for two decades as slippage, fading, tropism, the displaced and undue relation of a signifier to a system of signifiers. In the end, it is the moment of the referent between the whiteness of the page and the whirlwind galaxy of meaning that is the total overflow of the realist narrative.

As a textual swooning, the work is, as we have already said, sick. This sickness, as one might have suspected, already has a name, a proper name. During the fateful year of 1857, a certain doctor, B. A. Morel, published a book called the *Treatise on Degenerations* (*Traité des dégénérescences*) in which he explains in detail a sickness he calls "moral malaria," of which malaria is the physical version. He also develops a theory of "intoxicating miasma." One might think that this miasma is produced by the swamps and that the miasma itself was the active factor in the production of the illness. But Morel's comments are not as clear as that, for miasma is set in parallel with sickness, as if the miasma itself were a sickness. Morel writes:

Having arrived at this point in the theory, I am invincibly drawn to breaking the cords that tie me to the belief that such and such an agent of the outside world, electricity, iodine, moist air, the absence of like, etc. . . . possesses a special malfeasant property to produce goiter and cretinism.

I take refuge in the deleterious miasma related to the geological constitution of the soil. (674)

Bouvard and Pécuchet are sick with the illness that attacks the very writing of Flaubert in this last novel. The same symptomology is at work in all of them: the vaguely formed desire of a physical and textual elsewhere, the search for nonexistent meaning, a metaphysics that rejects the very bases of his own thought. From the badly buried *disjecta membra* of romantic desire in *Madame Bovary* to the painting of alterity in *Salammbô*, from the packages of desire all wrapped and ready to go in *L'Education sentimentale* to the hallucinations of *Saint Antoine*, Flaubert maintains flow at the center of his creation. But this flow goes way beyond a thematics of creation and a semioticity of stupidity in order to become, when all is said and done, a sickness whose symptom is the work itself. In the end, there is nothing beyond the mud. Mud, slip, slime, magma, miasma: so many loci where the explanation of facts becomes meaningless and where the relations between inside and outside are dissolved in the muck that the author had tried so hard to keep away. Everything flows, as Heraclitus says—especially realist narrative.

Flaubert's Polypary

In this part of the chapter, which I am devoting to an examination of seeing what fits and what does not fit in Flaubert's writing, I am going to start by examining some of the critical stances taken in the past two decades in studies of Flaubert. I would contend that there is a pattern in reading Flaubert, a pattern that does not fit the writing, but which, in a certain sense, aims to make the rupture of Flaubert's writing the entirety of the writing itself. Against that concept of rupture, I shall make three hypotheses. First, the ruptures in Flaubert's writing are, as they are for Balzac, found within the construct of the writing itself, as Carla Peterson has noted (175); Flaubert's writing as a watershed, distinct from what has gone before, is a famous idea but is a fictional construct. Second, the critical ploy used to read Flaubert, which amounts to a troping of the outsides of fiction by means of a textual protective railing, while providing the argument for the novel as rupture, is at the same time the best argument against that rupture. In other words, the critical stance used to see Flaubert's revolutionary status is both a means of reducing the validity of the fiction itself as self-sustaining enterprise and an argument against any ruptures in Flaubert's writing. Finally, I would contend that like Proust after him (as I have tried to show in *The Shock of Men*), Flaubert discomfits many a critical reader: as often as not, the reactions of the critic are an attempt to deal with the discomfort instead of addressing its origin. In Proust's case, the discomfiting factor is a scenario that gives no precedence to heterosexuality as a superior hermeneutic model; in Flaubert's case, as we shall see, it is Flaubert's obsessive enactment of a scenario of discomfort. For Flaubert, the locus of discomfort and the site of textual rupture are one and the same.

Over the past two decades, Flaubert's writing has received an enormous amount of critical attention. Subject in turn to the analytical tools of existentialist psychocriticism, structuralism, semiotics, and the various strains of poststructuralist thought, Flaubert's oeuvre seems always to provide new challenges and new answers. From being the writer who was considered to have given the world the summum of French realist fiction in *Madame Bovary*, simultaneously seen as a work of stylistic purity (a contradiction if ever there were one), Flaubert became the touchstone for all sorts of criticism that championed his work as that of the first modernist. Flaubert founded our modernity and provided the ideal field of study for all critical approaches that see an unbridgeable gap between representation and reality. How can Flaubert be the epigone of realism, the champion of aestheticism, the purveyor of truth, the founder of modernism, and the herald of postmodern reproaches to previous theories and praxes?

Part of the answer comes from the fact that as genre and praxis, the novel inscribes a truth that precedes the record or realization of that truth in so-called objective writing; this is one of the main theses, for example, of the early, seminal work by René Girard, *Mensonge romantique, vérité romanesque*, in which the critic maintains that novels often tell a truth (in this case, about the structures of desire) denied by science and social science. If we generalize from Girard's position, without ascribing the generalization to Girard, we see that

Madame Bovary may inscribe the truth that is reflected (or denied) alternatively in realist theory, in New Criticism, in thematic criticism, in structuralism, or in semiotics. The critic must simply place the appropriate grid on the writing or use the right optic to see what Flaubert has already inscribed in his fiction, which had remained hidden until the right critical apparatus came along. Just as Stendhal and Proust see the truth of the laws of desire better than their own contemporaries, and just as Girard sees what he perceives to be the truth about desire already inscribed in Stendhal's and Proust's novels, so too do many contemporary critics see Flaubert as a structuralist, semiotician, or poststructuralist, and so forth, *avant la lettre.* Yet this is only part of the answer, because there is another problem, symptomatic of a critically more interesting question of position and figurality in Flaubert's works. If a whole range of traditional and not-so-traditional critics are comfortable with Flaubert's works, the same cannot be said for the critics of the next generation. The more Flaubert becomes the touchstone for poststructuralist critics, and the more he is seen as the first modernist, the less critics seem comfortable with his work. At times one feels that the critics are going to great lengths both to feel comfortable and to posit Flaubert's production as an accessible whole.

In the wake of New Criticism, the biographical approach to literary criticism fell into disfavor. No longer were the author's life, comments, juvenilia, or correspondence means of entering his fictional world. Rather, the works were read for themselves, without the support provided by these supplementary writings. Yet even within the enormous amount of good criticism written in the past two decades about Flaubert's narratives, critics have not felt completely at home with Flaubert. Something in his writing upsets critical approaches that seek to interpret the work in an immanent fashion. Despite what would seem to be almost a warning about valorizing these secondary writings, critics still often begin their discussion of a problem in Flaubert's novels by detouring through the correspondence. The letters give the necessary clues to Flaubert's project; knowing that Flaubert wanted to write "the book on nothing [*le livre sur rien*]" seems to aid in understanding the fiction. In Flaubert's case, many critics temporarily put the intentional fallacy into brackets. Most significant, I think, is that this process occurs most frequently among the strong, original, thoughtful critics who are attempting to blaze new theoretical trails.

One of the most important narratologists, Gérard Genette, goes so far as to employ a quasi-religious vocabulary in speaking of the importance of the *Correspondance*; he writes of "the testimony [*témoignage*] of the *Correspondance*" (Genette and Todorov 8). And one of the most important French post-Freudians, J.-B. Pontalis, begins a study called "Flaubert's Illness" with Flaubert's letters and offers a symptomology for the man and for his works (277–312). If Genette's remark is cogent and those of Pontalis interesting though speculative, the same cannot always be said of other critics; some "use" of the correspondence along these lines can lead to a topsy-turvy reading, as Yvan Leclerc speaks of "the famous *first* letter of Gustave (which, by the way, was not the first). It must be reread as a piece dropped into the second volume [of *Bouvard et Pécuchet*]" (7). Much is at stake for these critics, who, despite their own critical caveats, use the letters as a strategy and momentarily commit an intentional fallacy that is usually erased as the critical mechanism is reestablished.

One of the best recent critics of Flaubert, Eugenio Donato, produced a series of studies that are landmarks in contemporary criticism. In an incisive article, "Flaubert and the Question of History: Notes for a Critical Anthology," he deals with problems of critical approaches to the question of the historical novel in Flaubert. Donato starts his study with four epigraphs, the first three of which come from Flaubert's letters to Louis Bouilhet. In the memorial volume of *MLN* dedicated to Donato, the first article, "Who Signs 'Flaubert?,'" is his; it too starts with quotes from a letter, this time to Maxime Du Camp (711). And the first paragraph of Donato's article, "The Crypt of Flaubert" (in Schor and Majewski 30), is a series of quotes from the correspondence. Finally, in his article on *Bouvard et Pécuchet*, "The Museum's Furnace," Donato even provides a meta-commentary: "Most readings of *Bouvard and Pécuchet* take their point of departure from Flaubert's remarks about the composition and significance of the work" (214).

Another recent example is a penetrating article by Jacques Derrida who deconstructs the question of philosophy in Flaubert. Derrida takes his epigraph from one of Flaubert's letters and comments: "It is March 1868 and Flaubert is writing to his niece, Caroline"

("Idea" 748). In a very different mode, Charles Bernheimer almost immediately starts his discussion of "The Psychogenesis of Flaubert's Style" with a reference to the correspondence. Bernheimer also notes the ease with which critics have used the correspondence as a clue to unraveling some of the difficulties of Flaubert's writing, in this case, specifically *La Tentation de Saint Antoine* (56). In "Flaubert's Conversion," Neil Hertz, following Sartre who follows Flaubert's own self-examination, refers to "what has become a famous letter" (63). On the previous page, Hertz comments on Sartre's preface to *L'Idiot de la famille*, where the subject matter is furthered by "the availability of so much material for interpretation in the early writings and in the correspondence." Finally, one could add to this assortment of critical readings the summum of the genre, the institutionalized version of the correspondence, published almost as a key to understanding Flaubert: *Préface à la vie d'écrivain*, edited by Geneviève Bollème. This book is nothing but excerpts from the correspondence.[4]

The second side-door has been the *Dictionnaire des idées reçues*. Françoise Gaillard, for example, starts a thoughtful article on the figure of history in Flaubert with the following exhortation to the reader: "Open the *Dictionnaire des idées reçues*" (Schor and Majewski 84). This side-door is especially useful since the piles of *idées reçues* and *bêtises* that are the marks of the dictionary inevitably correspond to passages in the novels, and specifically to the inscription, on a thematic level, of the *discours indirect libre*. So, for example, the dictionary's remark on Italy is "Must be seen immediately after marriage. —Is quite deceiving, not as beautiful as they say" (2:1014). The pithy enunciatorless dictionary definition corresponds almost verbatim to the remarks made in *discours indirect libre* to Madame Dambreuse after the marriage of her niece: "Moreover, it was rather good for the newlyweds to travel; later encumbrances, children would arrive! But Italy did not correspond to the idea they had of it" (2:401). Thus there seems to be a structural homology between the two kinds of discourse that offers a *relève* of questions of enunciation and inscription. And in that there is an intrinsic relation between *Bouvard et Pécuchet* and the *Dictionnaire des idées reçues* in form and content, the strategy is an extremely efficient means of getting access to such a problematic work. Anne Herschberg-Pierrot (13–33) uses both side-doors, as a sizable part of the first third of her book on the *Diction-

naire is devoted to the correspondence. Significant too is that it matters little whether what follows is effective: the technique itself seems
to be a bearer of some textual truth. Thus Yvan Leclerc (60) can
write the following without seeming to realize the irony of the complete *non sequitur*: "I have consulted a book I had at hand, *L'Essai sur
la physiognomie* by Lavater. Whether or not Flaubert read it matters
little . . . "

The third strategy of entry is an approach to the mature works
through early novels like *Novembre* or the first version of *L'Education
sentimentale*. It is an approach that has the added effect of being an
attempt to recuperate the whole of the production. The best known
examples of this strategy are Shoshana Felman's excellent studies of
Mémoires d'un fou and *Novembre* (*Folie* 170–213). These strategies
may work together in concert or may work against each other. Thus,
after a quote from Valéry, Felman begins her first study of Flaubert
in the same volume, "Illusion réaliste et répétition romanesque,"
with a quote from the correspondence (159). On the other hand,
Flaubert rereads his own *Novembre* in October 1853 and draws the
following conclusion: "But it is no good. There are monstrosities in
bad taste, and all in all, the whole is not satisfying. I see no way to rewrite it, I would have to do everything anew. Here and there a good
sentence, a beautiful comparison. But no stylistic weave [*pas de tissu
de style*]" (*Corr* 2:460). In that the question of style seems of primary
importance for the canonic Flaubert, *Novembre* seems rather to belong to a separate category. Yet there is a way of recuperating what is
beyond the demarcating line of style. Mark Conroy begins his study
of Flaubert with a telling remark that seems to validate these approaches through paratexts:

There exists, no doubt, a line between Flaubert's youthful and mature writings, but it is not a straight one. The justification, therefore, for resorting to
Flaubert's *écrits de jeunesse* at the outset is partially pragmatic (since Flaubert's
letters, so numerous on *Madame Bovary*, are much scantier on *L'Education
sentimentale*), and also partially philosophical (since many of the concerns
that motivated the young Flaubert to take up his pen are insistent in his later
work as well, and not only because *L'Education* itself has been a continuing
project). (43)

Conroy's remark is illuminating: since one paratext (the letters) is
more or less absent, another (the early writings) will have to be used.

Indeed, Michal Ginsburg's thesis in her study, *Flaubert Writing*, is grounded in the early writings: "The starting point for this study was my feeling that Flaubert's difficulty sustaining a narrative, so evident in such early works as *Les Mémoires d'un fou* and *Novembre*, is not entirely overcome in his mature works" (1).

It would seem then that both the critics who posit a break in literary production and those who see continuity take a holistic approach. This approach necessarily links the productions of the early and mature writer, even if a break is posited in a whole. In that this wholeness is posited a priori, there is an echo of the genetic structuralism of Lucien Goldmann, who, in his study, "La méthode structuraliste génétique en histoire de la littérature" (335–72), could "normalize" a break or *décalage* as a dialectical reversal. In taking one of these side-doors, then, the postmodern critical mode seems to recapitulate either traditional criticism or structuralism. Traditional criticism stressed the unity of the *oeuvre*, the natural, organic development of a writer, and especially, with the abundant use of the correspondence, the links, be they real or rhetorical, between the author's private life and the contents of his fiction. And with structuralism, there are presuppositions about the closure of a work and the interpretableness of structure; that these were the very bases for the critical revolt against structuralism, in which the key signposts are Foucault's *Les Mots et les choses*, Derrida's *De la grammatologie*, and Barthes's *S/Z*, ironizes the resemblance between poststructuralist critics and those who preceded. Of course these works were simultaneous with the institutionalization and dissemination of structuralism; the poststructuralist reaction began to be felt as these three works themselves were disseminated. But with or without this irony, does the critic have a choice today?

In a study more recent than the one on Flaubert, Derrida cautions that "the competence of the Joyce of the letters and conversations does not seem to me to enjoy any privilege" (*Ulysse* 122). That this lack of privilege should manifest itself for Joyce—for whom any paratext would undoubtedly be a welcome aid, if only it were usable—but not for Flaubert is itself a telling remark. But, by and large, the presence within poststructuralist criticism of various faults like an intentional fallacy, the adherence to an organic model, or recourse to a discrete metanarrative, remains disquieting, even in the service of a deconstructive strategy. The strength of poststructuralist readings has in most other cases been their ability to establish a discourse that becomes disruptive after a smooth entry into the writing. Flaubert, however, seems to elicit a willful suspension of the "rules" of poststructuralism, as if the critic felt obliged to invent the imaginary unity of the work that Flaubert himself did not aver; only then can the critic use his or her tools to undo that unity.

What is it in Flaubert that so often brings about an old-fashioned strategy of recuperation? In part this approach to Flaubert is made necessary by Flaubert's questioning of the concept of a grounded realist practice. As numerous critics point out, Flaubert is above all an archaeologist. Raymonde Debray-Genette, who starts her "Les Débauches apographiques de Flaubert" with a quote from the correspondence, points to the "apographic need," that is to say, Flaubert's ever-present need to recopy (Debray-Genette and Neefs 49–50).[5] So the approach of modern criticism seems mimetically to repeat the Flaubertian project of going from the readable fragment to the unreadable, mysterious, buried core. Current criticism often uses strategies of working from the margins toward a center that is subsequently destabilized by the very critical apparatus used to get to the center. Flaubert's fundamental questioning of the processes of narrative does two things to critics' strategies. First of all, Flaubert's works are always decentered by the narrative process, even before the critic attempts to inscribe this process of decentering in his or her reading. But poststructuralist readings, and precisely those of deconstruction, would see this decentering as the fundamental process at work in fiction. The process, however, is critical in Flaubert, since readers who do not share the presuppositions of deconstruction can still agree on the presence of this decentering mechanism.

Without recourse to a deconstructive strategy, one can consider two points from the early chapters of *Madame Bovary*. First, there is the description of Emma. Literally caught in the description of extremities such as nails, hair, heels, and spectacles (1:304–6), the description seems as separate as the details of which it is composed, what Thomas Pavel calls "the realist detour" (168). And a moment in the description that might mark a point leads to confusion instead of clarity: "What was beautiful was her eyes: although they were brown, they seemed black because of the lashes, and her gaze came frankly to you with candid daring" (1:305). The insinuation of *discours indirect libre* detours the narrative from the establishment of a base at a locus of neutral discourse. A second example of decentering in the narrative is the chapter devoted to Emma's education and upbringing (1:323–27). The result of the formation is a disordered grab-bag of romantic illusions, where the false neutrality of *discours indirect libre* joins the grafted subjectivity of Emma, whose originality as a subject consists in her lack of originality:

> In those days she had a cult of Mary Queen of Scots and enthusiastic veneration of illustrious or unfortunate women. Joan of Arc, Heloise, Agnes Sorel, the beautiful Ferronnière and Clémence Isaure, for her, stood out like comets against the dark immensity of history, where, here and there sprung out, though more lost in the shadows and without any relations to one another, Saint Louis with his oak, Bayard dying, some ferocities of Louis XI, a bit of Saint Bartholomew, the Bearnaise tuft, and always the memory of the painted plates lauding Louis XIV. (1:325)

Whereas in his description of Madame Vauquer and her boarding house, Balzac uses the details strung out diachronically to produce a whole coterminous with an ideological construct, Flaubert distributes the details so as to make a construct an impossibility (Culler). Like a fractal, Flaubert's work shows the absence of continuity in the detail as well as in the whole.

Moreover, since the writing is decentered, the margins and depths are not as neatly defined as the critic might like. Again Balzac provides the counterpoint in *Le Père Goriot*. Having described the Maison Vauquer and its residents, he makes the following statement about Paris: "But Paris is a veritable ocean. Take a sounding, you will never know its depth. Cross it, describe it! . . . there will always be a virgin spot. . . . The *Maison Vauquer* is one of these curious monstrosities" (3:59). Balzac has already dropped his plumb line and determined depth and his "virgin spot" has already been penetrated by the prose with which he has constructed a meaningful locus. Flaubert inscribes Balzac's Paris for Emma, but it exceeds any limits: "Paris, vaster than the Ocean, thus shimmered in Emma's eyes in a vermilion atmosphere" (1:344). Flaubert goes beyond Balzac; Flaubert's plumb line never touches bottom. His descriptions can never have neatly determined margins: "It was an existence above others, between heaven and earth, in storms, something sublime" (1:344).

Thus the strategy of using the letters, the early writings, or the *Dictionnaire des idées reçues* returns a lost possibility to the critic. Either through a perceived neutrality or a clear act of limitation these writings provide a base upon which the critic can build and from which he or she can work toward the center to perform the reversal that is the necessary *coup* for postmodern criticism. These strategies help explain the works and help move the critic from edge to center because the various kinds of paratexts are themselves readable. In that the letters, for example, seem to mime the imaginary, stable center of a novel, they are a useful means of entry into a destabilized universe.[6] The letters tell the critic: this is what is going on in the novel; this is the project. These works provide a sense of comfort and home to the critic. The critic reads over the addressee's shoulder to get at the "truth" of what Flaubert wanted to do in the novels. Obviously, there is always the possibility of a dialectical reversal of what a letter says: the novelist does not follow through with what he said he was doing or going to do. Yet, even so, the "truth" of the letter is still understood as such. The letters resolve the ambiguities to a certain extent, place them in perspective, and frame them in a clear discourse.

At the other end of Flaubert's production, the *Dictionnaire* is a collection of the signs of the sociolect, the remarks made by everyone to everyone, the signs of an ossified system against which the novels can be set up as oppositional discourse. Getting to the novels through one of these side-doors is a way of having a place to stand or sit while we struggle with the problems of Flaubert's narrative. The early writings also provide comfort: the confirmations of a teleology of Flaubert's writing are found in the very earliest writings. As Louis Althusser remarks of one of Flaubert's most notable contemporaries, the critics can "very schematically allow that the young Marx is not Marx or affirm that the young Marx is Marx" (49). The same applies here. All three are strategies of recuperation that involve the grounding of an author who seems to refuse it categorically, since the structures and systems of Flaubert's works, taken on a micro- or macroscopic level cannot be integrated into a comfortable system.

But why is the postmodern critic not at home in Flaubert? There is a problem of base or center that always puts into question this presumably neutral locus that is the idealization of representation. This idealized locus is where, in Benveniste's terms (239–42), the story tells itself and where there is no barrier to representation as an act and therefore no barrier between representation and represented. It is less the ground of reality than it is the implied narratability of the world and the implied possibility of bridging difference. In Derridean terms, this fictional representation, which is a unified performative and constative act, bridges the abyss of différance.

No pretext, however, is safe from inquiry in Flaubert's novels. Every presumably neutral locus is undone; every purported bridging of difference is demarcated as an act of imposed fictional representation. No aspect of the Flaubertian project, not even the writing project itself, provides an anchor for the writing. Specifically, three aspects of this writing undo the process of representation itself and re-mark the crisis: the extirpation of romanticism, the anatomy of realism, and finally, the total ontological questioning of writing as theory, project, and praxis. The first aspect is the removal of the encrypted remains of romanticism within narrative discourse. In *Littérature et sensation* (202), Richard says that "one should perhaps see in *Madame Bovary* less the process/trial [*procès*] of novelistic illusion than the process/trial of the novelistic incapable of sustaining its illusions to the end." It is clear that this process or trial occurs through a requestioning of romanticism and its use in narrative. Realism suffers from the weight of the languages of love and desire that remain from earlier sentimental fiction, the inherited audience of novel-readers, and the figures of desire that romanticism has left behind. Both *Madame Bovary* and *L'Education sentimentale* are attempts at dislodging these encrypted romantic remains; the first shows the fictional nature of romantic desire; the second shows the deceit, deception, and disappointment, in short, the *déception*, that come with a fidelity to an outmoded formula for the presentation of desire.

Only in *L'Education sentimentale* does Flaubert finally resolve this problem that had proven so tenacious in both *Madame Bovary* and *Salammbô*; Pavel goes so far as to assert that the project of *Madame Bovary* includes the maintenance of the moral code inherited from romanticism (*Mirage* 170). From a theoretical point of view *L'Education sentimentale* does not raise the same questions as the two earlier novels, or those of *Bouvard et Pécuchet*; it is this absolute difference from his other works that allows Flaubert to accomplish this part of the project. At times one is almost inclined to think that Flaubert writes *L'Education sentimentale* through a process of textual purging, especially noticeable if one compares the excesses of the first version with the rhetorical restraint of the final version. The final version seems to be a novel by Balzac or Stendhal stripped of the critical and ideological biases and, at least relative to Balzac, rhetorical excess. Certainly Flaubert makes a gesture in the direction of his immediate predecessors by solving the problem of authority and paternity before the story itself begins. Unlike a *Bildungsroman* of desire like *Le Rouge et le Noir*, for example, where Julien Sorel struggles with the authority figured by his father, in *L'Education sentimentale* the authority is dead even before Frédéric is born: "Her husband, a plebeian that her parents had made her marry, had died from a sword blow, during her pregnancy, leaving her a compromised fortune" (2:42). And it is certainly not Arnoux who will play the new Monsieur de Rênal.

With the question of previously existing authority dealt with a priori, Flaubert can submit this authority, in its incarnation as preexisting textuality, to a process of purification. As it does with so many other things, *Bouvard et Pécuchet* will put the very process of purification into question, as can be seen, for example, in the explosion of the alembic (2:761), in the ensuing chemistry and anatomy experiments, and in the questions relating to purity in architecture (2:800–802).

In *L'Education sentimentale*, romanticism is not found in any places from which it might be difficult to extirpate it. Flaubert reduces it to a series of packets with which he can deal in a summary fashion: "Then noticing a volume of Hugo and another of Lamartine on the bookcase, [Hussonet] waxed prolific with sarcastic remarks about the romantic school" (2:64). Despite the thematic differences among the points of view on romanticism ascribed to Hussonet, Frédéric, and Flaubert himself, their points of view can be solidified, moved, and abolished. Easily transportable, the pieces of the romantic praxis and ideology that Flaubert had combated can be disposed of. Thus, for example, Flaubert can easily encapsulate one of the great commonplaces of romantic writing, the excesses of Italy, by having Frédéric begin to write yet another Italian novel, which we understand ironically to be eminently disposable: "He began to write a novel entitled: *Sylvio, le fils du pêcheur*. The thing took place in Venice. He was the hero, Mme Arnoux, the heroine" (2:56).

Clearly there has been a process of genetic development from *Madame Bovary* and the antinovel *Salammbô*, both of which try to deal with these encrypted remains but cannot dislodge them. In *L'Education sentimentale*, Flaubert has discovered a way of moving packets of received information in a narrative context without doing damage to the narrative. He prepares the way for the little packets of stupidity in *Bouvard et Pécuchet*: "Pellerin read all the works of aesthetics to discover the true theory of the Beautiful" (2:68). Pellerin is Bouvard and Pécuchet *in statu nascendi*; at the end of the novel, "Pellerin, after having dabbled in Fourierism, homeopathy, seances [*tables tournantes*], Gothic art, and humanitarian painting, had become a photographer" (2:454). Thus there is at least a theoretical resolution to the double problem of authority and the weight of the past and of what authority has left in its wake. The problem is so regulated that writing can be moved in this system as a vehicle for desire or for vatic impulse:

—Oh! Who brings you back?

This rather simple question embarrassed Frédéric; and, not knowing what to answer, he asked whether by chance his notebook, a little notebook in blue leather, had been found.

—The one in which you put your love letters [*vos lettres de femme*]? said Arnoux.

Frédéric, blushing like a virgin, disallowed such a supposition.

—Your poems, then? answered the merchant. (2:74)

From the very first, a kind of novelistic idealism is posited that corresponds to the idealism in representation already discussed. For example, giving into the vagaries of bibliomancy [*le sort virgilien*], Deslauriers has picked up a volume of Plato: "a translation of Plato opened by chance elated him" (2:44). Yet Flaubert's choice of Plato is anything but a chance occurrence (Derrida, "Idea"). The ideality of the Platonic world is a necessary vehicle for Flaubert: with all problems of communication resolved and all white noise gone, the perfect message-bearing system will allow Flaubert to explore the mobility of desire. Whether there is no message, as in "Frédéric had little to narrate" (2:46), or a complete message, there is full communication and the act of representation is identical to itself. In this world there is no loss through writing or repetition. Three times Frédéric rereads the letter announcing his uncle's death but there is no loss in the message. What does dissipate is not narrative but desire: "No longer finding Mme Arnoux in the environment in which he had met her, she seemed to lose something, bear some sort of lowering in status, no longer be the same" (2:140). By the end of the novel this dissipation of desire will bring into question something only to be dealt with in *Bouvard et Pécuchet*, that is, the very possibility of an ideal system of communication.

Still, the question of an ideal system arises much earlier relative to intertextuality. Flaubert must dissolve or neutralize the accumulated scholarship and authority of his readings in order to melt them into *Salammbô* and *Bouvard et Pécuchet*. That very melting process is recuperable within the writing project itself; though arduous, it is neither problematic for Flaubert nor discomfiting for the reader. What is problematic is the corpus of works of his predecessor, Balzac, who has ideologically rewritten the world in *La Comédie humaine*. Flaubert seeks to rewrite Balzac's famous doubly centered discourse of throne and altar; Flaubert's project is to describe a world, even if it is only the world of realist discourse and not the world of objects, without the benefit of the transcendental signs to which Balzac has recourse to ground his semiosis.[7]

For lack of a better term, the third aspect of this project is the ontological critique of writing itself, resumable heuristically in the phrase (from the *Correspondance*), of the "livre sur rien." Brombert notes the use of this phrase:

Contemporary criticism is fond of quoting Flaubert's proclaimed desire to write a book with hardly a subject, a book about nothing at all ("un livre sur rien") that would be held together through sheer power of structure and style. . . . It is almost as though Flaubert coined the by now commonplace chiasmatic opposition between the story of an adventure and the adventure of a story. (Schor and Majewski 100)

This entails a total questioning of the meaning, function, status, and existence of writing—specifically realist writing. On every page, Flaubert incessantly re-marks the questions he is raising but never answering about the nature of writing fiction. And it is this constant questioning of the writing project, its place and its substance, that is seen in the permanent crisis in the writing, the effects of a style that as it develops knows less and less of what it marks and where it sits.

All these strands come together in a configuration that epitomizes the dislocation of Flaubert's writing. Nothing is safe in his writing; in short, nothing and no one important is at home. The metaphors and scenes describing home and hearth are constantly undone to reveal ideological contradictions, narrative double binds, epistemological aporias, and ontological abysses. In Flaubert's writing, the figure of home is primarily a figure of homelessness. It is not the *Heimkehr* of the eternal return, nor is it the heliotropic return to origins that marks Western metaphysics for Derrida (*Marges* 247–324). Homelessness is everywhere. On a thematic level, one easily remarks the frequent setting up and dismantling of houses in *Madame Bovary*, *L'Education sentimentale*, and *Bouvard et Pécuchet*. The event is simultaneously marked with an ease and a dis-ease. Setting up or dismantling a house is tantamount to a mathematical equation, yet there is always an awkward forcing of the situation, whether it is Emma Bovary's series of new beds, Frédéric's last turn as a petit bourgeois, or the scrambled geography of Bouvard and Pécuchet. Certainly, some of Flaubert's characters seem to be at home, but whatever their station in life, they are always in supporting roles: Homais, Madame Aubain, Dambreuse, or Hamilcar. The being-at-home of secondary characters is ironic: even when a secondary character has wealth, he or she is always dependent structurally on the primary character(s). Thus being thematically or economically at home means being structurally parasitic on a more independent set of signifiers. These secondary characters aside, for the protagonists at least even a homecoming means an imminent move, a dispossession, and a displacement.

This displacement is a necessary figure for Flaubert, who uses the move to cover a certain paradox of writing. At one level, the dispossession corresponds to an un-grounding of the narrative. The writing that would normally find a haven in the accreted praxis of novel writing and a comfortable spot for desire in the reinscribed fragments of romanticism is literally moved away from the comforts of too solidly entrenched interpretations. The decentering of the Flaubertian narrative does not automatically ensure the establishment of a new hermeneutics, since such an establishment would paradoxically imply that this decentering is itself a ground, that the difference is a base. Instead, the decentering brings into question any preexisting hermeneutics grounded outside the work. Secondly, the decentering figures both the crisis at work in the act of inscription and the paradox that produces this crisis: the inscribed event must constatively or performatively occur somewhere. Yet Flaubert elects to remove this somewhere, a removal that itself marks the permanent crisis in representation. Ultimately then, the displacement of textual hermeneutics leads to a permanent requestioning of the very ontology of Flaubert's textuality.

This hermeneutic disruption occurring implicitly, as well as the ontological mise-en-question, find their complement in the questioning of the reader's knowledge of the writing. There is thus an explicit epistemological problem that corresponds to the ontological, thematic, and hermeneutic displacement. Flaubert does his utmost to dispossess the readers, unseat them from their comfortable chairs, and unground the basis for reading that upsets any normative relation between writer, be he real, rhetorical, or imagined, and reader, be he or she singular or plural, real or rhetorical. There is an implicit challenge to any interpretation that relies on an agreement, be it pragmatic or dialectical, as that of a super-reader (Riffaterre 203), an interpretive community (Fish), or a horizon of expectations (Jauss 144–207). Just as the use of the author's correspondence to "get at the text" does not *necessarily* imply a weakness or fault, this challenge does not imply that these concepts are wrong or useless. On the contrary, the very ungrounding process used by Flaubert makes these dynamic constructs most useful; Flaubert's writings test the critical apparatus. Within the immanent textual structure, the figure of "home" is the emblematic sign of dispossession and disintegration; in the dynamic between writing and reader, the figure is a sign of discomfort and dislocation.

Every critical position is an ex-centric one, every point of criticism is necessarily ex-static. Flaubert is not very generous in providing a place for his reader to stand or to sit. The floors make the critic slide and the chairs are wobbly or out of reach. Not for Flaubert is Balzac's oft-mentioned armchair in the beginning of *Le Père Goriot* (3:50). And despite the ambiguity of the gender of Balzac's implied reader, we can still extrapolate a reading public that is female and bourgeois, an ideology of middle-class leisure, a set of expectations about a novel and about narrative fiction in general, and a dynamic between the author and his rhetorical reader. In other words, even if each individual addressee is situated at the point of rupture, those ruptures retrospectively may be seen to melt into a generalized sea of implied readership. As Fredric Jameson points out:

> To juxtapose the depersonalized and retextualized provincial houses of Flaubert with this one [in Balzac's *La Vieille Fille*] is to become perhaps uncomfortably aware of the degree to which the Balzacian dwelling invites the awakening of a longing for possession, of the mild and warming fantasy of landed property as the tangible figure of a Utopian wish-fulfillment. (157)

At one point, Flaubert does provide an armchair for his reader, but this singular armchair is at the end of the first version of *L'Education sentimentale* (371), where the author is trying to tie up loose ends for which he needs the reader's indulgence: "Will M. Renaud make his fortune? I don't know. Did Mme Renaud have another lover? That is what I don't know either." It is at this point by a present of enunciation, marked deictically not by tenses of narration but by the use of the future, the present, and the *passé composé*, that the narrator forcibly restrains the reader in his or her chair. It is both an appeal and an off-handed familiarity that contrast in every way with the writings of the mature Flaubert:

> Insofar as spectacle is concerned, don't yet get out of your armchair [*ne te lève pas encore de ton fauteuil*], before I have completely finished what I wanted to show you here, dear reader, regretting that you had less pleasure in watching it than I had in making it move, and wishing you only for the future, when you don't know what to do, hours as peaceful as those I spent blackening this paper. (*Education* 371)

Any reader will recognize the appeal to theatricality that is more a mark of Balzacian rhetoric than that of Flaubert, in whose work theater normally provokes discomfort (1:493–94), palpitations in Emma (1:498), and *bêtise* in Charles, who finds that the music of *Lucia di Lammermoor* ruins the words (1:496). Any reader will recognize too that this narrator, so frivolously comfortable with his scribbling, is not at all the tortured Flaubert of the correspondence.[8]

Flaubert's chairs are usually a vastly different lot. Lined up against the wall, they impose their uncomfortable order on anyone who dares sit on them. This facticity is both a false order and a masking of the theoretical crisis. The false order comes from the very array; the presumed order and lack of disarray of the objects implies order in the narrative and representability throughout a continuity. By implying order in the narrative, the seemingly ordered objects displace the crisis in writing: they seem to say that everything is solid, in order, and in its place; that there is no problem with grounding; that there is no hot seat for reader or writer. Yet the imposition itself forces the reader to notice the obvious: there is a progressive discomfort in Flaubert's seating arrangements. In *Madame Bovary*, a chair can be brought in for Charles to make himself at home in the classroom (1:293). In "Un coeur simple," Mme Aubain is at home, for she is the product of a half-century of accreted bourgeois respectability. But no one else, and certainly not Félicité or Loulou, is at home with her. The chairs are in a line: "In the room Mme Aubain occupied all day as she sat by the casement window in a straw chair next to the wainscoting, painted white, there were eight mahogany chairs lined up" (2:591). Significantly, when Mme Aubain has died, no one is at home: "Madame's armchair, her pedestal table, her footwarmer, the eight chairs, were gone" (2:619). By *Bouvard et Pécuchet*, there is no place to stand or to sit if a character or an implied reader wants to be at home in the center of things: "The living room was waxed so much that one could not stand up. The eight Utrecht chairs had their backs to the wall" (2:753).[9]

One is at home with Flaubert only in *L'Education sentimentale*, where the author needs a fixed system to explore the mobility of desire. Flaubert posits a model of inscription that is an ideal communicational system in which desire can roam and in which it can eventually dissipate. Thus, even if Flaubert does not go as far as the Balzacian rhetoric of the first version of the novel, it is imperative that the system be fixed and that its loci be comfortable. There is no better example than Rosanette's boudoir, where all is *luxe, calme, et volupté*:

He entered the boudoir, which was swagged in a pale blue silk with bouquets of wildflowers, while on the ceiling in a gilt-wood circle, Cupids emerging from an azure sky scampered on clouds shaped like eiderdown. These elegant touches, which would be pittances for those like Rosanette today, amazed him. He admired everything: the artificial morning glories embellishing the outline of the mirror, the curtains on the fireplace, the Turkish sofa, and in a recess in the wall, a sort of tent done in pink silk, with white muslin on top. (2:148)

There is no touch of the irony here that (de)constructs the Bovarys' wedding cake; there is only the understatement and modesty of the author's aside with his mention of today. Again, in *L'Education sentimentale*, the seat reminds us of the communicational system of fixed meaning: "the trunk for the wounded established on a chair" (2:325). This remains true even if this value has gone down: "In the armchair was a former fabulist, a ruin" (2:391). In *L'Education sentimentale*, the system is so constant and point of view is so at ease that it can be literally and emblematically inscribed at a vantage point. Even after desire has been nullified, Flaubert can reinscribe desire and fix it through an act of rememoration, naming, and seating. Mme Arnoux says to Frédéric: "I shall sit there, on the bench I named 'the Frédéric bench'" (2:450). And thus, when all is said and done, Frédéric and Deslauriers sit and chat by the fire (2:432) as they remember the marks of dissipated desire.

Yet normally in a Flaubertian narrative, having entered a room, one faces what Emma Bovary herself faces, the most discomfiting sign of homelessness: "From the first cold snaps, Emma left her room for the living room, a long room with a low ceiling, on whose mantle was a tufted polypary spread out against the mirror" (1:379). The polypary sits there in silence. In an excellent article, "Roman et objets: l'exemple de *Madame Bovary*," Claude Duchet calls the polypary a "metaphor for the bourgeois order" (Genette and Todorov 36–37).[10] While I agree with Duchet, I believe that the object is among the special objects in Flaubert's world that include Charles Bovary's cap, Salammbô's zaimph, and the *bahut de la renaissance* from *Bouvard et Pécuchet*. In that, as Duchet points out, it is a metaphor as well, there are implications for the figural level of the novel. It is perhaps only a supernumerary detail like the barometer of "Un coeur simple" that serves, according to Roland Barthes, to make the meta-narrative remark that "this is a realist text."[11]

One may hypothetically posit a degree-zero object, whether it is the barometer or something else, whose sole function is as a meta-narrative marker of "realism." One can also say that it is the deictic marker that says "this is a bourgeois text," which perhaps amounts to the same thing. Duchet says that, for all the objects of *Madame Bovary*, "a purely sociological classification permits us to distinguish three essential groups: the professional object, the domestic object, the object of leisure or of standing [the status symbol]" (Genette and Todorov 24). And yet the polypary is undeniably much more than that. It was once but is no longer home to a myriad of interdependent coelenterates. In that it so visibly marks an absence, it is a structure of death, disintegration, and dispossession. Moreover, the polypary is reflected in the mirror: it is thus doubly represented in the writing. With the image of death on the one hand and the immediate specularity of the image on the other, the polypary certainly insists far beyond the meta-statement "this is a realist text."

The polypary is a triple image: it is an image of homelessness that thematically and specularly corresponds to the unseating of the embedded traces of romantic desire. Second, it is an image of the novel itself, a dispossessed and homeless waif that refuses the comfortable communicational mode seen in the Balzacian intertext. Third, the polypary is the image of the critical position that corresponds ironically to the "livre sur rien," a phrase that itself, if applied, upsets the critical relation and the modes of perception of the writing by the critic, including the critic's reading of this very image. In short, the polypary is the represented and reflected sign of permanent disruption in Flaubert's novels. The polypary remarks the fact that there is no return, that home and ground are eternally absent, even where we most need and hope to find them. The polypary signs virtuality instead of verisimilar representation; it shows that representation, understood on a naive level, can only produce still life, or, in French, *nature morte*. The polypary is an abandoned ground, a wasteland, a sign of a permanent absence, a failure at representation, and an impossibility of recuperation and rememoration.

With the polypary we learn of the complete homelessness of the Flaubertian narrative. For there is no place to return, no base for the writing, which is always disruptive to home life. Who is at home in Flaubert? The eponymous and macaronic pun on his name notwithstanding, Homais is always where he belongs, as he is repetitively reinscribed by a series of signs that mark his self-stated and oft-repeated identity to himself:

And the sign, the whole width of the shop, has *Homais, pharmacien* in gold letters. Then, at the back of the shop, behind the great scales fixed to the counter, the word *laboratory* unfurls above a glass door, which, halfway up, repeats *Homais* again in gold letters on a black background. (1:357)

Homais's valueless iconicity is supported by the *bêtise* of public opinion; the apotheosis of this vacant sign of being at home comes with the *croix d'honneur*, sign of his permanent reinscription at his own locus: "He has a wealth of clients [*Il fait une clientèle d'enfer*]; authority handles him and public opinion protects him. He has just received the *croix d'honneur*" (1:611). In a different way, the Vaubyessard are at home, massively and historically; and the aura of this home in which Emma bathes for weeks is enough to keep her comfortable: "One of the women [the marquise herself] rose, came to meet Emma, and had her sit by her, on a love seat [*causeuse*], where she began to speak in a friendly way, as if she had known her for a long time" (1:334). Again, as the ironic reinscription of her windfall (*aubaine*) into presence, Mme Aubain of "Un coeur simple" is also at home. Over a period of fifty years, her presence gradually accretes, like that of the pictures in the chateau guaranteed by history, like that of the constant reinscription of "Homais, pharmacien," guaranteed by the sociolect. Her presence is also a consecrated one guaranteed by an aesthetic reinscription of identity with the stereotypical landscapes and etchings hanging on the walls (2:592). The narrative reinscribes representation as naturally belonging *to* this world and as being at home for itself *in* this world, as the harmonious joining *of* this world and its representations.

Flaubert too is at home in this world, at least in one specific way, since there is spiritual angst at the level of writing as an activity and there is a permanent crisis at the level of writing as product.[12] Presenting himself rhetorically at the neutral locus of narration, Flaubert is at home in his detailing and debunking of a cliché. The wealth of examples includes the inscription of received ideology of home and hearth that is the mark of the notary public, the guardian of ordered inscriptions:

Then through a clearing, a white house appears beyond a round lawn with a Cupid, finger to mouth, decorating it; two cast iron vases are at each end of the stoop; escutcheons shine on the door; it is the notary's house, and the most beautiful in the area [*et la plus belle du pays*]. (1:355)

Coming as it does after the strategically placed Cupid that is the apotheosis of petty bourgeois kitsch, the ironic phrase "and the most beautiful in the area" helps undo this received knowledge. The irony disengages the various parts of discourse from one another and from the illusion of representation.

Irony in the work dislocates the presumed relation between representational system and represented, and it nullifies the contract of readability. As Prendergast (202–3) puts it: "The absence of inverted commas maintains the *illusion* of the innocence or 'naturalness' of the writing. It superficially disguises its derivative character in order to proffer itself as pure 'representation,' in accordance with an aesthetic of naive realism."[13] Tony Tanner sees *Madame Bovary* as the paradigmatic novel of the violation of contracts at the level of theme and plot, but the contract between writer and reader is also violated (233–67). Following those lines, I am proposing that the violation of the contract between writer and reader is the phenomenological reflection of the violation of binding ties, cont(r)acts between writing as representation and the world it purportedly represents as an a priori verisimilar existence or as an a posteriori construct. The irony undoes both possibilities. Even more memorable is the Bovarys' wedding cake, which has a similar signification; its dismembered description ironically illustrates a maxim that will certainly *not* be the watchword of the novel: "Charbonnier est maître chez lui."[14] Charles will not be master of his castle: looking for his center, his place to sit, he too will wander from room to room. But what he finds is Emma's room, the room of displaced desire, where her love letters are hidden. After Emma's death, it is even clear to Charles that the room itself is a tissue of lies that states nothing more than *her* own disruption of home: "but the bedroom, her bedroom, stayed as it had been" (1:605).

Emma's room is a key locus of the question of home and its dislocation in Flaubert's novels. At a moral or even extramoral level, the return to a locus that stays the same, Emma's room, but which is never quite the same, being always a contradiction in its very construction, allows the narrative to dissociate truth and morality. Because the discourses of truth and lying and right and wrong have become unlinked, whole new fields of novelistic endeavor become possible. Zola and Proust, for example, do not have to justify their subject within their works, morality having been dissociated from truth (in the sense of rectitude). Moreover, because of the dissociation of truth and lying from a semiotics and semantics of value, it will eventually be possible in the novel to explore the problematics of meaning, which henceforth does not reside in a conjunction of discourses and ideologies: only a few years separate *Bouvard et Pécuchet* from Edouard Dujardin's *Les Lauriers sont coupés*.

In Emma's room we also discover a phenomenology of reading. Flaubert theatricalizes a certain mise-en-scène in the revelations in Emma's bedroom. There is a double figure at work: the figure of the secret of the room is discovered, but it is linked to the figure of the wrong *destinataire*, Charles reading his late wife's mail. Both the secret and the nondestinataire are longstanding and complementary narrative devices. Here, the double figure of secret and misreader is the sign of the rupture at the very level of the production of the narrative. The position of the misreader, whether parasitic or frankly oppositional, signals the disarray of the communicational model, the disjunction of values, and the disintegration of writing and its strategies. In the figure of Charles reading Emma's love letters we can easily see the figure of the displaced reader, the critic, the Baudelairean "hypocrite lecteur," who reads Flaubert's letters to Louise Colet in order to understand his or her own malaise with *Madame Bovary*. Again, the relation between reader and author can be seen as the phenomenological version of what is occurring within the writing.

So this is no simple reversal of a maxim, whereby Emma is the master of the house instead of Charles. Emma's displacement and unsettling functions are signs of something far more radical than a mere reversal of roles. Like Frédéric and Deslauriers, who are creatures of desire as well, and like the narrative itself, Emma is always finding a new bed: "For the fourth time in her life she slept in an unknown spot. The first was the day she entered the convent, the second, the day she arrived at Tostes, the third, at Vaubyessard, the fourth, this one; each figured in her life like the inauguration of a new phase" (1:369). Each new bed corresponds to a change in state, whether this change is a legal, moral, or emotional one; yet at the same time that there seems to be a willful act, Emma is moved around like an object. Each of her displacements is a sign of an economic system that uproots women as objects; it is a system that does not allow them ever to be at home anywhere. Home is not "a woman's place"; it is the locus of accreted and codified meanings and ideological structures into which she is thrust or from which she is pushed out. Home is where she is stranded (Gilbert and Gubar 107–83).

Thus the figure of the feminine is itself a disruption of the universe of the novel. But if the novel is understood through naive realism, the position of the woman as commodity happens also to be sociologically true in the world that the novel represents. Perceived as a natural truth, however specious and odious that may be, this sociological truth is in turn reinscribed in the novel and in the nineteenth century novel in general. The truth within the narrative is echoed and grounded by the superposition of this external "truth." The figure of the feminine is both disruptive immanently as a paradigm and theory of textuality and relationally through a reassociation of representation and represented. This conjunction too will be examined by Flaubert in *L'Education sentimentale* so he can extirpate the interwoven truths and lies fostered by a power structure backed by morality. Now, while I am not implying that Flaubert was a feminist before the fact—it would be a fatuous position to take—I am saying that within the crisis of textuality, the figure of the feminine is explicitly and implicitly put into question. Already in *Salammbô*, Flaubert attempts a fragmentation of the feminine when viewed from a phallocratic position; it is a dislocation accomplished through his technique of tesselated descriptions:

Amidst the menservants and itinerant salesmen wandered [*circulaient*] women of all nations, brown like ripe dates, greenish like olives, yellow like oranges, sold by sailors, chosen from the slums [*bouges*], stolen from caravans, taken in the sack of cities, whom one tired out with love as long as they were young, whom one besieged with punches when they were old, and who died in the retreats, in the gutters, among the chattel, with the abandoned beasts of burden. (1:758)

On the level of desire, Emma's situation is echoed by that of Frédéric in *L'Education sentimentale*. He too is displaced by desire; accordingly he too is never at home:

He went out in the world and had other loves. But the permanent memory of the first made them insipid to him; and then the vehemence of desire, the very flower of feeling was lost. . . . Years passed; and he withstood the idling [*désoeuvrement*] of his mind and the inertia of his heart. (2:448–49)

Thus many of Flaubert's characters, including Frédéric and Deslauriers, are figures of feminine desire. In Flaubert's novels, no creature of desire is ever at home; desire itself is always mobile and always displaced. If to possess is to be masculine since possession implies a fixity, to desire is to be feminine because it means to be displaced and "moved." To desire is thus to be moved away from fixed signs, from meaning, and from significations.

Bouvard and Pécuchet, who desire knowledge, are also not at home. Bouvard's room is a series of empty reflections, false significations, and slippages that will be ironically reinscribed on a large scale when he inherits from his so-called uncle who is "really" his father:

Bouvard's room, well polished, with percale curtains and mahogany furniture, enjoyed [*jouissait*] a balcony with a view of the river. The two main ornaments were a liquor tray in the middle of the dresser and daguerrotypes of friends the length of the mirror; an oil painting [of his uncle] was in the alcove. (2:717)

Mechanized versions of art, the daguerrotypes contrast with the so-called natural, that is to say romanticized, representations in "Un coeur simple." The daguerrotypes reflect no one special and reflect nowhere; their representational value is so reduced that they have no image to give. And the uncle/father is ex-centric: the one position that would authorize home and hearth, validity and history, is put to one side in an alcove that is out of the direct line of sight and decidedly off-center. Home then becomes the spot where writing functionally agrees with what it "represents," so that by the time of *Bouvard et Pécuchet* not even Homais, though anchored in *Madame Bovary*, would be at home.

In *Bouvard et Pécuchet*, the world becomes a vast polypary, endlessly reflected in the funhouse of a hall of mirrors, where even death itself, still meaningful in *Madame Bovary*, occupies a meaningless niche: "Their house looked like a museum. . . . When one had crossed the threshold, one encountered a stone trough (a Gallo-Roman sarcophagus), then one's eyes were struck by the hardware" (2:798). By this last novel, the only reason to set up a home for the eternally homeless is that it provides a functional literality that marks something, though incorrectly, once and for all. When Bouvard and Pécuchet begin to converse and ultimately set up house together, this economic and literary state is prompted by nothing more than the fact that their names are written in their hats. Similarly, there is nothing more than a functional reason when it is a question of Bouvard and Mme Bordin setting up a home together. Bouvard makes a most unemotional proposal of marriage from which desire, the *trou-blion* of home life and textual safety, is clearly barred: "Our linens have the same mark, a "B"! We shall unite our initials [*majuscules*]" (2:876).

Faced with the polypary, Emma is as *unheimlich* as is the polypary itself; she too produces a reflection that betrays the deadness of the situation. Perhaps Emma is at home once, when she is still at Les Bertaux, or more exactly when she has returned to Les Bertaux from the convent school. For it is this return to her father's house that marks, in its repetition, the possibility of being at home: being at home means being at home again. Home is essentially a state of repetition and reinscription, something that Flaubert seeks endlessly to avoid, since repetition implies ground and the crisis that he is eternally inscribing refuses both this ground and its safety. So Emma's home is only hers for a while, since it is soon to be left for the marriage bed. Les Bertaux temporarily provides a state of home and boundedness, something that Flaubert demonstrates with an excess of description. Home, or the comforts of realism, is not where there is a supplement of useless details, as Barthes would have it, but where the object always exceeds the space allotted to it. It is where the "thing" cannot be fit simply into a niche in a vestibule, an opening in a polypary, or a room in a house:

The shovel, the pincers, and the bellows, all of colossal size, shone like polished steel, while along the walls extended an abundance of cooking equipment, in which the clear flame of the household [*foyer*] sparkled unequally with the first light of day coming through the windows. (1:304)

Home is where the object does *not* fit; it is also where the reflection and representation exceed, multiply, and ultimately refuse the prosaic framing of Flaubert's commas. As Debray-Genette puts it: "The describer is a prisoner of the object he causes to be born, caught in his own trap" (221). It is that way at Les Bertaux, with the unequal reflections of light; it is the same at the chateau: "The candles of the candelabra elongated the flames on the silver covers; the cut crystal, covered with a dull vapor, sent pale rays back and forth" (1:335). Even the first chapter of *Salammbô*, "Le Festin," shows the same figure, the excess of identity that characterizes the novel and its centeredness, before Salammbô herself, the figure of feminine desire, appears: "The craters, edged with convex mirrors, multiplied the enlarged image of things" (1:712).

Home is marked by the excess of object over representation and of image over inscription. But most of the world represented in Flaubert's narratives does not have the luxury of this excess of the nonrepresentable. As Derrida points out in "Envoi" (*Psyché* 139), "To think the limit of representation is to think the unrepresented or the unrepresentable." This unrepresentable is both what one *cannot* and what one *must not* represent. Homelessness is the usual state, where everything does have a place, where nothing is in excess, and where everything can be described. The state of homelessness is the one that fits the novel and in which, in turn, the novel fits. In this case, things can be added and subtracted by simple mechanical formulas. Thus the operative law of the universe of homelessness is a mathematical equation that turns into a zero-sum problem, after which there nothing is left. The universe of homelessness is one of accounting; it is a world of debts with few, if any, credits. If Emma does not pay the debt that she has incurred, all her things will be seized (1:558). The possessions are seizable because these objects have never been at home. Since the Bovarys' house is not a home, even the things that in other narratives or other situations might provide the excess of reflection can be disposed of: "He had to sell the silver piece by piece; afterwards, he sold the living room furniture. The apartments became bare" (1:605).

This excess always upsets things and is itself unseated; the very nature of the excess turns home into homelessness. Again, the exception is *L'Education sentimentale*, where the excess of desire is accompanied by the possibility of instant and complete translation. In *L'Education sentimentale* there is a faithful representation that does not exist elsewhere in Flaubert's work: "This bit of paper represented fifteen big bags of money to him" (2:211). Like paper money for the fool in *Faust II* (ll.6161–72), this paper can buy for Frédéric a quantity of things and services then enumerated by Flaubert, including a wealth of possibilities.

Absent elsewhere, the possibility of mutation and translation in *L'Education sentimentale* is less a yielding to the capitalist model of representation against which Flaubert always struggled than it is the assumption necessary to the demonstration of the mutations of desire. Still, excess is often reduced according to the normal model. Similarly, the Arnoux's house, factitious creation that it is, somehow never lives up to the excess of its original production. There is an excess of desire that is initially seen in Frédéric's first vision, be it image, fantasy, or representation, of Mme Arnoux. This excess is also seen in the hybrid state of art and industry that is the excessive sign of the present of production of *L'Art industriel.* This excess will be undone and unseated by the author throughout the novel. Hence, the Arnoux's house can be dismantled, and the effects sold in a liquidation sale (2:442).

Normally, however, the excess does upset things, because it is a mechanical excess, not an organic one. Where there is no uncanny reminder of the illusions of representation, the object can easily become a fragment, a detail to be separated, sold, or distributed. And whoever can master the economic system can participate in the exchange and thus can be said, at least temporarily, to be "at home": Frédéric "bought, all at once, the coach, the horse, the furniture, and two jardinieres taken from Arnoux's, to put at either side of his living room door" (2:159). Where there is an excess, where not everything can be represented, since there is always an image in excess that is an effect greater than the piece, there is a home with a *génie du lieu*. At home, things double, exceed, pass, and go beyond the place conveniently assigned to them, yet they remain there as well, not slipping away, displaced like the homeless objects and characters of the works:

A straight double stairway, with a red carpet and copper rods, stood against the high walls in shiny stucco. At the bottom of the steps, there was a banana tree whose wide leaves fell over the plush of the staircase. Two bronze candelabra had porcelain globes hanging on chains; the vents of the gaping heaters gave off a heavy air; and all that was heard was the tick-tock of a large clock, standing at the other end of the entryway, under a panoply. (2:50–51)

If for Flaubert home is characterized by an excess, both of objects and of meaning, a Benjaminesque aura that goes beyond translation into a narrative of representation, the state of homelessness is characterized by the complete framing of objects, whether or not there is meaning. Thus at Tostes, which is *not* home for Emma, there is a hodgepodge of empty shells of objects; even if they are devoid or voided of meaning, at least they are in their proper places. They are not covered with the patina of authenticity, the mildew of the excess of life, but rather with the dust of fragmentation and fall-out; there is a "quantity of other dusty things whose use was impossible to guess" (1:320).

The process of textual displacement discussed above functions in the realist narratives of Flaubert's mature production. With *Bouvard et Pécuchet*, there is an imperative for metanarration, even at the levels of theme and plot. This last novel is a studied debunking of the ideology that underlines every narrative process that can possibly be inscribed in the writing. The book is geared to producing an anatomy of the process of representation through the means offered by narrative discourse. Nowhere is the establishment, and hence the artificiality, of house and home more evident. Certainly, Flaubert shows us the fiction of the entire situation. Reinscribing the heterogeneous group of objects at Tostes, Flaubert has Bouvard and Pécuchet first acquire "a bunch of things 'that might possibly be useful'" (2:725) for determining sense and meaning. Dusted off, they are still the same inscribed objects of *Madame Bovary* and the belatedly famed barometer of "Un coeur simple." Yet this *tas de choses* is ultimately no different from Frédéric's possible acquisition of Deslauriers himself, considered throughout, but ultimately deferred until the homoerotic end of the novel: "He got the idea to have Deslauriers move in. But how would he welcome *her*, his future mistress" (2:159). Thus the last novel recapitulates and repeats but does not return the structuring of desire and communication that is one of the basic laws of desire in *L'Education sentimentale*.

Reinscribed too in *Bouvard et Pécuchet* is the most tenacious ideology of Flaubert's novels: the act or theory of representation that sees object and constructed world as being naturally related to the world on which they are the mark of culture. The house sits naturally amid the gardens, landscapes, and *terres* of the park:

They returned by the hollow under the beech wood. From that side, the house showed its courtyard and its front.

It was painted white with yellow accents [*des réchampis de couleur jaune*]. The shed and the storeroom, the wash house and the woodshed formed two lower wings. The kitchen led into a small room. After that, there was the hallway, a larger second room, and the living room. The four bedrooms on the second floor gave onto the corridor that faced the courtyard. Pécuchet took one for his collections; the last was going to be the library; and upon opening the cupboards, they found other books, but did not give in to the whim to read the titles. The most important thing was the garden. (2:731)

Ironic reinscription of the entire set-up, this situation of the house shows the fiction of trying to establish a home. At best what can occur is a sterile representation of a home. Mastery of the economic systems and of the representational systems produces a collection of synecdoches that never quite add up to a whole, for their house, as we know, "looked like a museum" (2:798).

Flaubert's conclusion on the figure of the "home" is ironic. We have noted that Flaubert himself is only really at home in the state of breaking up a home by dismantling objects and debunking ideologies. Yet how can he be home in a state of homelessness? Flaubert is at home when his is the only position safe from destruction, when he can control what moves and what does not move, what is bought, described, sold, detailed, or fragmented. In the few scenes at home (Les Bertaux, Mme Aubain's house, Vaubyessard), Flaubert is quick to get the reader or critic out the door. For at home, there may always be a place for the reader; at least metaphorically, the reader may find an adequately comfortable chair. What that means is that there is always a position other than that of the invisible enunciator that is a safe one. Thus there is a comfortable ideological position, a haven of throne and altar; there is a spot that implicitly resists the *livre sur rien*. Since the reader, akin to Emma and Frédéric, is also a figure of desire, he or she too must be uprooted. Like Emma, the reader is chattel to be moved according to Flaubert's inscription of the rhetorical reader at any point of the narrative. Without this constant displacement that is ironically necessary for the stability of Flaubert's writing, the novel too becomes a museum: Flaubert's novel would turn into the Louvre depicted by Zola in *L'Assommoir*, a locus of fixed meaning and mechanized viewing.

Oddly enough, then, the difference between home and homeless-ness in Flaubert is one that depends on the failure of representation. Representation of home is exceeded by the natural image of things; home is that which cannot ultimately be inscribed in the novel. Homelessness, which we normally take as complete uprooting, is that which is organized by framing, by narrative, even a process of narrative destruction that is that of fragmentation, detailing, and dis-membering, into discrete packets separated by commas. In Flaubert home has no home, is homeless, and the homeless are always every-where to be found, at home, in the novel.

Reference Matter

Notes

CHAPTER I

1. It is in this light that one may consider the work of textual geneticists partly to be a reaction against the unanchored textuality of poststructuralism.

2. Indeed, as early as 1979, Rodolphe Gasché provided a brilliant critique of the taming of deconstruction in his article "Deconstruction as Criticism."

3. As Thomas DiPiero has effectively shown in his work on the early French novel, the breakdown was long in coming. Writing of Furetière, DiPiero notes pithily that the author "allows the disjunction separating the referential and the analytico-ideological domains to take hold" (175). My point here is that, with the nineteenth-century novel, these two domains are supposed to be coterminous; when the breakdown occurs, it is a radical one.

CHAPTER 2

1. Stendhal's remarkable *Vie de Rossini* has recently been reissued in paperback. This availability may spur some to read the work and discover its amazing construction of the character of Rossini, who seems at times the germ of many novelistic creations. The original antihero, Stendhal's Rossini is a combination of narrative perfection, hedonism, sloth, and magic. See my short article "Rossini's Castrati."

2. We should not imagine, however, that what is "natural" is any less ironic for Stendhal: "This evening, I saw, or thought I saw, the triumph of

the natural in a young person who truly seems to have a great personality. . . . She would only have to change her manners a bit, but she thinks of it as something lowly with consequences for the rest of her life, to move away from the natural for one moment" (255). On the role of nature in Stendhal, as well as his relation to Rousseau and the latter's ideology of nature, see Crouzet.

3. Now obviously many modern novels do not have one or several of these characteristics. These absences may be seen as the negations of part of the ideal form of the genre but they could also be the return of the suppressed negations found within the genre, even at its origins. More generally, however, one could quarrel with any aspect of this definition that neglects the dichotomy between theory and praxis, the dialectics of form, and a myriad of other indications about which many thousands of pages have been written.

4. For example, the theories proposed in *Le Rouge et le Noir* are versions of and justifications for the acts of representation in that novel, as I have pointed out in my article "A Chronicle of Production."

5. By no means am I suggesting that my far-from-comprehensive sketch is anything more than a heuristic bit of shorthand. The literature on the evolution of the novel is voluminous. See especially Ian Watt's landmark study, *The Rise of the Novel*; Julia Kristeva's work *Le Texte du Roman*; Thomas Di-Piero's study of the French novel; Percy Adams's study of the interrelationship between travel literature and the evolution of the novel; and English Showalter's study of the evolution of the novel.

6. I am using these works as examples and I do not mean to suggest a linear approach to understanding the development of the eighteenth-century English novel. No such version could account for the complexities of the novel, either in England or in France; no such explanation could illuminate *Tristram Shandy*, for example. At the same time, Stendhal, perspicacious reader that he is, has an understanding of what he likes and what he does not like in the literature of his forebears and contemporaries, and he clearly can see, in some of this writing, germs that may eventually prove to be useful.

7. The imposition of the dialectical reading can have all sorts of modifications depending on the point of view of the critic who sees perhaps more of a struggle between text and context in the real world than between text and reception or between text and ideal. Thus there are various ways of modifying the dialectic of accounting for a change in direction or of avoiding a teleology of narrative form.

8. Ann Jefferson's argument misses the mark because she relies too heavily on analogy: "The would-be novelist is indeed in a closely analogous position to the would-be lover, and furthermore, . . . fiction itself is specifically

responsible for the predicaments of the lover" (47). Following the excellent work of René Girard, Jefferson sees fiction as a mediating device that works on the levels of theme and plot, but the work does not help us understand what is at stake on a theoretical level.

9. Stendhal even suggests that as far as maneuvers are concerned we could compare Lovelace and Tom Jones (238n).

10. Those words are what Julien Sorel reads on the paper found in the church (*Romans* 1:240). In the section of the preface to "Les Cenci" in the *Chroniques italiennes* (*Romans* 2:679), where Stendhal is writing about Don Juan, he uses the same expression: "Making fun of the judge: is it not the first step, the first attempt made by every little beginning Don Juan?" The separation of truth and representation is changed here into a separation of authority and action, or official and unofficial truth.

11. The references to Madame de Lafayette are 38, 97, 216; to Scott, including *The Pirate, The Bride of Lammermoor, The Heart of Midlothian, Old Mortality, Rob Roy*, and *Ivanhoe*, are 48, 55, 64, 89, 94, 96, 106, 122, 140, 150, 157, 252, 272; to Rousseau 104, 145, 156, 218, 226, 253, 261, 308, 338; to Madame de Staël 60, 81, 156, 230, 333; to Laclos 85, 86, 226; and to Richardson 90 and 163. Oddly, inclusion in this list seems to be the only reference to *Tom Jones* in the work.

12. The word "wayward" is in English in Stendhal's work. Jefferson (61) comments that the "'waywardness' . . . links the lover, the novelistic text in which he may be represented, and its happy reader. It is in this sense that *De l'amour* may be considered a novelistic text." The problem is far more radical in Stendhal: the position of the reader is by no means unproblematic, nor is the "novelistic text" a closed, readable act of writing at this point.

13. As will be seen in the discussion below, I find the defining moment for Fabrice's independence (not as a person but as a function within the construction of the narrative) to be precisely the moment at which he establishes semiotic independence, that is to say, the time he spends in prison.

14. Stendhal rejected an alternate version of the sentence just quoted: "This book decided Fabrice's personality" (2:1384). It is too close to being an unironic repetition of Julien Sorel's Koran to be a valid means of continuation, a problem Naomi Schor (135–46) discusses in relation to *Lamiel*.

15. Shoshana Felman problematizes the novel as she underlines the fact that Fabrice's linguistic apprenticeship is both a search for meaning and a search for a someone to receive his messages: a *destinataire* (196); thus this apprenticeship involves both the contents or themes of the work and the narrative forms that structure and modify these contents. Among other studies of semioticity in the work are those done by Peter Brooks, who pays special attention to Fabrice in prison; William Berg; and Lois Ann Russell, who

provides a thematic discussion of writing. Vivian Kogan's work, while interesting, is unfortunately marred by a conflation of signified and referent.

16. It matters for the development of the novel as a whole, but at this point, what is important is the fact that this mark is the inscription of difference.

17. As a parallel, one might think of how language and accent are presented in films. Quite often, during the heyday of Hollywood, if an American film was set in Russia, for example, the Russian characters would have "Russian" accents even when they talked among themselves. Despite the fact that they were presumably speaking unaccented Russian, it was presented as accented English.

18. Examples from Balzac and Proust will illuminate the means by which realist praxis pairs power and authority with correct writing. Balzac's Vautrin is not merely the successful and powerful figure he is because he can successfully penetrate others and read their minds, but also because he is adept at remarking and rewriting what is already there. Proust's Marcel eventually overcomes the solitary pleasures of reading and the masturbatory fantasies and modes, both theoretical and other, of perception that go with it. Finally, in a double act of inscription, the performance of the Vinteuil Septet, which has come into being because of the act of reading turned into writing accomplished by Mlle Vinteuil's friend, Marcel changes from reader to writer and begins the long process in *Le Temps retrouvé* that moves toward the act of inscription that proleptically becomes the book that we read.

19. Rabine (132) considers the prison "a sort of Stendhalian signature," with descriptive factors including the mountains, stream, and the view from above that recapitulate the beginning of the novel. Thus the prison scene is the novel of the novel and the laboratory for fiction-making. Victor Brombert ("Esquisse" 260) points out that one of the felicitous aspects of the metaphorical prison is that it brings knowledge: "Finally, the metaphoric prison turns out to be happy to the extent that it brings knowledge. Thus the young Marcel, in *Combray*, discovers that the obscure freshness of his room offers 'the complete spectacle of the summer' to his mind." On the thematic level the Tour Farnèse is, according to Brombert (247), a "fortress of dream and of the contemplation of love" and thus is found "on the side of love."

20. *Le Rouge et le Noir* shows both systems at work. On the one hand there is a post-Rousseauistic system that depends on a transcendental signified: ardor, desire, love, and ambition. On the other hand, from the very beginning, there is a structuring of the narrative to control flows, to determine paths, to participate in the master plot of an economy of exchange that depends on the transcendental signifiers' precedence: the name-of-the-father, the capital of the new society, the proper writing, as I have shown in my article "A Chronicle of Production."

21. In a syllepsis, two different kinds of complements or modifiers, usually one concrete and one figurative, are yoked to one word.

22. The development of this space of representation allows for movement to occur within a system. The theorization of the system is the equivalent of the development of the ontological and epistemological groundings of the work. The ontological structuring of a system and its theorization give the potential for the existence of the system. Thus the establishment of a channel of communication is precisely the opening up of a potential space that can itself be theorized. The theorization of the means by which this occurs is the development of the epistemological ground for the system, where it becomes evident how what is, is knowable. For this, the communication must firmly establish itself as grounded in a system. As is the case with the *Rouge*, each of these theoretical presuppositions brings with it an implicit means of undoing itself. The establishment of a ground for the potentiality of communication in prison is based on the presence of the preexisting law; but this law is now to be occluded in order for the system to exist.

23. Béatrice Didier (213) reminds us that for Stendhal, the Italian language is the language of the mother, the language associated with her and with an Oedipal psychobiography as well. At a certain point, Stendhal relearns Italian, "which is nothing other than the maternal language, obliterated by death, the language of the unconscious which unites him to the mother." Thus the strategic reappearance of Italian at this point would be a reminder of the latent Oedipal relations between Gina and Fabrice, repressed anew by the insistence of the otherwise unnecessary translation into French.

CHAPTER 3

1. I should like to thank Éric Bordas for his illuminating comments on this white-handed reader. I shall address the problem of this reader in the part of this chapter devoted to misreading.

2. For a discussion of impotence and emasculation in French romanticism, see Margaret Waller's excellent book *The Male Malady*. To a great extent, the Balzac of the philosophical works invokes the same model of impotence and emasculation that Waller describes.

3. See Lucienne Frappier-Mazur for an excellent catalogue of the metaphoric descriptions of Balzac's characters.

4. As Roland Barthes has shown in *S/Z*, these neuter or neutral figures are fundamental to an understanding of "Sarrasine" and, I would add, other works like it in the *Etudes philosophiques*. They are points of reversal or symbolic changes within the system and are the marks of a romantic ideology.

5. Thus writing can be seen as difference in the panoply of meanings that Derrida gives it (*Ecriture* and *Marges*).

6. Indeed, as William Paulson points out, one-quarter of the novel consists of recycled material, a process he relates both to a Balzacian aesthetic and to a vitalist philosophy (33).

7. Some editions of *Illusions perdues*, including the Intégrale edition, reprint the titles Balzac gave to his novel in serial form. One section is entitled "Study on the Art of Singing Palinodes" (511). Balzac's ironic version of palinody shows the complex relations among three types of writing: journalism, the theater, and "more serious" literature, such as Lucien's *Les Marguerites*. See Richard Terdiman's excellent work (117–46) for a study of journalism in Balzac's Paris in which the critic illuminates the complex nature of writing such palinodes.

8. In his introduction to this novel in the Intégrale edition, Citron says that this novel *Olympia* was in fact, "an old text, entitled *Fragments of a Novel Published during the Empire* [*Fragments d'un roman publié sous l'Empire*], intended for a collection of *Fantasies* that never saw the light of day. The novel appeared in September, 1833, in a periodical, the *Causeries du monde*." Thus from the beginning, these fragments are no more than fragments.

9. As Citron (3:220n) points out in a note to the Intégrale edition, Balzac will produce two more exceptions to this rule: *Modeste Mignon* and *Les Paysans*. Even then, these exceptional amalgamations are rare in Balzac's work.

10. This femininity and aristocratic origin have recently been successfully challenged by Franc Schuerewegen in *Balzac contre Balzac* (15–32) and by Stéphane Vachon in his comments on the phrase "main blanche" in his edition of *Le Père Goriot*. Their work underlines the simple fact that the indeterminacy of the reader in such important areas makes him or her not a neutral narratee, but always a bad reader.

11. Thus I am not in agreement with Mary Ann Piwowarczyk (162) who feels that the most serious objection to Prince's formulation concerns the zero-degree narratee's knowledge of referents, and more specifically, knowledge of proper names. For a close reading of Prince's article as well as that of Piwowarczyk, and of Iser's book, see Ray. I do not mean to suggest a criticism of Prince's work here. Rather, I am trying to use what I perceive as a critical blind spot to develop my own consideration of the functions of the reader in Balzac.

12. The fascinating articles published on this matter are too extensive to mention. The entire issue of *GLYPH* 7 (1980) is devoted to selected papers from the Strasbourg Colloquium on Genre and many of the articles engage this issue. See especially Lacoue-Labarthe and Derrida ("La Loi du genre"). See also Derrida (*Eperons*) on the question of writing the feminine in Nietzsche.

13. If it is easy enough, however, to hypothesize the existence of a queer reader for works such as *Le Père Goriot* and "La Fille aux yeux d'or" because of their content, it is certainly almost as easy to posit a queer reader for any other Balzac work. On reading Balzac queerly, see Michael Lucey, "Balzac's Queer Cousins." In general, on the problematics of narrative and homosexuality, I refer the reader to my two books on twentieth-century French literature and homosexuality: *The Shock of Men* and *Alcibiades at the Door*.

14. Just as anyone who reads the *peau de chagrin*, i.e., the skin, is diminished, anyone who reads the *Peau de chagrin*, i.e., the novel, is supposedly magnified or enlightened.

15. Once again, it is clear that this zero degree in Balzac brings into question, as has already been mentioned, the absolute division perceived in literary history between Balzac and Flaubert. Without making direct reference to Flaubert in this part of his study, Prendergast (88) notes the very Flaubertian nature of the systems at work. Speaking of the various "deals" in *Illusions perdues* and *Splendeurs et misères des courtisanes*, he says, "Deals, pacts, contracts are thus shadowed by the spectre of forgery. . . . Much of the action turns on fabricated publications, falsified documents, on the drama of the *signature*." He adds, "The signature, guarantee of contract, here guarantees nothing. It founds a process of circulation and exchange in which things are not as they appear, not what they *represent*" (89).

16. This narratological function finds a "pure" rhetorical version in the combination of contrasts called an enthymeme, which is a rhetorical term denoting several things, including maintaining the truth of a proposition from the assumed truth of its contrary, an abbreviated syllogism, and a pairing of contrasts or what Chaneles and Snyder (91) call a "clash of contraries" (Lanham 41). Genette relates the enthymeme both to an invasion of the story by the discourse and to a willful act of detouring the writing toward the author*s goal: "those enthymemes characteristic of Balzacian discourse, which gladden connoisseurs and some of which barely dissimulate their function of filling in holes [*colmatage*]" ("Vraisemblance" 11). In a completely different perspective, Naomi Schor arrives at a conclusion about proper and improper as central functions of Balzacian narrative. In her study of the relations between fiction and interpretation, Schor relates the acts of hermeneutic interpretation and misinterpretation to an act of exclusion in *Le Cousin Pons*. She says that "interpretation as practiced by the secondary characters is a form of persecution, the hermeneutic object is a scapegoat" ("Fiction," in Suleiman and Crosman 169n).

17. From the point of view of contemporary criticism, Balzac's mention of the torrent is not at all a chance occurrence. Mehlman writes of Diderot's use of the word *cataracte*: "as a discursive machine, the 'cataract' is thus fun-

damentally political, allowing one to effect a transgression while affirming the terms of the barrier" (22). See also Michel Serres's study ("Noise") of one of Balzac's most self-reflexive works, "Le Chef-d'oeuvre inconnu."

18. Naomi Schor (*Reading in Detail* 141–47) relates the sublime in Balzac's *Le Curé de Tours* to "the last vestige of classicism" (147). In relating the sublime to the theatrical, as opposed to the novelistic and specifically the realistic, I am taking a similar position.

CHAPTER 4

1. I would like to thank Ross Chambers for reminding me of this scene as well as for giving me the useful expression *nec tecum nec sine te* used often below. More generally, I would like to express my gratitude to him here for his generous, insightful, and helpful commentary on this whole part of the study.

2. On literary hauntings, see Esther Rashkin, Avital Ronell, and Jacques Derrida (*Spectres*).

3. Making the same error in his Latin quote, Edgar Allan Poe notes in "The Purloined Letter" (697): "It is all very well to talk about the *facilis descensus Averni*; but in all kinds of climbing, as Catalani said of singing, it is far more easy to get up than to come down."

4. This seems all the more plausible if a passage from Dante (later quoted by T. S. Eliot in *The Wasteland*) is interpolated here, in which it is clear that the existence of talk is predicated on the nonexistence of the return: "If I thought that my answer were to one who might ever return to the world, this flame would shake no more; but since from this depth none ever returned alive, if what I hear is true, I answer you without fear of infamy" (*Inf.* 27:61–66).

5. Villers-Cotteret is moreover the town of Alexandre Dumas to whom the *Filles du feu* is dedicated. So the danger of the vulgar is coupled with an ambiguous reference to another writer to whom homage is paid.

6. The well-known passage from Homer reads as follows: "There are two gates through which the insubstantial dreams issue. One pair of gates is made of horn, and one of ivory. Those of the dreams which issue through the gate of sawn ivory, these are deceptive dreams, their message is never accomplished. But those that come into the open through the gates of the polished horn accomplish the truth for any mortal who sees them." William Beauchamp (98–99) points out the reference to Homer and mentions a poem by Gautier as well, "Au Sommeil."

7. Daniel Couty (15–17) reminds the reader of the difference between the book of memory and the book to come, with references being made to chapters 1 and 42 of the *Vita nuova*. Michael Pitwood (230) discusses the influ-

ence of Dante on Nerval among others, and alludes to this reference to the *Vita nuova*. He goes on to relate the references to Dante in *Aurélia* to Nerval's personal concerns and especially to his obsession with a Beatrice-like goddess (232–34).

8. The passage is as follows:

> Sunt geminae somni portae, quarum altera fertur
> cornea, qua veris facilis datur exitus umbris,
> altera candenti perfecta nitens elephanto,
> sed falsa ad caelum mittunt insomnia manes.
> his ibi tum natum Anchises unaque Sibyllam
> prosequitur dictis portaque emittit eburna,
> ille viam secat ad navis sociosque revisit (*Aen.* 6:893–99).

9. According to Freudian theory, the backward glance at representability (*Rücksicht auf Darstellbarkeit*) is one of the primary processes involved in the organization of the dream. In a dream, the dream-work weaves together the heterogeneous strands that make up the dream through the constraints of the considerations of representability and of secondary revision. The dream world and literary world seem most clearly related through the process of inscription of the figure that defines both the dream and the literary work. In his exceptional work *Discours, figure*, Jean-François Lyotard places great stress on the notion of figurability as it relates to the considerations of representability and to secondary revision: "The *Rücksicht auf Darstellbarkeit* is the arrangement of an initial text, which has two goals according to Freud: to illustrate this text, but also to replace some of its parts with figures" (249). The eruption or interruption of the figure within the work is for Lyotard (51) the presence of nonlanguage in language. For Julia Kristeva (*Révolution* 60), the considerations of representability are the index of a figurability that is the articulation between the semiotic and the thetic. This thetic aspect is that cut (*coupure*) that produces the position of signification (41). Yet though there is a mimetic aspect relating writing to dream for Nerval, as there is one relating writing to folie, the eruption always occurs within the frame of writing, and the eruption of the figural and of the thetic is refigured as writing. For more on this matter, see Laurence Porter 66–67, 70–73. Freud's discussion of the material can be found in the *S.E.*: 5:343–44, 488–503; and in the *G.W.*: 2–3:349, 492–507.

10. The Italian word order will become important to the argument that continues. Here is the whole passage:

> . . . volsimi a la sinistra . . .
> per dicere a Virgilio: "Men che dramma
> di sangue m'è rimaso che non tremi:

conosco i segni de l'antica fiamma."
Ma Virgilio n'avea lasciati scemi
di sé, Virgilio dolcissimo patre,
Virgilio a cui per mia salute die'mi;
né quantunque perdeo l'antica matre,
valse a le guance nette di rugiada
che, lagrimando, non tornasser atre.
"Dante, perché Virgilio se ne vada,
non pianger anco, non piangere ancora;
ché pianger ti conven per altra spada."

11. In his introduction to *Faust II*, Nerval himself makes an analogy between the descent of Orpheus into the underworld in search of Eurydice and
Faust's own search for the soul of Helen.

12. Freccero (208) has referred to the crucial importance of this passage
in Dante's work. Following the passage from the direct quotation of Virgil
to the translation of "agnosco veteris flammae vestigia," to the "Eurydice"
passage, he notes: "The progression from direct quotation to direct translation to merest allusion is an effacement, further and further away from the
letter of Virgil's text, as Virgil fades away in the dramatic representation to
make way for Beatrice. It is then, for the first time, that the poet is called by
name: 'Dante!' The intrusion of Virgil's words into Dante's text is at that
point the mark of poetic maturity."

CHAPTER 5

1. Alain Corbin masterfully shows how the struggle against the *flou*, mud,
miasmas, and the like continues from the middle of the eighteenth century
through Haussmann's sweeping reforms of the city of Paris. Corbin (28)
notes that "mud, or more exactly the vapors that arise from mud, becomes
the object of an anxious discourse" by the middle of the eighteenth century.
This anxiety still continues a century later; Haussmann's project can be understood purely in ideological terms. Georges Knaebel, whom Corbin
quotes (307), notes that for Haussmann, "there is the city that one beauti-
fies, in which the bourgeois is given in representation, at the interior of
which nothing must shock the senses—which explains the expulsion of the
dirty, the poor, the unclean, the nauseating—and the 'non-city.'"

2. I have discussed this buzzing in my book *Flaubert and Sons*.

3. In a passage on fumigation, Corbin (78) makes a list that could have
come directly from *Bouvard et Pécuchet*: "Fumigation with paper, old shoes,
and other smelly substances calms the rise of vapors and cures amenorrhea.
Smoke from cephalic powders strengthens the brain. Fumigation with as-

tringent mixtures heads off a cold. . . . Fumigation with cinnabar cures the pox."

4. In her reading of Flaubert, Janet Beizer devotes one chapter to Flaubert's letters to Louise Colet, one chapter to Colet's novel *La Servante*, which the critic sees as a "surrogate for all her missing letters to Flaubert" (101), and one to *Madame Bovary*. Recently, Martine Reid has published a solid reading of the letters for themselves in her book *Flaubert correspondant*.

5. Neefs, by the way, begins his contribution to the same volume, "L'imaginaire des documents," with a quote from the *Correspondance* as well (175).

6. The first version of *L'Education sentimentale*, for example, gives horizons as limits and not as extensions into the infinite: "While you were reading a book you liked, savoring each word, tasting each sentence, and turning around in your head as you would turn a juicy fruit on your tongue, entering the author's thought [*pensée*], and dreaming, at the horizons it lets you discover, you undoubtedly have jumped from pain at the sounds of an organ grinder starting his song, or from the noise of a door opening to let in an unexpected visit" (*Education* 1:307).

7. Erich Auerbach succinctly gives the classic formula for the difference between Balzac and Flaubert: "It was in conformity with [Balzac's] emotional, fiery, and uncritical temperament, as well as with the romantic way of life, to sense hidden demonic forces everywhere and to exaggerate expression to the point of melodrama. In the next generation, which comes on the stage in the fifties, there is a strong reaction in this respect. In Flaubert realism becomes impartial, impersonal, and objective" (482).

8. See, however, the amusing letter that Flaubert writes to his niece Caroline, April 24, 1857: "I thank you for having written me such a nice letter. Your spelling is better than in those you sent me on previous trips, and the style is good as well. If you sit long enough in my armchair, put your elbows on my table, and take your head in your hands, you may wind up a writer" (*Corr.* 2:707).

9. In the *Dictionnaire des idées reçues*, Flaubert says, "Waxing. Only good if you do it yourself" (2:1004).

10. Sartre (2:1664) mentions a polypary in the letters.

11. Barthes's detail may not have been the most appropriately chosen one, since the barometer represents a moment in discourse that attempts to translate the world exactly into signs. This is a process not at all alien to Barthes himself: "the metro I take, with complicated changes—but I am stubborn—to see the barometric pressure on Avenue Rapp in order to set my new barometer" (*Incidents* 104).

12. In a letter of August 14, 1853, to Louise Colet, Flaubert writes: "As

for *Bovary*, impossible even to think about it. I must be *at home* to write" (*Corr.* 2:391).

13. Prendergast's remark correctly separates the question of irony from the semantic fields in which critics often put it. There have been many cogent studies of irony in Flaubert, though critics rarely see it as a rhetorical figure whose function dis-orders the readability of the writing. Irony is a question in the fields of representation and theory. Along these lines, Prendergast criticizes the concept of readability in Barthes's readings of Flaubert: "One can equally argue that the story does not 'remain readable' (i.e. representational) as a ruse designed to throw into sharper relief the ironic deconstruction of the conventions of narrative representation."

14. As Tanner (352) points out, "detailing is dismembering." The detailed description of the cake breaks down both the cake as an object and as an ideology. For other discussions of the debunking of ideological and discursive systems, see Tanner's pages on Binet (254–65) and my *Flaubert and Sons* (19–68).

Bibliography

Adams, Percy G. *Travel Literature and the Evolution of the Novel*. Lexington: The University Press of Kentucky, 1983.

Alighieri, Dante. *The Divine Comedy*. Trans. Charles S. Singleton. Second printing, with corrections. Princeton: Princeton University Press, 1977. 6 vols.

Althusser, Louis. *Pour Marx*. Paris: François Maspero, 1973.

André, Robert. *Ecriture et pulsions dans le roman stendhalien*. Paris: Klincksieck, 1977.

Auerbach, Erich. *Mimesis: The Representation of Reality in Western Literature*. Trans. Willard R. Trask. Princeton: Princeton University Press, 1953.

Bachelard, Gaston. *The Poetics of Space*. Trans. Maria Jolas. Boston: Beacon Press, 1969.

Balzac, Honoré de. *La Comédie humaine*. 7 vols. Paris: Seuil (Intégrale), 1965–66.

———. *La Comédie humaine*. Ed. Pierre-Georges Castex et al. Paris: Gallimard (Pléiade), 1976–81. 12 vols.

———. *Le Père Goriot*. Ed. Stéphane Vachon. Paris: Livre de Poche, 1995.

Barthes, Roland. *Incidents*. Paris: Seuil, 1987.

———. "L'Effet de réel." *Communications* 11 (1968): 84–89.

———. *Le Plaisir du texte*. Paris: Seuil, 1973.

———. *S/Z*. Paris: Seuil, 1970.

Bastet, Ned. "Un Langage en liberté surveillée: de quelques procédés d'écriture dans *Aurélia*." *Cahiers Gérard de Nerval* 3 (1980): 22–30.

Beauchamp, William. *The Style of Nerval's* Aurélia. The Hague: Mouton, 1976.

Beizer, Janet. *Ventriloquized Bodies: Narratives of Hysteria in Nineteenth-Century France*. Ithaca, N.Y.: Cornell University Press, 1994.

Bell, David F. *Circumstances: Chance in the Literary Text*. Lincoln: University of Nebraska Press, 1993.

Benveniste, Emile. *Problèmes de linguistique générale*. Vol. 1. Paris: Gallimard (TEL), 1966.

Berg, William J. "Cryptographie et communication dans 'La Chartreuse de Parme.'" *Stendhal Club* 20 (1978): 170–82.

Bernheimer, Charles. *Flaubert and Kafka: Studies in Psychopoetic Structure*. New Haven: Yale University Press, 1982.

Berthier, Patrick. "La dot de Dinah." *Romantisme* 13.40 (1983): 119–28.

Blin, Georges. *Stendhal et les problèmes du roman*. Paris: Corti, 1954.

Brombert, Victor. "Esquisse de la prison heureuse." *Revue d'Histoire Littéraire de la France* 71.2 (1971): 247–61.

———. *The Romantic Prison: The French Tradition*. Princeton: Princeton University Press, 1978.

Brooks, Peter. "L'invention de l'écriture (et du langage) dans *La Chartreuse de Parme*." *Stendhal Club* 20 (1978): 183–90.

Cervantes, Miguel de. *Novelas ejemplares*. Ed. Juan Bautista Avalle-Arce. Vol. 3. Madrid: Editorial Castalia, 1982.

Chambers, Ross. *Mélancolie et opposition*. Paris: José Corti, 1987.

———. *Story and Situation*. Minneapolis: University of Minnesota Press, 1984.

Champfleury, Jules. *Les Excentriques*. Paris: Michel Lévy, 1852.

Chaneles, Sol, and Jerome Snyder. *"that pestilent cosmetic, rhetoric."* New York: Grossman, 1972.

Conroy, Mark. *Modernism and Authority: Strategies of Legitimation in Flaubert and Conrad*. Baltimore: Johns Hopkins University Press, 1985.

Corbin, Alain. *Le Miasme et la jonquille*. Paris: Champs-Flammarion, 1986.

Couty, Daniel. *"Aurélia*: de l'impuissance narrative au pouvoir des mots." *Cahiers Gérard de Nerval* 3 (1980): 15–17.

Crouzet, Michel. *Nature et Société chez Stendhal*. Lille: Presses Universitaires de Lille, 1985.

Culler, Jonathan. *Flaubert: The Uses of Uncertainty*. Ithaca, N.Y.: Cornell University Press, 1973.

Dällenbach, Lucien. *La Canne de Balzac*. Paris: José Corti, 1996.

———. "Reading as Suture." *Style* 18.2 (1984): 196–206.

Debray-Genette, Raymonde. *Métamorphoses du récit. Autour de Flaubert*. Paris: Seuil, 1988.

———, and Jacques Neefs, eds. *Roman d'archives*. Lille: Presses Universitaires de Lille, 1987.

de la Carrera, Rosalina. "History's Unconscious in Victor Hugo's *Les Misérables*." *MLN* 96.4 (1981): 839–55.

de Man, Paul. *The Rhetoric of Romanticism*. New York: Columbia University Press, 1984.

Derrida, Jacques. "An Idea of Flaubert: 'Plato's Letter.'" *MLN* 99.4 (1984): 748–68.

———. *La Carte postale de Socrate à Freud et au-delà*. Paris: Aubier-Flammarion, 1980.

———. *De la grammatologie*. Paris: Minuit, 1967.

———. *La Dissémination*. Paris: Seuil, 1972.

———. *L'Ecriture et la différence*. Paris: Editions du Seuil, 1967.

———. *Eperons*. Paris: Flammarion, 1978.

———. "La Loi du genre / The Law of Genre." Trans. Avital Ronell. *GLYPH* 7 (1980): 176–232.

———. *Marges de la philosophie*. Paris: Minuit, 1972.

———. *Spectres de Marx. L'Etat de dette, le travail du deuil et la nouvelle Internationale*. Paris: Galilée, 1993.

———. "Structure, Sign, and Play in the Discourse of the Human Sciences." In *The Structuralist Controversy*. Ed. Richard Macksey and Eugenio Donato. Baltimore: The Johns Hopkins University Press, 1970.

———. *Ulysse gramophone*. Paris: Galilée, 1987.

Descombes, Vincent. *Grammaire d'objets en tous genres*. Paris: Minuit, 1983.

Destruel, Philippe. "*Angélique* et la bibliothèque de Babel." *Romantisme* 34 (1985): 21–32.

Didier, Béatrice. *Stendhal autobiographe*. Paris: Presses Universitaires de France, 1983.

Didi-Huberman, Georges. *La Peinture incarnée*. Paris: Minuit, 1985.

DiPiero, Thomas. *Dangerous Truths & Criminal Passions: The Evolution of the French Novel, 1569–1791*. Stanford: Stanford University Press, 1992.

Donato, Eugenio. "Flaubert and the Question of History." *MLN* 91.5 (1976): 850–70.

———. "Who Signs 'Flaubert'?" *MLN* 99.4 (1984): 711–26.

———. "The Museum's Furnace: Notes Toward a Contextual Reading of *Bouvard and Pécuchet*." *Textual Strategies*. Ed. Josué V. Harari. Ithaca, N.Y.: Cornell University Press, 1979. 213–38.

Dumas Fils, Alexandre. *Diane de Lys*. Paris: Librairie Nouvelle, 1855.

———. *La Dame aux camélias*. Paris: Calmann-Lévy, 1961.

Eagleton, Terry. *The Ideology of the Aesthetic*. London: Basil Blackwell, 1990.

Eco, Umberto. *Lector in Fabula*. Milan: Bompiani, 1979.

————. *The Role of the Reader*. Bloomington: Indiana University Press, 1979.

Eisenzweig, Uri. *L'Espace imaginaire d'un récit*. Neuchâtel: La Baconnière, 1976.

Epschtein, M. "Stilprinzipien des Realismus bei Stendhal und Balzac." *Kunst und Literatur* 26 (1978): 705–25.

Felman, Shoshana. *La "Folie" dans l'oeuvre romanesque de Stendhal*. Paris: José Corti, 1971.

————. *La Folie et la chose littéraire*. Paris: Seuil, 1978.

Fish, Stanley. *Is There a Text in This Class? The Authority of Interpretive Communities*. Cambridge, Mass.: Harvard University Press, 1980.

Flaubert, Gustave. *Correspondance*. Ed. Jean Bruneau. Paris: Gallimard (Pléiade), 1973–80. 2 vols.

————. *L'Education sentimentale. Version de 1845. Oeuvres complètes*. Vol. 1. Paris: Seuil (Intégrale), 1964.

————. *Oeuvres*. Ed. A. Thibaudet and R. Dumesnil. Paris: Gallimard (Pléiade), 1951–52. 2 vols.

————. *Préface à la vie d'écrivain*. Ed. Geneviève Bollème. Paris: Seuil, 1963.

Foucault, Michel. *Dits et écrits 1954–1988*. Paris: Gallimard, 1994. 4 vols.

————. *Les Mots et les choses. Une archéologie des sciences humaines*. Paris: Gallimard, 1966.

————. *Surveiller et punir. Naissance de la prison*. Paris: Gallimard, 1975.

Frappier-Mazur, Lucienne. *L'Expression métaphorique dans la "Comédie humaine."* Paris: Klincksieck, 1976.

Freccero, John. *Dante: The Poetics of Conversion*. Cambridge, Mass.: Harvard University Press, 1986.

Fried, Michael. *Absorption and Theatricality: Painting and Beholder in the Age of Diderot*. Berkeley: University of California Press, 1980.

————. *Courbet's Realism*. Chicago: University of Chicago Press, 1990.

Gaillard, Françoise. "Une Inénarrable Histoire." In *Flaubert et le comble d'art. Nouvelles Recherches sur Bouvard et Pécuchet de Flaubert*. Ed. Pierre Cogny et al. Paris: SEDES, 1981. 75–87.

Gasché, Rodolphe. "Deconstruction as Criticism." *GLYPH* 6 (1979): 177–215.

————. "The Mixture of Genres, The Mixture of Styles, and Figural Interpretation: *Sylvie*, by Gérard de Nerval." *GLYPH* 7 (1980): 102–30.

————. *The Tain of the Mirror*. Cambridge, Mass.: Harvard University Press, 1986.

Genette, Gérard. "Vraisemblance et motivation." *Communications* 11 (1968): 5–21.

————, and Tzvetan Todorov, eds. *Travail de Flaubert*. Paris: Seuil (Points), 1983.

Gilbert, Sandra M., and Susan Gubar. *The Madwoman in the Attic: The Woman Writer and the Nineteenth-Century Literary Imagination.* New Haven: Yale, 1979 (rpt. 1984).

Ginsburg, Michal Peled. *Flaubert Writing.* Stanford: Stanford University Press, 1986.

Girard, René. *Mensonge romantique, vérité romanesque.* Paris: Grasset, 1961.

————. *La Violence et le sacré.* Paris: Grasset, 1972.

Goldmann, Lucien. *Pour une sociologie du roman.* Paris: Gallimard (Idées), 1964.

Gordon, Rae Beth. "Dentelle: Métaphore du texte dans *Sylvie*." *Romanic Review* 73 (1982): 45–66.

Herschberg-Pierrot, Anne. *Le Dictionnaire des idées reçues de Flaubert.* Lille: Presses Universitaires de Lille, 1988.

Hertz, Neil. *The End of the Line: Essays on Psychoanalysis and the Sublime.* New York: Columbia University Press, 1985.

Hoffmann, E. T. A. "Nachricht von den neuesten Schicksalen des Hundes Berganza." In *Werke*, vol. 1. Zurich: Stauffacher-Verlag, 1965.

Homer. *The Odyssey.* With a translation by A. T. Murray. Cambridge, Mass.: Harvard University Press (Loeb), 1919 (rpt. 1960).

Iser, Wolfgang. *The Act of Reading.* Baltimore: Johns Hopkins University Press, 1979.

————. *Prospecting: From Reader Response to Literary Anthropology.* Baltimore: The Johns Hopkins University Press, 1989.

Jakobson, Roman. "The Dominant." *Readings in Russian Poetics.* Ed. and trans. Ladislav Matejka and Krystyna Pomorska. Cambridge, Mass.: MIT Press, 1971. 82–85.

James, Henry. *The New York Edition of Henry James.* New York: Charles Scribners' Sons, 1907–17. 20 vols.

Jameson, Fredric. *The Political Unconscious: Narrative as a Socially Symbolic Act.* Ithaca, N.Y.: Cornell University Press, 1981.

Jauss, Hans Robert. *Literaturgeschichte als Provokation.* Frankfurt: Suhrkamp Verlag, 1970.

Jean, Raymond. *La Poétique du désir.* Paris: Seuil, 1974.

Jeanneret, Michel. *La Lettre perdue. Ecriture et folie dans l'oeuvre de Nerval.* Paris: Flammarion, 1978.

Jefferson, Ann. *Reading Realism in Stendhal.* Cambridge: Cambridge University Press, 1988.

Johnson, Barbara. *The Critical Difference: Essays in the Contemporary Rhetoric of Reading.* Baltimore: The Johns Hopkins University Press, 1980.

Jones, Grahame C. "Réel, Saint-Réal: Une épigraphe du 'Rouge' et le réalisme stendhalien." *Stendhal Club* 25 (1983): 235–43.

Kadish, Doris Y. *Politicizing Gender: Narrative Strategies in the Aftermath of the French Revolution.* New Brunswick: Rutgers University Press, 1991.

Kamuf, Peggy. *Signature Pieces: On the Institution of Authorship.* Ithaca, N.Y.: Cornell University Press, 1988.

Kogan, Vivian. "Signs and Signals in *La Chartreuse de Parme.*" *Nineteenth-Century French Studies* 2 (1974): 29–38.

Kristeva, Julia. *La Révolution du langage poétique.* Paris: Seuil, 1974.

———. *Soleil noir.* Paris: Gallimard, 1987.

———. *Le Texte du roman.* The Hague: Mouton, 1970.

Lacan, Jacques. *Ecrits.* Paris: Seuil, 1966.

Lacoue-Labarthe, Philippe, and Jean-Luc Nancy. "Genre." Trans. Lawrence R. Schehr. *GLYPH* 7 (1980): 1–14.

Lanham, Richard A. *A Handlist of Rhetorical Terms: A Guide for Students of English Literature.* Berkeley: University of California Press, 1969.

Lanson, Gustave. *Histoire de la littérature française.* Paris: Hachette, 1903.

Leclerc, Yvan. *La Spirale et le monument. Essai sur Bouvard et Pécuchet.* Paris: SEDES, 1988.

Lucey, Michael. "Balzac's Queer Cousins and Their Friends." In *Novel Gazing: Queer Readings in Fiction.* Ed. Eve Kosofsky Sedgwick. Durham: Duke University Press, 1997.

Lukács, Georg. *Studies in European Realism.* New York: Grosset and Dunlap, 1964.

Lyotard, Jean-François. *Discours, figure.* Paris: Klincksieck, 1974.

Mandelbrot, Benoît. *Les Objets fractals.* Paris: Flammarion, 1975.

Marin, Louis. *La Critique du discours.* Paris: Minuit, 1975.

Mehlman, Jeffrey. *Cataract: A Study in Diderot.* Middletown, Conn.: Wesleyan University Press, 1979.

Miller, J. Hillis. *The Ethics of Reading.* New York: Columbia University Press, 1987.

Montello, Josué. *Un Maître oublié de Stendhal.* Paris: Seghers, 1970.

Morel, Bénédict Auguste. *Traité des dégénérescences physiques, intellectuelles et morales de l'espèce humaine.* Paris: J. B. Baillière, 1857 (rpt. New York: Arno Press, 1976).

Mozet, Nicole. "Au commencement est l'imprimerie." In *Balzac: Illusions perdues. L'oeuvre capitale dans l'oeuvre.* Ed. Françoise van Rossum-Guyon. Groningen, Netherlands: CRIN, 1988. 23–33.

Nerval, Gérard de. *Oeuvres.* Vol. 1. Paris: Edition Garnier Frères, 1966.

Newmark, Kevin. *Beyond Symbolism.* Ithaca, N.Y.: Cornell University Press, 1991.

Nietzsche, Friedrich. *Werke in drei Bänden.* Ed. Karl Schlechta. Munich: Karl Hanser Verlag, 1966. 3 vols.

Pasco, Allan H. "The Unheroic Mode: Stendhal's *La Chartreuse de Parme*." *Philological Quarterly* 70.3 (1991): 361–78.

Paulson, William. "De la force vitale au système organisateur: *La Muse de département* et l'esthétique balzacienne." *Romantisme* 17.55 (1987): 33–40.

Pavel, Thomas. *Le Mirage linguistique. Essai sur la modernisation intellectuelle.* Paris: Minuit, 1988.

Peterson, Carla L. *The Determined Reader: Gender and Culture in the Novel from Napoleon to Victoria.* New Brunswick, N.J.: Rutgers University Press, 1986.

Pitwood, Michael. *Dante and the French Romantics.* Geneva: Droz, 1985.

Piwowarczyk, Mary Ann. "The Narratee and the Situation of Enunciation: A Reconsideration of Prince's Theory." *Genre* 9 (1976): 161–77.

Poe, Edgar Allan. *Poetry and Tales.* Ed. Patrick F. Quinn. New York: The Library of America, 1984.

Pontalis, J.-B. *Après Freud.* Paris: Gallimard (Idées), 1968.

Porter, Laurence M. *The Interpretation of Dreams.* Boston: Twayne, 1987.

Prendergast, Christopher. *The Order of Mimesis: Balzac, Stendhal, Nerval, Flaubert.* Cambridge: Cambridge University Press, 1986.

Prince, Gerald. "Introduction à l'étude du narrataire." *Poétique* 14 (1973): 178–96.

———. "The Narratee Revisited." *Style* 19.3 (1985): 299–303.

Proust, Marcel. *A la recherche du temps perdu.* Paris: Gallimard (Pléiade), 1987–89. 4 vols.

———. *Contre Sainte-Beuve.* Paris: Gallimard (Pléiade), 1971.

Rabine, Leslie. "Ideology and Contradiction in *La Chartreuse de Parme*." *SubStance* 21 (1978): 117–39.

Rashkin, Esther. *Family Secrets and the Psychoanalysis of Narrative.* Princeton: Princeton University Press, 1992.

Ray, William. "Recognizing Recognition." *Diacritics* 7.4 (1977): 20–33.

Reid, Martine. *Flaubert Correspondant.* Paris: SEDES, 1995.

Richard, Jean-Pierre. *Littérature et sensation.* Paris: Seuil, 1954.

Riffaterre, Michael. "Describing Poetic Structures: Two Approaches to Baudelaire's *Les Chats*." *Structuralism.* Ed. Jacques Ehrmann. New York: Doubleday Anchor, 1970. 188–230.

Ronell, Avital. *Dictations: On Haunted Writing.* Bloomington: Indiana University Press, 1986.

Rougemont, Denis de. *Love in the Western World.* Trans. Montgomery Belgion. New York: Harper and Row, 1956 (rpt. 1974).

Rousseau, Jean-Jacques. *Les Confessions.* In *Oeuvres complètes*, vol. 3. Paris: Gallimard (Pléiade), 1955.

Rousset, Jean. "L'Inscription du lecteur chez Balzac." *Le Statut de la Littéra-*

ture. Mélanges offerts à Paul Bénichou. Ed. Marc Fumaroli. Geneva: Droz, 1982. 241–56.

Russell, Lois Ann. "Les Jeux de l'écriture dans *La Chartreuse de Parme.*" *Stendhal Club* 25 (1982): 67–75.

Saint-Réal. "De l'usage de l'Histoire." In *Oeuvres,* vol. 3. Paris: Chez Les Libraires Associés, 1957.

Sartre, Jean-Paul. *La Nausée.* Paris: Gallimard (Folio), 1938.

———. *Les Carnets de la drôle de guerre.* Paris: Gallimard, 1983.

———. *L'Idiot de la famille. Gustave Flaubert de 1821 à 1957.* 3 vols. Paris: Gallimard, 1971–72.

Schehr, Lawrence. *Alcibiades at the Door: Gay Discourses in French Literature.* Stanford: Stanford University Press, 1995.

———. "A Chronicle of Production: The Creation of an Enunciative Framework in *Le Rouge et le Noir.*" *Australian Journal of French Studies* 22.1 (1985): 43–59.

———. "Le *Faust* de Nerval: Poésie et Vérité." *Romanic Review* 82.2 (1991): 146–63.

———. *Flaubert and Sons: Readings of Flaubert, Zola, and Proust.* New York: Peter Lang, 1986.

———. "Rossini's Castrati." *Lusitania.* Forthcoming.

———. "*Salammbô* as the Novel of Alterity." *Nineteenth-Century French Studies* 17.3–4 (1989): 326–41.

———. *The Shock of Men: Homosexual Hermeneutics and French Writing.* Stanford: Stanford University Press, 1995.

———. "Stendhal's Pathology of the Novel," *French Forum* 15.1 (1990): 53–72.

———. "The Unknown Subject: About Balzac's 'Chef-d'oeuvre inconnu.'" *Nineteenth-Century French Studies* 12.4 (1984): 58–69.

Scholes, Robert. "Reading Like a Man." *Men in Feminism.* Ed. Alice Jardine and Paul Smith. New York: Methuen, 1987.

Schor, Naomi. *Breaking the Chain: Women, Theory, and French Realist Fiction.* New York: Columbia University Press, 1985.

———. *Reading in Detail: Aesthetics and the Feminine.* New York: Methuen, 1987.

———, and Henry F. Majewski. *Flaubert and Postmodernism.* Lincoln: University of Nebraska Press, 1984.

Schuerewegen, Franc. *Balzac contre Balzac. Les Cartes du lecteur.* Paris and Toronto: SEDES/Paratexte, 1990.

———. "Lire dans ou hors du lièvre. Deux lectures du *Réquisitionnaire* de Balzac." *Littératures* 12 (1985): 61–75.

———. "Muséum ou *Croutéum*? Pons, Bouvard, Pécuchet et la collection." *Romantisme* 17 (55) (1987): 41–54.

Serres, Michel. *Le Passage du Nord-Ouest*. Paris: Minuit, 1980.

———. "Noise." *Sub-Stance* 40 (1983): 48–60.

Showalter, English, Jr. *The Evolution of the French Novel: 1641–1782*. Princeton: Princeton University Press, 1972.

Stendhal. *De l'amour*. Ed. V. del Litto. Paris: Gallimard (Folio), 1980.

———. *Romans et Nouvelles*. 2 vols. Paris: Gallimard (Pléiade), 1952.

Suleiman, Susan R., and Inge Crosman, eds. *The Reader in the Text*. Princeton: Princeton University Press, 1980.

Tanner, Tony. *Adultery in the Novel: Contract and Transgression*. Baltimore: The Johns Hopkins University Press, 1979.

Terdiman, Richard. *Discourse / Counter-Discourse: The Theory and Practice of Symbolic Resistance in Nineteenth-Century France*. Ithaca, N.Y.: Cornell University Press, 1985.

Tritsmans, Bruno. "Nerval et l'indétermination textuelle." *Poétique* 60 (1984): 423–36.

Tynianov, Iurii. *Archaisty i Novatory*. Leningrad: Priboi, 1929.

Vannier, Bernard. *L'Inscription du corps. Pour une sémiotique du portrait balzacien*. Paris: Klincksieck, 1972.

Virgil (P. Vergili Maronis). *Opera*. Ed. Frederick Hirtzel. Oxford: The Clarendon Press, 1900 (rpt. 1956).

Waller, Margaret. *The Male Malady: Fictions of Impotence in the French Romantic Novel*. New Brunswick: Rutgers University Press, 1993.

Watt, Ian. *The Rise of the Novel: Studies in Defoe, Richardson, and Fielding*. Berkeley: University of California Press, 1957.

Weber, Samuel. *Unwrapping Balzac*. Toronto: University of Toronto Press, 1979.

Wolff, Erwin. "Der intendierte Leser." *Poetica* 4 (1971): 141–66.

Index

In this index, an "f" after a number indicates a separate reference on the next page, and an "ff" indicates separate references on the next two pages. A continuous discussion over two of more pages is indicated by a span of page numbers, e.g., "57–59." *Passim* is used for a cluster of references in close but not consecutive sequence.